C-2014

4-3-15

3-

Why?

A courtroom drama of self-discovery

A novel by

R. H. King, Jr.

Walden Road Publishing

Walden Road Publishing
669 Walden Road, Winnetka, Illinois 60093
Copyright © 2014 by Robert H. King, Jr.

Printed in the United States of America

First edition, 2014

Cover design by Robin Katz, blackbird design

ISBN: 978-0-9903400-03

For Robin, the love of my life.

You have kept me on my toes all these years.

WHY?

A Courtroom Drama of Self Discovery

Chapter 1

When I opened my satchel-style briefcase, I found two semi-automatic pistols perched on top of the mid-term exams that I was supposed to administer to my freshman English class. I had put the finishing touches on the exams late last night and stacked them carefully in the briefcase. Nothing had been on top of them. I had no idea how those guns got in the briefcase, or why they were there. But I sensed that something bad was about to happen.

The twenty-five students in my class sat patiently in their Dartmouth Hall class room, waiting for me to pass out the exams. That's what Dartmouth professors are supposed to do: give lectures, grade papers, pass out exams. They do not carry weapons around in their briefcases. Those pistols sat on top of the exams like vipers guarding their lair. They glimmered with a black, foreboding sheen. For some reason, I was both drawn to, and repulsed by, the menace they communicated. I couldn't take my eyes off them. I just stood there, trying to figure out what I was supposed to do next.

With no conscious direction from me, I saw my hands disappear into the briefcase. I could feel them grasping the two weapons. The gun handles had a textured surface and were cool, almost soothing, to the touch. I tried to make my hands let go of the guns. It felt like my hands were frozen to the gun handles. My hands slowly lifted out of the briefcase, each grasping a pistol and aiming them out towards my class. Inside my head I was yelling "STOP," but my hands were not listening. It was if they belonged to someone else, and I was helpless to command them. Finally, I could feel my fingers wrap around the triggers, and then I knew it was too late. I began firing.

The rapid fire of the guns sounded like small claps of thunder that echoed off the confined space of the class room. I involuntarily flinched with each pull of the trigger.

Above that din, I could hear voices shrieking "What the . . .
," or shouting "Look out," along with screams and the
screeching of chairs as they twisted and fell. This was
almost immediately followed by the dull thud of
backpacks, and then bodies, plunging to the floor. All I
saw were the barrels of the pistols, which each seemed to
be six feet long, pointing out towards the classroom.
Everything else was a blur. By the time that I ran out of
bullets and stopped firing, the screaming had stopped,
replaced by some sobbing and moaning. Everyone in the
room was slumped over their desks or on the floor, dead,
dying or playing possum.

My hands dropped the guns back into the briefcase.
I stared at those trembling, traitorous hands in utter
disbelief. As if in a trance, I found myself turning and
leaving the classroom. I walked down the hall towards the
main doors. My field of vision seemed to narrow to a small
tunnel directly in front of me. I could, however, hear doors
to other class rooms creaking open a crack as I passed by.
Students or their professors peered out, no doubt attracted
by the unusual sound of gunshots. A murmuring of
concerned voices generally escalated to a small din. No
one ventured out into the hall, however, afraid of being shot
themselves. I could hear the scrapping of the old wooden
windows opening within other class rooms, as occupants
either tried to escape or to call out for help.

I walked out of the door of Dartmouth Hall. I
flopped down on the front steps. What had just happened?
How could I possibly have fired those guns? I felt dizzy
and sick to my stomach. I was so glad that my family
wasn't alive to see this. My parents would be embarrassed
beyond belief. My brother would be stunned that his milk-
toast twin was capable of such a violent act. I was also
glad that my ex-wife was not present to witness my descent
into oblivion. It would seemingly validate her recent
decision to leave me for someone else.

As I sat there, I could feel something in the breast pocket of my blazer and found a pack of cigarettes. I hadn't smoked since college, and I wasn't sure how the cigarettes found their way into my coat. With quivering hands, I pulled out a cigarette. Old habits die hard, and I reached into my pants pocket for a lighter, and was surprised to find one there. Today was full of mysteries. I lit the cigarette, inhaled the smoke hungrily, exhaled slowly, and took in the view around me. There really isn't a prettier or more serene place on earth than Hanover in the fall. Fall mornings had a clean, bracing crispness, with the hint of frost on the grass. The trees were at the height of turning into a pallet of blazing colors. People were milling about on the college Green directly below me, unaware of what had just transpired. Later in the afternoon, there would probably be pick-up football games taking place on the Green. I knew that I would not be there to see them.

I did not have an escape plan, because I had no idea that I was going to be involved in the shooting. No, that wasn't exactly accurate. I must have subconsciously realized that firing those guns at someone was a possibility when I put the guns in my briefcase. But I had no memory of even owning guns, much less putting them in my briefcase. If those weren't my guns, though, how did they get in my briefcase? No one else had access to it between the time I packed it up with the mid-term exams and the time I left for class. Those guns must have been mine. And I must have put them in the briefcase. But why? Certainly not to shoot my class. After all, I had spent a good deal of time last night perfecting the mid-term exam questions. Now there was no one to take the test.

When the police arrived, I immediately raised my hands and laid on my stomach. Despite offering no resistance, the police pounced on me. One officer jammed his knee in the middle of my back, sending bolts of pain up and down my spine, and held my head roughly down on the

pavement.   Another officer stuck his hands in all my
pockets, and then ran his hands up and down the entire
length of my body, presumably searching for weapons.
Finally satisfied that I posed no further risk, an officer
roughly cuffed my hands behind my back. The officers
yanked me to my feet and lead me away to a waiting police
car. They told me that I had the right to remain silent and
to an attorney, just like I had heard hundreds of times on
the television.   Behind me, I could hear shouting and
crying, as people discovered the carnage I had left behind
in my class room.   I knew that there would be many
students dead or seriously wounded.

For some reason, the police officers felt the need to
turn on the siren for the short, three block trip from the
steps of Dartmouth Hall to the Hanover police station.
Maybe the officers were overcome by the excitement of the
moment.   Maybe they wanted to proclaim the importance
of their cargo: a real criminal had been apprehended in
Hanover! Or maybe they wanted to call people's attention
to themselves: look at us, real police officers doing real
police work! Whatever the reason, the din the siren created
inside the police car was deafening, making my head throb.
From the back seat of the police car, I could barely hear
one of the officers radioing the police station to alert the
other officers that a major crime had been committed, and
the criminal suspect was on his way to the station.

Hanover has a population of approximately eight
thousand people, comprised primarily of Dartmouth
College professors, administrators and other employees,
and the owners and employees of the various service
industries that had grown to serve the college.   The ten-
person Hanover police force was housed in a recently
refurbished and modernized police station. I had been a
guest there once before for a few hours when I was student.
One night after a drunken binge had turned into an empty
beer bottle throwing contest between my dorm and the one

across the alley, the Hanover gendarmes had taken several of the participants into custody. No charges had been filed. The police station had a light and airy reception area, complete with comfy chairs for visitors. Behind the main counter, there were several desks with computer screens and keyboards. Notwithstanding the modern appearance, it was still a small-town operation. The biggest emergency this police station usually experienced was when a fight broke out at a Dartmouth hockey game, or when a frat party got out of hand. Drunken disorderly conduct was the meat-and-potatoes of the Hanover police force. Today, the situation was very different, and the local constables were sailing in largely uncharted waters.

The police hustled me into the police station through the side door and took me to a processing room behind the neat row of desks. The room was all white and lit by bright fluorescent bulbs. It reminded me somewhat of a hospital. Along one wall was a bench with handcuffs attached to metal rings secured to the bench. An officer led me over to the bench and handcuffed me to one of the metal rings. He told me to sit quietly. I complied. I looked around the room to get a sense of what was likely to happen next. Directly across the room, I could see two holding cells and a nearby door labeled "Solitary." On the same side of the room as the bench to which I was handcuffed, there was a door labeled "Interview Room" and another door with the label "Toilet." Despite the seriousness of my situation, I found myself smiling a little to myself, surprised that there was no label where I sat saying "Bench."

An officer came over and detached my handcuffs from the ring on the bench and led me across the room to still another door that was not labeled. Inside the room, there was a chest-high machine of some sort, with a small ledge that jutted out with a LCD screen. The officer directed me to approach the machine and give my hand to another officer whose job it apparently was to operate the machine. That officer took my hand and, one by one, rolled my thumb and fingers across the LCD screen. Probably a finger-printing machine of some sort, which could apparently electronically send my prints to the FBI centralized database without the fuss or muss of inking my fingers. I suppose the police wanted to see if I was wanted for any other crimes, or perhaps was a terrorist of some kind. I sighed. They would be disappointed. In over thirty years of driving, I had accumulated only four tickets. I was no master criminal.

An officer then placed me in the room marked "Solitary." This room, too, was painted stark, brilliant white. The room had a stainless steel toilet with no seat, a stainless steel sink and a bed bolted to the floor. It was illuminated by two sets of fluorescent lights housed in protective aluminum casing in the middle of the ceiling. I walked over to the bed and sat down. The adrenaline rush that had surged through my body in the last hour had expended itself, and I suddenly felt massively fatigued. I laid down on the coarse blanket that was neatly placed on the bed and closed my eyes.

A short time later, I was stirred from my sleep by a commotion occurring outside my cell. People were speaking in elevated tones. Where was the Chief? Had he been informed of the crime? Who was securing the crime scene? Questions flew back and forth between the police staff like a ball in a tennis match. Yes, the Chief had been informed. But it was Wednesday, the Chief's golf day, and he had to be called off the golf course to give him the news. He would be here once he showered and changed. Two officers had been left to rope off the crime scene and take statements. The state police hadn't been called yet, but the county coroner was in route to take charge of the bodies and perform the obligatory autopsies, although there was little question concerning the cause of death. The Hanover police department did not have a public relations officer, nor anyone with training on how to deal with the media that would most certainly soon be descending on Hanover. The staff concluded, by default, that the Chief would handle media relations when he got here.

I shut out the officers continuing conversations, and contemplated what was to come next. In most mass killings of the last few decades, the shooter had committed suicide or was killed by the authorities, leaving people to speculate upon his motive. Or he was a stark, raving lunatic with wild eyes and a menacing grin who was so mentally deranged that no lucid communication was possible. I, on the other hand, was still alive, and apparently rational. I was sure to be interrogated by police detectives, psychologists and the like, who would all be asking the same questions. No one would ask whether I had committed the crime. That was obvious. No, the question that would be asked, in a thousand different ways, from a thousand different perspectives, was: why? Why would a well-educated and established professor with no criminal record or history of mental instability slaughter his own students? It was a question that needed answering — that I needed to answer. But at that moment, I had no answer. For them, or for myself.

Chapter 2

My eyes slowly opened, and I had trouble rousing myself from what must have been a deep sleep. I felt groggy and disoriented, like I did when waking after a hard night of drinking. I couldn't immediately recall what day of the week it was. I blinked my eyes several times, trying to lift the mental fog. I stared up at an unfamiliar ceiling. Where was I? And then I suddenly sat bolt upright. I looked around quickly and took in my surroundings. The reality of where I was flooded back into my mind: I was in a cell in the Hanover Police Department. The reason I was there also came jarringly back into focus: I had shot a class room full of students. I was being held as a common criminal in jail. No, not as a "common" criminal — as a mass murderer, who was undoubtedly about to be put through the meat-grinder of the criminal justice system.

I heard the clanking of the cell door as a police officer entered. The officer re-handcuffed me, and led me to the "Interview" room. The room was rectangular in shape with a long metal table bolted to the floor in the middle of the room. I was beginning to notice this obsession with bolting things to the floor; did they really think that people would steal things from the police station? A single lamp hung from the ceiling, centered on the table. The walls here were also glaringly white. A large, gray-haired man dressed in full police regalia sat on one side of the table. He had dark bags under his eyes and a ruddiness to his complexion that made it appear that he had been on a bender for days. This was, I assumed, the Chief of Police. He had some manila file folders on the table in front of him that he was leafing through. He did not immediately look up when I entered the room, apparently engaged by the information in the files.

I was ushered to a chair facing the Chief, and my handcuffs were removed before I sat down. The police officer remained immediately behind me, so as to make sure that I would stay seated and cause no trouble, I assumed. The Chief broke the silence:

"Professor, my name is Tom Dodds. I'm the Hanover Chief of Police. I was told that you have been informed of your constitutional rights, is that correct?"

"I was told that I have the right to remain silent and to have an attorney."

Chief Dodd's brow furled. "You should also have been told that if you want an attorney and cannot afford one, one will be appointed by the court to represent you. Do you understand these rights?"

"I think so."

"I want to ask you some preliminary background questions, just to confirm some of the information we have. Are you agreeable to proceeding?"

"I guess so. Let me just tell you, Chief Dodds, that I am horrified by what happened yesterday, and can't explain it. I am not a violent person. I just couldn't stop myself once I found those guns in the briefcase. And I don't even know where those guns came from . . ."

"Hold on, Professor. I don't want to talk with you about that just now. This is just a discussion to get some of the basic facts down. I don't want you to talk about the shootings until you've had a chance to decide whether you want a lawyer or not. Because anything you say can be used against you later in court. Understand?"

I nodded my head. "I understand. What do you want to know?"

"Well, let's start with just confirming who you are and where you live. You are Professor Daniel Jackson, correct?"

"Yes."

"You are a visiting professor at Dartmouth College?"

"Correct."

"You live at 28 West Wheelock Street in Hanover, right?"

"Yes."

"Are you married?"

"No. Divorced, just last year."

"Does your ex-wife live nearby?"

"No. She lives in France now."

"Do you have any children?"

"No. We never had any."

"Are your parents still living?"

"No. They both passed away more than twenty years ago."

"Any siblings?"

"I had a twin brother, but he died in a car accident when I was in college."

"Have you ever been arrested before?"

"I assume you know from my fingerprint check that I have not."

"Is there anyone we should contact to tell them that you have been arrested?"

I thought about that for a minute. I didn't really have any close friends here in Hanover. My best friend in the world, Tim Davidson, currently lived in Rutland, Vermont, not too far from Hanover. Tim had been my freshman year roommate at Dartmouth. Although we had come from very different backgrounds and upbringings, we had forged a strong friendship. Tim was an only child of a well-to-do family in New York City. His father was a successful Wall Street banker, and his mother taught English at the city college. Perhaps in silent rebellion, Tim had been a religion major, and always knew that he wanted to become an Episcopal priest. His nickname during college was "Reverend," but not because he always followed the straight and narrow. To the contrary, he liked to party as much as the next guy, and had the beer gut to prove it. He certainly didn't look priestly. He rode a

Harley motorcycle, had a goatee and shaved head. At six foot six, and well north of three hundred pounds, Tim was an imposing figure. The only thing he was missing was the tattoos.

Our friendship had been cemented when he literally saved my life one winter weekend freshman year. A group of guys on our floor at the dorm decided to go party-hopping on Frat Row one Saturday night. It was mid-January, and the temperature was plummeting into the teens as we ventured out at about nine o'clock. Tim was an experienced drinker, whereas I was not. So when we went drinking, Tim always kept an eye on me to make sure that I wasn't getting into trouble. After visiting several of the frat houses and partaking of their open kegs, our group decided to make the long, cold walk back across campus to the dorm. When the group got back to the dorm, Tim had the brilliant idea to count noses to make sure that everyone had made it back okay. One nose was missing: mine.

Tim dutifully put back on his coat and started re-tracing the group's path from Frat Row. About halfway along the route, Tim found me. Apparently, I had felt the call of nature and stopped by a snow bank to take a piss. But in my drunken state, I had gotten frustrated fumbling with my zipper and finally just undid my belt and yanked my pants down around my knees. I guess I must have passed out in the act of pissing, because Tim found me face down — and dick down — in a snow bank. If Tim had not found me and hauled me back to the dorm over his shoulder, I could have frozen to death, or at a minimum, surely had severe frost bite in a most unforgiving place. That incident became the stuff of dorm legend; Tim bragged that he had saved his first soul. Tim and I became inseparable companions thereafter, often playing chess and drinking scotch in the evenings after studying.

After college, Tim went to Yale Divinity graduate school, and ultimately became the rector of an Episcopal church in Vermont. Although I was ashamed to be reaching out to Tim under these circumstances, I was confident that he would give me whatever support he could. "Chief Dodds, there is someone whom I would appreciate you notifying of my situation. It's Father Tim Davidson at the Episcopal church in Rutland, Vermont."

Chief Dodds raised his eyebrows slightly, but dutifully made a note on his pad of paper, and continued:

"Professor, I received word last night that your arraignment will be held at the West Lebanon courthouse at 11:00 a.m. tomorrow morning. You'll be transported there by our officers. Do you think that you will want to hire a lawyer to represent you at the arraignment?"

I had some familiarity with criminal procedure, but I thought it better to find out precisely what the Chief was talking about. "What happens at the arraignment?"

"Well, that's when the State will formally charge you with the commission of specified crimes. And you get a chance to plead guilty, or not guilty, to those crimes."

"Do people normally have a lawyer at an arraignment?"

"I can't give you legal advice, as to whether you should or shouldn't have a lawyer there. But if you're asking me if criminal defendants have lawyers there, I would say that more often than not, that's the case, if they can afford one. If you can't afford an attorney but want one, you can tell the judge that tomorrow and, if you qualify, the court will appoint a lawyer to represent you before you enter your plea."

Although college professors are not rich, I did make a living wage. And, despite the divorce, I did have some money saved up, as well as some retirement funds. I doubted that I would qualify to have a lawyer appointed for free.

"I'm not rich, but I don't think that I will qualify financially for appointed counsel. I think that I will want to get an attorney, talk with him before the arraignment, and have him there to represent me. How will I go about doing that?"

"I thought that you might say that. So I took the liberty of contacting the State bar association to get a list of criminal defense lawyers in the area. I also contacted the Boston bar association to get a list from them, just in case you thought you needed a lawyer from the big city." He handed me the file folder with lists of names and phone numbers.

I was actually touched by the Chief's concern.

"Thank you, Chief Dodds. That was very thoughtful of you. I have to admit that I am surprised that you'd go to all that trouble for me, after what happened yesterday."

The Chief's countenance darkened. "What 'happened' yesterday? What 'happened' yesterday is that you massacred fifteen students, and left five seriously wounded. I didn't do this for you. I want to make sure that there is no suggestion your constitutional rights weren't observed, so that when you get convicted, there is no ground for appeal." He took a breath, and then said slowly, in a clipped tone: "To be very, very clear, I hate what you did out there — what you 'allegedly' did — and I hope that you burn for it."

I was taken aback by the ferocity in the Chief's voice, but I had asked for it. Mass murders are not usually popular. And by my math, I apparently had missed five students entirely, as they were not among the dead or wounded.

"I understand Chief. Still, I am grateful. I'm not sure how I should proceed from here. Am I allowed to call one or more of these lawyers to talk to them to see if they will take my case? Or am I only allowed one phone call?"

The tenseness in the Chief's face subsided somewhat. He sighed. "Usually, you only get one phone call. But this is a different circumstance. When you are ready, I will allow you to use a phone that will be brought into the interview room. Understand, however, that I will have someone listening in on the line to make sure that nothing improper happens. So don't say anything that you don't want used against you in court."

"I understand. Give me an hour, and then I will be ready to make my calls." The Chief hoisted himself from his chair and left the room. The police officer re-handcuffed me and escorted me back to my cell to review the list of lawyers and select which ones to call.

I may not know a lot about the law, criminal law in particular, but I did understand that any lawyers who had offices around the Hanover area would not have much, if any, experience in defending persons accused of murder, much less mass murder. There were probably some attorneys in the Manchester area that had some experience defending murderers, but not a lot. No, I'd be better off looking in Boston. So I flipped through the Boston bar association listing of attorneys. It was conveniently broken down by subject matter expertise, so I turned to the criminal law section. I read through the pedigrees of several of the lawyers listed and began making a list.

I called out to the police officer watching my cell and asked to be taken to the interview room to make my calls. The officer led me out in handcuffs and took me to the room. A telephone had been placed on the rectangular table. One of my hands was handcuffed to the chair and then I was left alone. I began calling the names from my list. The initial conversations were quite short. As soon as I introduced myself and explained that I was the person accused of killing the fifteen Dartmouth students, I got a terse "not interested" and a click as the receiver was pounded down. This surprised me, as I thought most lawyers were publicity hounds and liked the limelight.

Apparently, there were some kinds of defendants even lawyers wouldn't represent, limelight or not.

After about a dozen failures, I found a listing for a Gus Stanton, a Dartmouth grad who had attended Harvard Law School. From his year of graduation, I surmised that he was in his late sixties or early seventies. I'd give him a try before throwing in the towel. I dialed Mr. Stanton's phone number. After several rings without an answer, I felt sure it would go to an answering machine. But suddenly, someone snatched up the receiver on the other end of the line and said gruffly "Stanton here."

"Mr. Stanton, my name is Dan Jackson. I am a professor at Dartmouth College. I am being arraigned tomorrow morning for the murders of fifteen students. I need a lawyer. Can you represent me?"

The phone was silent for some time. "Jimmy, is that you, you son of a bitch? I don't have time for this kind of nonsense. Leave me the fuck alone. You'll get your money in good time."

"Mr. Stanton, I am not Jimmy. I am Dan Jackson. I really am. I am sitting right now in the Hanover jail. I need legal help. Will you help me?"

Again, there was a long pause. I heard a long sigh. "Okay. Let's start over. You are telling me that you are that crazy professor that shot his students yesterday, is that it? How did you get my number?"

"I have been told that there are police officers listening in to this conversation, so I must be guarded in what I say. I am going to be arraigned tomorrow morning for those shootings. I got your name from a Boston bar association listing, and saw that you are a Dartmouth grad like me. Can I ask if you've had experience defending people accused of murder in New Hampshire?"

"So this is on the level?" There was another long pause. Then Stanton spoke: "Sure, I've handled several murder cases in New Hampshire and other New England states, too. But judging from the news stories, you don't need a lawyer, you need a shrink, or, better yet, a priest. I don't know that anybody can help you."

"I am told that normally criminal defendants have lawyers at the arraignment, and I assume I will need a lawyer to negotiate a plea deal, or for the trial, if it comes to that. I would think being a lawyer in a high profile case would be appealing to you."

"Well, it's not. Just a lot of stress. I've been doing this for over forty years — it's a little late in my career to worry about high profile cases. That's a young man's game."

"Would it make a difference to you if I told you that I could pay you?"

"How much money do you have?"

"Some. How much will it take?"

"That depends. In a case like this, there probably won't be a trial. Some plea deal will be offered, and we'll have little choice but to take it. In that case, it would cost probably no more than twenty-five thousand dollars. I would need a retainer in that amount to hold and bill against. If, on the other hand, you had a defense and there was going to be a trial, it would be more expensive."

"How much more expensive?"

"Well, I'd have to do more investigation, interviewing of witnesses, maybe even get an expert to testify. If that was the road this case took, it would cost upwards of $100,000, and I'd still need that $25,000 retainer up front. But I don't see the need for a trial in a case like this, based upon what I know so far, unless there is some defense. And that's something we would need to explore face to face, not over the telephone with the police listening in."

"Who decides whether there is a viable defense?"

"Well, after I had gathered more facts, I'd give you my advice. But ultimately, it's your decision as to whether you go to trial, regardless of whether I think there is a defense or not. As a criminal defendant, you have the right to make the prosecution prove that you are guilty beyond a reasonable doubt."

"So if I decide to go to trial, you'd still stay my lawyer?"

"Yes, as long as you can pay the freight, but that's something that is better discussed after we both know more."

"One more thing, Mr. Stanton. Can I ask how many murder trials you've defended?"

"I guess I've had about twenty five over the course of my career."

"May I ask how many you won?"

"Look, Professor, you'd better understand something upfront. The deck is stacked against most murder defendants. The state doesn't prosecute cases on a whim. It only goes after people that it believes it has the goods on — in other words, who really are guilty. So you're not going to find any criminal defense lawyer with a great win/loss ratio. Most murder defendants get convicted. I've gotten a few off, but not many. All I can tell you is that I've been around the block a few times, and I know all the tricks. You'll have as good a chance with me as you will with most anybody else you'd hire."

"I don't want to sound like a jerk, but I really don't know much about choosing a lawyer. Could you tell me about one of the cases that you won?"

The line was quiet for a moment, and then Mr. Stanton cleared his throat and started:

"It was several years ago. It was a case here in Massachusetts. A young black man was accused of murdering a white cab driver in Boston. The driver had been found in his cab in the North End, with two bullet wounds to the head. Some witnesses identified my client out of a line up as someone who had been seen running from the scene. But there was no physical evidence tying my client to the crime, and no evidence tying him to the murder weapon, which was found in a dumpster a block away from the cabbie's car. And there was something else that didn't fit: the cabbie's wallet was found on the body with fifty dollars in it, so this probably wasn't a robbery."

"If it wasn't a robbery, what was it?"

"I found one of the cabbie's buddies who told me that the cabbie played the numbers, and owed big money. So the killing was probably a mob hit, which was consistent with the double tap to the head. I was able to get the so-called eyewitnesses to admit on cross-examination that it was dark, and that they couldn't really be sure it was my client — as opposed to some other black guy — who fled from crime scene. My client also had a good alibi — he was coaching basketball for disadvantaged kids in Roxbury at the time of the murder, and had a ton of witnesses to corroborate that fact. However, because he was a black man accused of killing a white guy in the North End, a gaggle of black alibi witnesses probably wouldn't have gotten my guy off. But when I put on the cabbie's buddy to testify about the gambling, and got the arresting police officer to admit that the murder was consistent with a mob hit on a delinquent gambler, I was able to put it all together for the jury in my closing. They acquitted my client after a three-day trial."

I thought for a moment. I really wouldn't know a good lawyer from a bad one, or be able to discern whether one lawyer was better than another. But Mr. Stanton's success story seemed to indicate that he was resourceful and had good instincts. The thing that didn't fit from my limited experience was how a well-credentialed person like Mr. Stanton ended up in a solo criminal defense practice, as opposed to being a partner in some prominent, white-shoe corporate law firm. I did know one thing: several lawyers had been uninterested, to put it politely, in representing me.

Beggars can't be choosers, and a bird in the hand is better than two in the bush, as my father used to say. I decided that I better grab Mr. Stanton while I could. "I can get you the twenty-five thousand dollar retainer. How much do you charge an hour?"

"Three hundred dollars."

Until now, I had been aghast at what plumbers charged per hour. "That's a lot, but I guess that will be fine. So will you take my case?"

Again there was a long pause on the line. "Well, all right. I will get my things organized and drive up to Hanover this afternoon. We can meet this evening, and then we'll take care of the arraignment tomorrow. Make the arrangements to get me the retainer wire transferred to my bank account. Do you have something to write with?"

"Yes."

"Okay. Wire the money to Bank of Boston, account number 3567 for Law Offices of Gus Stanton. I won't leave for Hanover until I confirm that the money has reached the account."

"Understood. I will see you later tonight. Thank you, Mr. Stanton."

I called my bank in Hanover and made the necessary arrangements to have the $25,000 wired to Mr. Stanton's account. I then rang the police operator to tell her that I was done with my phone calls. As I was led back to my cell, I couldn't help wondering if I had hired the right lawyer, and whether he could help be unravel the mystery of why I had shot those students.

Chapter 3

At about four o'clock that afternoon, an officer came to my cell, handcuffed me and took me to the interview room where I had met with Chief Dodds earlier in the day. The officer removed the handcuffs, told me to sit down, and then exited the room. Moments later, the door swung open again, and there stood Tim Davidson.

Tim had on old, faded blue jeans, held up by a pair of suspenders draped over a red flannel shirt. He was not wearing his priestly collar, and could have easily been mistaken for a lumber jack. I stood and he engulfed me in a bear hug. I struggled to fight back the tears. Eventually, Tim put his hands on my shoulders, gently pushed me back and looked deeply into my tear-filled eyes.

"Dan, I'd like to say that it is good to see you, but I don't like seeing you like this, in here. Have a seat and get a hold of yourself."

I shook my head affirmatively and sat down, taking in some deep breaths to help calm me. I put my head in my hands for a few moments, and then looked at Tim.

"God, Tim. I shot my students. I don't know why I did it. When I saw those guns in my briefcase, I just couldn't stop my hands from grabbing them and firing. You know me. I am not a violent person. I couldn't have done this. It has to be a dream."

Tim looked down at his hands, which were folded on the table in front of him. He softly asked:

"Dan, why did you put the guns in your briefcase in the first place?"

"I didn't. Well, I mean that I don't remember putting them in my briefcase. Hell, I don't even remember owning any guns of any kind. It's all insane. It has to be a nightmare."

Tim shook his head. "Dan, it won't do any good to avoid facing reality. This isn't a dream. I saw fifteen minutes of coverage on the shootings on the Today show this morning. Your picture was plastered all over the screen. You killed fifteen of your students and wounded five others. If you're dreaming, then I'm having the same dream. How likely is that?"

I had to acknowledge that seemed unlikely. "Not very, I guess. But what if you are just part my dream."

Tim rolled his eyes, and waived his hands around the room. "Does this whole situation really feel like a dream?"

I thought about that question for a moment. Yesterday, when my hands gripped the guns, I could feel the textured surface of the handles and the coolness of the metal against my skin. That was real. The sound of the guns thundering in the class room had hurt my ears, and I felt myself flinch with each shot. That was real. The moaning and sobbing of my victims was all too real, and haunted me. The tears that I could feel running down my cheeks at this very moment as I remembered my horrible deed were real. Tim was right. This was no dream.

I gave a long, deep sigh. "No, Tim. I guess this doesn't really feel like a dream."

"And let's say that it was a dream. There's something called 'lucid dreaming' that I recall we heard about in our abnormal psychology class. That's where the person dreaming knows that he is in a dream and can manipulate and control the course of the dream. If you think this is a dream, can you control it? Do you think that you could just get up and walk out that door?"

I had to admit, my confinement definitely felt real. There was no way that the officers were going to allow me to walk out of here. I was a prisoner. That was real.

"No, I don't feel in control of any of this."

"All right, then. Enough talk about dreams. Let's get back to reality."

"Okay, but what am I supposed to do now?"

Tim paused for a moment, as if looking for the right words. He then responded:

"This isn't easy for me to say, but I am your best friend, and somebody's got to say it. Dan, you committed a terrible crime. You have to acknowledge it. Only then will you be able to begin the process of seeking redemption and forgiveness. I know that you are not really into religion, but there is more at stake here than just you. There is your soul. I don't want you to loose either yourself, or your soul."

"You saved my soul once already. Remember that winter night freshman year?"

Tim smiled. "Yes, I do. But I'm not suggesting that I can save your soul this time. You have to save it yourself."

"So you're saying that I should just confess and plead guilty?"

"Is there any doubt in your mind that you shot those students?"

The answer to that question didn't require much thought. "No, but I don't know why I did it. That's what is driving me nuts. I need to understand why this happened."

"Why you did it is irrelevant. By focusing on 'why,' you are just looking for an excuse, a dodge — something that will allow you to blame something or someone else for your own conduct. 'Oh, I was drunk, or depressed, or high,' or 'the devil made me do it — those might be reasons 'why' you shot your students. But those are just excuses. You shot those students. You need to admit it and seek forgiveness. Otherwise, you will be perpetually tormented by this act. Surely you don't want to turn this into a circus by hiring a lawyer and trying to plead not guilty, do you?"

"Tim, I am not sure what I should do. But I do want to try to find out why I did this. And I do think that I need legal advice on what my options are. I called a bunch of lawyers from lists that Chief Dodds gave me, but most of them weren't interested in representing me. I finally found a Dartmouth grad who went to Harvard Law School who agreed to represent me, and he said that I might have a defense. I wired him a twenty-five thousand dollar retainer this morning."

Tim shook his head. "What's this lawyer's name?"

"Gus Stanton."

"Does he have any experience defending murder cases?"

"He says that he does. He's coming up tonight to discuss the case and help me prepare for the arraignment tomorrow morning."

Tim sighed. "Well, I guess you have to have some lawyer for the arraignment, but I want to check this guy out. I don't want you to be stuck with some guy who will lead you down the primrose path into thinking that there is some way out of this other than to take responsibility for your actions. The Boston Diocese has lawyers that it uses from time to time, and I'll reach out to my friends there to see what I can find out from them about your Mr. Stanton."

There was a knock on the door, and the officer stuck his head in, telling us that time was up for the visit. Tim and I stood and hugged again. As Tim turned to leave, he said: "Dan, I know that things seem bleak right now, but I will be here for you. Please think about what I have said, and talk with this Stanton guy about what would happen to you if you just pleaded guilty and accepted your punishment. Please don't allow him to trick you into thinking that you can walk away from this by engaging in cheap lawyers' tricks. Promise me that you won't go down that path without talking with me first."

"I promise."

"And I promise you that no matter how long you have to be in prison, I'll be there every step of the way to help you get the redemption that you need."

I just nodded my head and gave Tim a small smile. Then I was re-cuffed and returned to my cell to await my next visitor, my lawyer, Mr. Stanton.

Shortly after I finished my dinner, one of the officers came into my cell and told me that Mr. Stanton was here to meet with me. I was handcuffed and escorted to the Interview room. A man, who must have been Mr. Stanton, was seated in the chair facing me, with a battered leather briefcase on the table next to him.

He appeared to be of average height, and although slightly chunky, not obese. He had on a gray suit that looked like it had been stashed all balled up in the trunk of a car. He had on a gold and black regiment striped tie, loose at the neck. The top button of his shirt was undone, exposing a small tuft of curly gray chest hair. He wore oval wire-rimmed glasses held together with small pieces of duct tape on the temples. His hair was long, gray and pulled tightly back into a pony tail. It looked like it had been last cut with garden shears. He had a bushy gray mustache that appeared to be at war with his mouth. Deep lines creased his forehead. Stanton's outward appearance was tired, old and beaten. However, his eyes were not. They were a luminescent hazel color and seemed to twinkle. I hoped his eyes reflected some legal acumen that his outward appearance otherwise did not.

The officer removed my handcuffs, and I shook hands with Mr. Stanton and sat down. Mr. Stanton told the officer that handcuffing me to the chair was unnecessary, so the officer turned and left. Mr. Stanton looked me over carefully.

"Professor Jackson, let's get right to it. I got the wire transfer of the twenty-five thousand dollar retainer to my account. Thank you. Even before I received notification of that, I began my investigation into the case. I have looked over the initial police reports, and inspected the crime scene before coming here to the police station. I must tell you, right now it doesn't look good."

I nodded my head slightly, to show that I understood. Mr. Stanton continued:

"The police have recovered two semi-automatic pistols in a briefcase bearing your initials that you left behind in your class room. According to the police report, the guns were purchased using your credit card just last week at Hal's Gun Shop in West Lebanon. The owner of Hal's positively identified a photo of you as someone who bought guns at the store, although without checking the receipts he couldn't remember what guns you had purchased. The briefcase and pistols have your fingerprints all over them. Ballistic reports have confirmed that the bullets that killed the students were fired from your guns. Five students escaped injury in the shooting, and have given statements to the police identifying you as the shooter."

I pursed my lips and again nodded my head slightly. None of this was surprising. "Maybe I should just plead guilty. I mean, I did shoot my students. I deserve to be punished. I am ready to take responsibility for my actions. What is the likely sentence for a crime like this?"

"For multiple murders, life imprisonment. But let's not get ahead of ourselves just yet." Stanton grabbed a legal pad from his briefcase, on which he had written a series of questions. "I need to explore what type of defense we can mount. I don't suppose that any of your students had threatened you prior to this incident?"

"No."

"Were you romantically involved with any of them, and maybe got jilted?"

"No."

"Had any of the students angered you in any way?"

I thought about that for a moment. I had gotten poor to mediocre student reviews for my teaching of the

Shakespeare course last semester, but none of my current students had been in that class. "No," I responded.

"Do you have a drinking problem?"

"I don't think so. I mean, I drink, but usually not to excess."

"Had you been drinking the night before the incident?"

"I had some wine with dinner, I think."

"How much?"

"I don't really remember. But probably only a glass or two."

"Had you been drinking the morning of the shooting?"

"Of course not. My class starts at 10:00 a.m."

"Just asking. Do you use drugs?"

"No."

"Have you ever been seen by a psychiatrist?"

"Only a couple's therapist right before my divorce."

"Was it someone here in town?"

"Yes. Dr. Robert Mistrum."

"Did Dr. Mistrum indicate to you that you were suffering from any emotional or mental instability?"

"He said that I was an emotionally closed off person, in part because of the way I was brought up by my parents. He said that made it hard for me to express my emotions. He also suspected that I had not been nursed by my mother, which caused me to have a breast fetish. My ex-wife had big boobs, which is why Dr. Mistrum thought I was attracted to her. Really, it was all nonsense."

"Was the divorce amicable? Will your ex-wife be a potential character witness for you?"

"Hardly. She lives in France now. There's no way she'd ever voluntarily come back here to help me, even if she was so inclined, which she wouldn't be."

"Okay. I am just exploring all possible avenues. Have you ever been hospitalized for any extended period for any reason?"

"I spent sometime in the hospital here in Hanover when I was in college, recovering from injuries I suffered in a car accident."

Scranton scribbled notes on his legal pad, and sat quietly for a moment. "Well, that rules out some possible defenses, like self-defense or a crime of passion. I normally don't ask my clients whether they committed the crime, because I don't want that to influence my efforts on their behalf. But in this case, Professor, you know and I know that you shot those students. And what I'm trying to figure out is why did you do it?"

That was the very question that I wanted to have answered. "I honestly don't know."

"You don't know? What do you mean you don't know?"

"I don't know why I did it. I really don't. When I opened my briefcase and saw the two guns, I just picked them up and started shooting. I don't know why."

"Why did you buy the guns in the first place?"

"I don't know. I don't really even remember buying them."

"Well, do you remember thinking about shooting your students?"

"No. I finished preparing the mid-term exam the night before. Why would I do that if I was intending to kill all my students?"

"Do you remember putting the guns in your briefcase?"

"Not really. I can't think of any reason as to why I would do that. But I can't think of any reason why I would buy the guns, either, and don't remember doing so."

"Are you having any trouble remembering any other events during the weeks leading up to the mid-term exam?"

"I remember finishing up the mid-term exam the night before, but don't have a specific recollection of much else from the week or even the month before the shooting."

Stanton was quiet again, staring at me intensely. I believe he was trying to judge whether I was telling him the truth. He drew in a long breath, and slowly exhaled, making a slight whistling sound through the gap between his front teeth. "Professor, about the only defense that is coming to my mind is an insanity defense."

"I don't think that I am insane. I mean, I don't think that I am Napoleon. My pants are on correctly, and my fly closed. I don't see dragons flying about, and don't hear voices. I know that I shot those students, and I know that it was wrong to do so. I don't see how I can claim to be insane."

"I understand your reaction, but hear me out. Most states have a very strict definition of what constitutes insanity, requiring that, as a result of a severe mental disease or defect, the defendant was unable to appreciate the nature and quality or wrongfulness of his act. Only certain types of mental defects count. For example, getting drunk or high doesn't cut it. Under that definition, even if you were suffering from a qualifying mental affliction, but you still knew that shooting people was wrong, you couldn't really sustain the insanity defense."

"Then obviously, I don't qualify for an insanity defense."

"Not so fast, Professor. New Hampshire doesn't use that definition. It is the only state that uses what's called the Durham Product Test, which requires the defense to prove that the defendant committed a crime as a result of a mental disease or defect, and it's up to the jury to decide what constitutes a mental disease or defect. Under the New

Hampshire test, the jury can basically do what it wants, instead of being bound by a strict definition of mental illness. And most people would think that almost by definition, a person who guns down fifteen people for no apparent reason is nuts, no insult intended."

"It sounds to me like the New Hampshire rule is easier to satisfy than the rule followed in other places. Is that right?"

"Well, in theory, I would agree that not being hemmed in by a strict definition of mental disease or defect gives a defendant more running room. I mean, theoretically, even self-induced drunkenness could qualify. But I have to tell you, no defendant tried for murder in New Hampshire has ever successfully been acquitted by reason of insanity. Ever."

"But why is that? I would think that giving the jury such latitude would result in more acquittals."

"Remember that normally the jury will first hear, as part of the prosecution's case, all the sordid details of the murder — and that by pleading the insanity defense, the defendant admits he committed the murders. That tends to inflame the jury against the defendant. So while it's true that the jury has more discretion, unless the defendant is somehow sympathetic, the jury doesn't choose to exercise that discretion in the defendant's favor. Very few murders claiming insanity are sympathetic. I mean if you have a wife who was habitually beaten by her husband, and finally lashed back, you might have a sympathetic defendant. But your circumstances don't fit that fact pattern."

"Mr. Stanton, do you think I have a viable insanity defense under the New Hampshire rule."

Mr. Stanton was quiet again, lost in thought for several minutes. "Maybe. I'm thinking right now that the very fact that you don't know why you shot those students may be the basis of our insanity defense. Of course, we'll have to find a psychiatrist to agree with that and agree to testify as an expert on your behalf. But that shouldn't be too difficult."

"Why not?"

"You can almost always find an expert who will testify as to anything, as long as he's paid. If you plead not guilty by reason of insanity, the State will also have the right to have you examined by a physiatrist. But I think once I teach you the ropes, you'll be able to handle the State's psychiatrist. So getting back to tomorrow, do you want to enter a plea of guilty, not guilty, or not guilty by reason of insanity?"

"What's the difference?"

"Well, obviously if you plead guilty, the only thing left for the court to do will be to determine your sentence, which as I said, would almost certainly be life imprisonment. If you plead not guilty, then we go to trial, but I don't know what kind of defense we could realistically mount. If we're going to pursue an insanity defense, we have to give the State notice of that defense at the earliest opportunity, and then you will have to be examined by a psychiatrist for both the defense and prosecution. There are also other consequences. If you are found not guilty by reason of insanity, you are not set free, but rather sent to the State mental hospital until a judge determines that you are no longer a threat to the community."

I pondered this for a minute. Tim told me that I needed to accept responsibility for this terrible event. That meant pleading guilty. But pleading guilty also probably meant never finding out why this all happened. I desperately needed to know that.

"If I plead guilty, will it be possible for me to get psychiatric treatment to try to find out why I did this?"

"The state prison system does have doctors and psychiatrists on staff, but as you might imagine, there's a long line of prisoners in need of their help. But yes, you'd be able to receive treatment while in prison."

"Well, if the sentence that I would receive is life imprisonment, then I guess I am prepared to plead guilty."

"Professor, I hate to see you throw in the towel so quickly. If you plead not guilty by reason of insanity, then at least you'll get a chance to be examined by a psychiatrist to see if you really do have a mental illness. If it turns out that after the examination the insanity defense is not viable, you could always change your plea to guilty at that time. But at least the insanity plea would give us a fighting chance to win the case."

"No offense, Mr. Stanton, but this isn't about winning from my perspective. And if I can get access to professional counseling in prison, I am prepared to accept my punishment."

Mr. Stanton frowned slightly, but only for a moment. "Then here is what will happen. I will talk with the prosecutor before the arraignment to work out a plea deal for a life sentence in return for a guilty plea. The judge will have the indictment specifying the charges. We will get a copy of it tomorrow morning before the hearing. He will ask if we waive reading of the indictment, and we will. Then he will ask for your plea. I will tell the judge about the plea deal and the recommended life sentence. The judge will then ask you if you understand the plea arrangement, and understand that by doing this you are waiving your right to a trial. You should make it clear to the judge that you do understand, and that you are doing the deal of your own free will. Once he is satisfied that you understand the arrangement, the judge accepts the plea and schedules another hearing in a week or so for formal sentencing. Do you have any questions?"

"Why can't the judge just sentence me at the arraignment?"

"He needs to get some additional information about your personal history and any recommendations from the prosecution and defense. In your case, it will be essentially a formality because a life sentence is the maximum sentence available for murder. I suppose he could impose fifteen life sentences to be served consecutively, but it really won't matter. Your sentence will be life without possibility of parole. That will be the deal. You will spend the rest of your life in prison. Period. You do understand that, right?"

I stared down at my hands, and said in a small, trembling voice: "It's what I deserve. Yes, I understand."

"Okay then. I will take care of everything. One more thing: you shouldn't talk to anyone about the shootings or the charges. Have you spoken to anyone?"

"Chief Dodds asked me some background questions, but wouldn't let me talk about the shootings at all. I also met with my friend, Father Tim Davidson this afternoon."

"Who is this Father Davidson?"

"Probably my best friend in the world. He lives in Rutland, Vermont."

"Is he your priest?"

"I am not much of a church goer. So not really."

"Well, from now on, you can't talk to him about the shooting or the case unless you and he can swear that he is your spiritual advisor. Communications between a priest and his spiritual advisee are privileged under New Hampshire law, and he can't be forced to testify about what you tell him. Otherwise, if he is just visiting you as your friend, he could be forced to testify about everything you say to him. Understand?"

"But if I am pleading guilty, what difference does it make?"

"Look, Professor, in this business nothing is a sure thing, so I try to take as much risk out of the equation as possible. Just do like I tell you until we have this all put to bed, okay?"

"Sure, Mr. Stanton. I understand."

I reached across the table and shook Mr. Stanton's hand. I had a strange sense of relief, having made the decision to plead guilty and accept my punishment. I knew it would make Tim happy. It was difficult to really envision what spending the rest of my life in prison would entail, but at a minimum, it would give me time, and perhaps access to professional help, to try to figure out why I had shot my students.

Chapter 4

The next morning I was transported in a Hanover police car to the courthouse in West Lebanon. I sat handcuffed in the back seat between two officers. As we drove by the front of the courthouse, I could see a fairly large crowd of television vans from various networks was waiting for me, with a forest of antenna stretching up to the sky. Dozens of people, presumably reporters, milled about. But my police car drove passed the assembled throng, turned the corner and took me through a side entrance to the courthouse. Once inside the courthouse, the officers took me to a holding cell adjacent to the courtroom. At the appointed time, a deputy led me into the courtroom.

It was not what I expected. Three of the walls were painted a blizzard white. The judge's bench was on a raised dais at the back of the courtroom. The wall behind the bench was covered from floor to ceiling with highly polished wood paneling that glistened in the morning light. At either end of the back wall, a State of New Hampshire flag and a United States flag stood securely in their stanchions. Two rectangular wooden tables with scarred surfaces were situated some fifteen feet from the judge's alter, and parallel to it, so that the lawyers sitting at those tables were directly facing the judge.

Another fifteen feet back was a railing with a hinged gate that separated the working courtroom space from the peanut gallery and looked like a communion rail from an Episcopal church. The benches in the audience section of the courtroom looked like pews and were packed with people. As I glanced over in their direction, I saw the faces of the mothers and fathers of my dead students glaring at me with abject hatred. I looked away quickly. I did not blame them. I also saw Tim sitting in the front row on the aisle, dressed in his black priest's suit. This time, he was wearing his white priest's collar, which seemed to shine like the beacon in a New England lighthouse. At least there was one friendly face in the courtroom.

Mr. Stanton was seated at one of the counsel tables. The officers led me there and un-handcuffed me. I sat next to Mr. Stanton. The deputies pulled up chairs directly behind me, ready to pounce should I make any menacing move. Mr. Stanton shook my hand. He leaned over and whispered in my ear: "There's been a surprise."

"What?" I whispered in return.

"It's the indictment. In addition to the fifteen charges of murder and five charges for aggravated battery and attempted murder, the State has charged you with kidnapping."

"Kidnapping? What are they talking about?"

"Technically kidnapping includes forcibly restraining someone from leaving a confined area. They are claiming that for the few moments after you drew the pistols and began shooting, your students were technically kidnapped."

"That's silly. It was only a matter of seconds. Why would they bother with that when they have the murder charges?"

"They want to up the ante. If they can prevail on the kidnapping charges as well as the murder charge, it becomes what is called capital murder. Only persons convicted of capital murder can receive the death penalty."

This did up the ante. I had been prepared to be punished for what I did, but not executed. "So am I to assume that the plea deal is off?"

"Yes, unless you want to agree to an execution."

I was not going to agree to my own execution. That left only two alternatives: not guilty, or not guilty by reason of insanity. If I pleaded not guilty by reason of insanity, two psychiatrists would examine me, according to what Mr. Stanton had told me. Surely one of them would help me understand why I committed these crimes. In any

event, as Mr. Stanton had pointed out, there was a certain
logical appeal to the insanity defense because what I had
done sure seemed crazy. I knew that Tim felt that why I
committed the crimes was irrelevant, and that I had
promised him that I would talk with him before agreeing to
try to present a defense to the charges. But even Tim
wouldn't expect me to just accept the death penalty. And
there was really no time to consult with Tim at this point in
any event.

"I think I want to plead not guilty by reason of
insanity."

"Then this is what will happen. The judge will ask
if we waive a reading of the indictment, and I will say yes.
Then he will ask for your plea. You have to stand and say
'not guilty by reason of insanity.' The judge will then set a
schedule for the case, and set a trial date. I will ask that
you be set free on bail, but frankly I doubt that will happen.
And then you will be held in some jail to await trial. Any
questions?"

"How long will I have to wait for trial?"

"Six months wouldn't be unusual."

"Is it possible to get a quicker trial date?"

"We will need time to develop your defense and
have you meet with a psychiatrist of our choosing, and the
prosecution will also need time to have you examined and
develop its case."

"I want to go to trial as quickly as possible. Like in
thirty to sixty days. Can you do that?"

Mr. Stanton thought for a moment. "Yes. We'll
have to get right to work to find a shrink to examine you.
But I know of some potential candidates who are
sufficiently flexible in their views to serve our purposes.
Yes, it's possible."

"Then let's do it."

"I'll tell the judge that. But ultimately, it's up to the
court to decide."

"Okay, just do your best. I am anxious to get this resolved."

Our whispered conference was abruptly interrupted when the bailiff entered the courtroom from a door behind the judge's bench and said in a loud voice: "All rise! This session of the New Hampshire District Court, Second District, is now in session. Draw near and you will be heard. The Honorable Judge Cyrus Winston presiding." During the bailiff's speech, the judge himself had entered the room, ascended some steps leading up to the bench, and stood before his chair. The bailiff continued: "Be seated and come to order. State versus Dan Jackson."

Judge Winston was so short and slight that his over-sized chair virtually engulfed him as he sat down. Although lacking in physical stature, his presence exuded power and wisdom. In his judicial robes, he looked like a wizard, absent the pointy hat, ready to administer legal spells. He had a solemn and business-like demeanor. In a loud, squeaky voice, Judge Winston croaked: "Is the prosecution ready?"

A deep baritone voice from my left spoke: "Carl Johnson for the State is present and ready."

This was the prosecutor who would be handling my case. I glanced over at him. He was about six foot two with an athletic build, had shiny, neatly coiffed dark hair and a pronounced, square jaw. He was dressed in a neatly tailored navy blue suit, white button-down shirt and a solid blue tie. He briefly looked over at Mr. Stanton with a sneer on his face.

Mr. Stanton rose to his feet. "Gus Stanton for the defendant is present and ready."

Judge Winston then took over. "All right, we are here this morning for the defendant's arraignment. The defendant has been charged with fifteen counts of murder in the first degree, five counts of aggravated battery, five counts of attempted murder in the first degree, and twenty-

five counts of kidnapping. Has the defendant been
provided with a copy of the indictment?"

Mr. Stanton responded, "We have Your Honor.
And the defendant waives formal reading of the
indictment."

"Very well, Mr. Stanton. Is the defendant ready to
plead to the indictment?"

"He is, Your Honor."

Mr. Stanton pulled at my elbow and I stood.

"How do you plead, Mr. Jackson?"

In a surprisingly calm, firm voice, I said "Not guilty
by reason of insanity, Your Honor."

A buzz went through the crowded courtroom. I
could hear comments like "Oh come on!" and "Bullshit!"
being blurted out. I glanced over at the prosecutor, who sat
silently with a small smirk on his face, shaking his head. I
stole a glance back at Tim, who had a deep frown on his
face, his arms folded across his huge chest. Judge Winston
struck his gavel on the bench three times. He bellowed:
"Order in the courtroom! I will have order!." The room
fell quiet.

"The next order of business is the question of bail.
Mr. Johnson, what is the State's position?"

The prosecutor rose to his feet. "Your Honor, in
light of the horrific nature and extent of this crime and the
potential that the death penalty could induce the defendant
to flee, the State believes that bail should be denied.
Moreover, in light of the insanity plea, there is the public
safety to consider. The State believes that the defendant
should be bound over to the state prison in Concord until
trial."

"Mr. Stanton, what says the defense?"

"Your Honor, the defense recognizes the
seriousness of the charges, but believes that in view of the
defendant's ties to the area and his lack of prior criminal
record, there is no reason to believe that he is a flight risk,

and that any such risk can be ameliorated by a bond in an appropriate amount."

As Mr. Stanton had predicted, Judge Winston wasn't buying it. Judge Winston squinted down at Mr. Stanton, and then at me. "The Court agrees with the State, and for the reasons set forth by Mr. Johnson, bail will be denied, and the defendant will be bound over to the men's state prison facility in Concord, New Hampshire until trial. Are the State and defense ready to discuss scheduling?"

Mr. Stanton rose again: "The defense is ready, Your Honor. We would request an early trial date. We do not anticipate much, if any, motion practice. We recognize that the State will have the right to have Mr. Jackson examined by a psychiatrist, and we are hopeful that can be accomplished with dispatch. We would like a trial date within 30-60 days."

A gasp arose from the crowd, and again Judge Winston pounded his gavel for silence. The prosecutor rose: "Your Honor, I think 30 days is a bit ambitious, but we will be happy to accommodate the defense request for a trial date sixty days out."

Judge Winston looked down at the calendar on the bench. "Very well. Trial is set for January 5. The state will disclose all evidence and witnesses, including expert witness reports, by December 1. Any motions challenging evidence or witnesses will be filed by December 15, with oppositions by December 30. Motions will be argued on January 5 starting at 9:00 a.m. sharp, and we will begin picking a jury immediately upon conclusion of the hearing on the motions. Have a good day."

With that, the bailiff cried out "All rise," and Judge Winston strutted from the courtroom. Mr. Stanton turned to me and leaned closer. "I will start talking to some psychiatrists we might want to use as an expert. I will try to pick one during the next few days, and then arrange a meeting between the three of us. I am actually glad that they will be taking you down to Concord to be held before trial; it's an easier drive from Boston. So I'll be in touch. Until then, don't talk with anyone else but me about this case, unless your priest friend becomes your spiritual advisor."

"Tim is actualy here in the courtroom. Would it be possible for me to speak with him briefly before I am taken away?"

Mr. Stanton motioned to one of the officers who came over to counsel table. He whispered something in the officer's ear, and then pointed over towards where Tim was seated. The officer nodded his head, went over to Tim, whispered in his ear and then led him up to counsel table. I shook Tim's hand and in a low voice said: "Look, this didn't go exactly as I had planned. I was going to plead guilty until they charged me with capital murder which is punishable by death. I can't plead guilty to that. The insanity defense will give me some time to try to figure out why I did this, and maybe get me psychiatric help. Don't be mad at me."

Tim smiled slightly. "I understand. But I hope you understand that just because you raise an insanity defense doesn't mean that you will avoid facing the death penalty if you lose. I'm worried that your lawyer is unduly influencing your decisions. I will come to visit you in Concord in a day or so, when I have more information on your Mr. Stanton."

"Sure. I'll look forward to it. And thanks, Tim. I need you more now than ever."

I was handcuffed and led away. Officers put me into a State Police car for the trip to my new home in the men's state prison facility at Concord. On the trip, I began wondering whether the psychiatrist Mr. Stanton hired would be able to uncover why I had committed these crimes. If the process of preparing my insanity defense could resolve that question, I would be satisfied, even if, as

Tim had ominously predicted, the defense was ultimately unsuccessful.

Chapter 5

My new "home" at the men's state prison in Concord was not much different than the Hanover police station, only a little smaller. It was an eight foot by ten foot rectangle. The cement walls were painted a winter white. There was a bed bolted to the floor with a thin plastic-covered mattress, a stainless steel toilet with no seat, a small stainless steel table bolted to the wall, and a chair. A single light bulb in the ceiling, covered with mesh wire, was the only illumination. When the guards sounded lights out at 10:00 p.m. each night, that one light went out and plunged the cell into total darkness. The lights went back on at 6:00 a.m. every morning.

Although most prisoners were two to a cell, I had been placed in isolation. The guards told me that it was for my own protection. The prison population had its own definition of Dante's Circles of Hell, and mass murderers, particularly of children or teenagers, were in the inner circle, along with child molesters. I would not be safe in the general prison population, because one of the inmates in a "higher" circle — like a rapist, wife murderer, or bank robber — might well feel that I deserved a shiv in my gut. So I had no roommate, ate in my cell, and had private exercise time of one hour a day.

Today, however, the routine would be altered. Mr. Stanton and the psychiatrist he had retained to serve as an expert witness for my defense were scheduled to visit me. At the appointed time, the guard led me to the interview room. When I entered the room, I saw Mr. Stanton and another elderly gentleman sitting next to him. Mr. Stanton rose, shook my hand and said "Dan, I would like you to meet Dr. Albert Van DeMere. He is the expert psychiatrist that I have retained to help us develop an insanity defense." Dr. Van DeMere rose from his chair as if he was unfolding himself. He was tall, at least six foot four. His clothes hung on his skeletal frame. He had a bald head, large sad eyes and wore a monocle. He reminded me of Mr. Peanut, and, if anything, appeared to be much older than even Mr. Stanton. I shook Dr. Van DeMere's boney hand.

We all sat down, and Mr. Stanton began shuffling some papers. He looked up and started: "I have been discussing the facts of the case as I know them thus far with Dr. Van DeMere and explaining to him what we had discussed as the basis of an insanity defense — namely that you don't know why the shootings occurred. Dr. Van DeMere thinks that there may be a good psychiatric basis for that defense, but would like to ask you some questions to explore that a bit further. Dr. Van DeMere?"

"Professor Jackson, over the course of my career, I have made an intense study of what are called 'disassociative disorders.' Disassociation is the mind's reaction to a stressful or traumatic event, and impairs the normal state of awareness. It can limit or alter one's sense of identity, memory or consciousness."

"I am not sure that I understand what you are talking about."

"Well, Professor let me give you some examples. There is disassociative amnesia, where one is unable to recall important personal information. It is commonally encountered in hospital emergency rooms and is usually caused by a single, stressful event, like a car accident. Forgotten details might include one's actions immediately before the stress-producing event. Then there is dissociative fuge, which usually involves the creation of a new, either partial or complete, identity to replace the personal details that are lost in response to some traumatic event. A person with this form of dissociative disorder remains alert and oriented, but will be unconnected to his former identity, and think that he is someone else. There is also dissociative identity disorder, sometimes called multiple personality disorder. This form of the disorder is believed to be caused by severe trauma, and results in distinct, coherent identities existing within one individual that are able to assume control of the person's behavior and thought."

"I don't think that any of those describe my situation at all."

"Quite so, Professor. But there is another form of dissociation that is called a 'Depersonalization disorder.' It is a syndrome where the patient has persistent or recurrent feelings of being disconnected from his physicality, feeling as though he is not completely occupying his body, or feeling detached from his own thoughts or emotions. Some patients describe it as a difficulty relating oneself to reality and the environment, as though one is in a dream. Many mental conditions that have heretofore been categorized as schizophrenia or bipolar disorders I believe are better understood as various forms of depersonalization disorder, and better treated from that perspective."

This all sounded like a bunch of pyscho-gobleliguke to me, much like the junk that I'd heard from the marriage counselor before my divorce. "Can I ask you a few questions, Dr. Van DeMere?"

"Yes."

"You mentioned that you've studied this syndrome over the course of your career. I was wondering if you would mind telling me a little bit about your medical background and training."

"Certainly. I attended the University of West Virginia, were I was a pre-med major. I then got my medical degree from the American Caribbean Medical School. I did my residency work in psychiatric medicine in Mobile, Alabama, and ultimately developed my own private psychiatric practice in Boston. I was actively engaged in the practice for about forty years, and retired about three years ago. Now, I do an occasional engagement as an expert witness or consultant."

I was not particularly impressed by Dr. Van DeMere's credentials, but I was willing to assume at the moment that he was the best that Mr. Stanton could get. After all, Mr. Stanton hadn't exactly been my first choice, either. I continued:

"What do you charge to act as an expert witness?"

"I charge two hundred dollars an hour for non-courtroom time, and two hundred fifty dollars an hour for in-court testimony."

That was five hundred dollars an hour for this little audience with Mr. Stanton and the good doctor! I better move this along. "Based upon what you've been told, do you think that I have this 'depersonalization disorder?'?"

"I, of course, cannot make a definitive diagnosis without examining you further, but I believe that it might possibly explain why you don't know the reason for the shootings. Your mind has created a detached reality where the reason for your conduct is not available to you. You are merely an observer of your conduct, without an ability to understand what motivates it. Think of your mind as a computer with an almost infinite set of file folders full of thoughts, learning and memories. A person with depersonalization disorder only has access to a certain set of folders in his mind that make up his detached reality."

"But it wouldn't explain why I shot those students, would it? It would only explain why I don't know what motivated me to kill them?"

"Well, that's right, but based upon what Mr. Stanton has told me . . . ."

Mr. Stanton interrupted Dr. Van DeMere. "Look, Professor, at this point knowing why you did it probably won't help us get you off. In a criminal case, motive is usually important to the prosecution when it is trying to put together a circumstantial case, not necessarily to the defense."

"I don't understand what you mean."

"In a lot of cases, the prosecution may have a dead body, but no direct evidence linking the defendant to the crime. Then the prosecutor is forced to use what is called circumstantial evidence — evidence that tends to suggest the defendant did it, but isn't like an eyewitness saying: 'He did it.'"

"I'm not sure I understand."

"Let me give you an example. Let's say that you wanted to prove that I had been in a hotel swimming pool. You didn't have any eyewitnesses, but you had wet footprints leading from the pool to my hotel room, and a wet bathing suit that belonged to me that had been found in my hotel room. Those wet footprints and wet bathing suit are circumstantial evidence that I was in the hotel swimming pool. Understand?"

"I think so."

"Well, in a murder case, when the prosecution tries to prove a circumstantial case, it generally relies upon evidence of two types: motive and opportunity.   The prosecutor tries to prove that the defendant had a motive to commit the crime and the opportunity to do it, and leaves it to the jury to connect the dots. But for our defense of this case, motive is not helpful. If we knew why you shot those students, it might undermine our insanity defense that is premised on the fact that you don't know why you did it."

"But I would like to find out why I did it."

"Professor, if we are successful in sustaining this defense, you'll have plenty of time with the State shrinks at the State mental hospital to explore that to your heart's content. But right now, we have to focus on a defense that may save your life, and it isn't aided by finding out why you shot those kids. Okay?"

"But is my ignorance of why I did it a real defense?"

"As I explained to you previously, under New Hampshire's unique standard for insanity, it could be. In any event, it's all we got, so we don't have much choice. Forget about finding out why. In this case, ignorance is bliss."

This was a disappointing turn of affairs, but I supposed Mr. Stanton knew what he was doing. I turned to Dr. Van DeMere. "What do you need to know to decide whether I have this disorder?"

"Well, I would like to ask you some questions to see if the diagnosis fits."

"Fire away."

"Mr. Stanton tells me that you don't have any recollection of planning to shoot the students, is that right?"

"Correct."

"And you don't recall why you purchased the guns?"

"No. I don't even have a clear recollection of purchasing the guns, but I must have."

"When you did the shooting, did you have the feeling that you were watching yourself from outside your body?"

I thought for a moment. "Yes, I have to say that is what it felt like. I had the feeling that I was watching a movie of myself."

"Did you have any emotional response to the shootings?"

"I was horrified as I watched my hands reach into the briefcase and withdraw those guns. I felt incredible frustration that I couldn't control my hands and stop my fingers from pulling those triggers. And I guess I felt disbelief that I could do such a thing. It just didn't make any sense."

"Good. These are all classic symptoms of depersonalization disorder. Now, the next step. The disorder is normally associated with some severe emotional trauma. In the past six months or so, have you had any emotional crisis?"

"You don't want to go all the way back to my childhood to see if I was a bed-wetter?"

"Professor, please.   You may have a very low regard for my profession, but try to take this seriously."

"Sorry, doctor. No offense intended."

"There is a method to my madness, Professor. According to the police reports, and Mr. Stanton's investigation to date, you have never had any sort of suggestion of mental illness, or any sort of abnormal behavior prior to the shootings. So there is no need to delve into the distant past. If you had suffered some traumatic event in your distant past sufficient to cause the disorder, it would have manifested itself well before now, I believe. What I am interested in is the near term. Have you had any emotional trauma in the last six months?"

"I went through a messy divorce this year that was pretty traumatic for me."

"How long had you been married?"

"Twenty-five years. We had been high school sweethearts, and got married after my first year in grad school. So we were together for almost thirty years."

"Was it you or your ex-wife who wanted the divorce?"

"My ex-wife."

"What is your ex-wife's name?"

"Nancy."

"Did Nancy tell you why she wanted a divorce?"

I sat back in my chair for a moment and stared at the ceiling, gathering my thoughts. Although it had been almost ten months ago, I remembered that night like it was yesterday. Nancy and I were eating dinner at the kitchen table in my house in Hanover. Nancy lived in our house in Boston where she worked, and had come up to spend the weekend with me. I got up from the table to see if she wanted any more wine, but Nancy put her hand over the glass, motioning that she wanted no more. As I returned to my seat, Nancy said "Dan, I have something to tell you. I know it is going to upset you." I asked what it was. She took a deep breath and continued: "I have been having an affair with someone else for a long time. I have fallen in love with that person. Although I do love you, I am not in love with you anymore. I want to end our marriage." It was as if someone had punched me in the stomach. I couldn't breathe. The room started to spin around me. I clutched the sides of the table with both hands, afraid I might topple over. "Can I ask who it is?" Nancy met my gaze, and then looked away. "It's Beth."

Beth? That was unbelievable. I had first met Beth back in college. She had been Nancy's freshman year roommate at Holy Cross, a school Nancy had chosen so that she could be close to me at Dartmouth. Beth was, to my way of thinking, not a very attractive looking woman. She was short and a little on the stocky side. She carried the extra weight in her boobs and her ass, though, so she was somewhat curvaceous. She had short, muddy-colored hair, and never wore make-up. She had no sense of humor or "sparkle" about her, as far as I could see. By contrast, Nancy was a tall, blond-haired beauty with a light-the-world-on-fire personality.

I would come down to Holy Cross to spend the weekend several times during the semester, and Beth would obligingly find other quarters so that Nancy and I could sleep together. Beth never seemed to have a date, though, and often hung out with us. After college, Beth got a graduate degree in French literature from Harvard, and moved to Paris to teach at the Sorbonne. She had married a man who also taught at the Sorbonne about fifteen years ago, which to my mind proved the adage that there was a lid for every pot. However, the marriage only lasted for four years.

Nancy and Beth had stayed in touch over the years, primarily by mail and telephone. Beth would drop in for a

short visit on occasion when she was in the States, and
stayed with us a few times. In the last ten years or so,
Nancy and Beth had started going on vacations together.
There was a trip to South America, where Beth was
speaking at some conference, a skiing trip in the Alps for
another conference, and a hiking safari in Africa. I never
thought anything about it. I didn't like hiking or skiing,
and was sort of relieved that Nancy had someone else to go
with. It never occurred to me that Nancy and Beth were
lovers.

Surprisingly, I maintained my cool that night. I
remember asking how long the affair had been going on.
Nancy explained that she and Beth had always had an
attraction to each other, and had done some sexual
experimentation together in college, but had set it aside.
On one of Beth's visits to our home about a decade ago,
while I was at school teaching, Beth had confided to Nancy
that she still had feelings for Nancy. Nancy told Beth that
she was feeling alone and empty in our marriage,
something she had never said to me. Beth had reached over
and begun gently stroking Nancy's face, and then caressing
her breasts. According to Nancy, one thing lead to another,
and they were in bed together — in my bed together. It was
after that encounter that the vacations started, and
unbeknownst to me, almost weekly phone calls.

From my perspective, Nancy wasn't really a
lesbian. At worst, she was bi-sexual, which meant that I
was not categorically eliminated as a potential lover. I was
also surprised to find that, notwithstanding the shock of
hearing her confession of infidelity, I still loved her, and
didn't want to lose her. I remember asking her if there was
anything that we could do to save the marriage, but she
shook her head no and looked away. I asked her if she
would at least come to a marriage counselor with me, and
eventually she said that she would, I think out of pity for
me.

The marriage counseling was a disaster and sealed my fate. Dr. Mistrum, the marriage counselor, seemed like a caricature of a shrink. He was a fat little man, had a receding hair line and a Freud-like goatee. He always seemed to be siding with Nancy, suggesting that she had to be "true to her feelings." But what about my feelings? My desire to save the marriage was characterized by Dr. Mistrum as "controlling" and "limiting." He focused his questioning of me almost entirely on my parents and my upbringing, indicating he found me "emotionally closed" and unable to show my feelings. Each session ended with Nancy in tears and me fuming. After a month of those fruitless sessions, I threw in the towel, hired a lawyer and went through with the divorce. It became final in September, and Nancy moved to France to be with Beth.

My reminiscing was interrupted by Dr. Van DeMere. "Professor, are you still with us?"

"Oh, yes. Sorry. Just lost in thought for a moment. What was your question again?"

"Did Nancy tell you why she wanted the divorce?"

"It turns out that she had been having an affair with a woman lover named Beth for the last decade. She wanted out of the marriage to be with her."

Dr. Van DeMere's eyebrows arched noticeably. "Did you have any inkling that Nancy was a lesbian?"

"I don't think she was. I mean, she always seemed to enjoy sex with me."

Scenes from our sexual experiences shot through my mind to buttress my response. Initially, our sexual encounters were limited to lengthy making-out sessions on the couch in Nancy's parents' house that sometimes led to mutual undressing and heavy petting. It wasn't until college that we finally went all the way. After that, we sort of plodded along, sticking primarily to the missionary position. I had assumed the sex was satisfying to her. She never complained. She made all the right noises at the right times.

Dr. Van DeMere continued: "If your sex life was satisfying, why do you think that Nancy left you for another woman?"

That was a question that I had asked myself a hundred times. Dr. Mistrum had suggested that it was because I was unable to provide Nancy with the emotional intimacy she required. Without such emotional intimacy, he admonished, sex was just a physical response. With such emotional intimacy, sex became a bonding, satisfying expression of love. Again, my parents were to blame in Dr. Mistrum's eyes. "I am not really sure. She obviously found something she needed in that other relationship that I did not provide."

"In a normal week, how often would you hold hands with Nancy?"

I thought back. We had stopped holding hands back in college. "We weren't really the hand-holding type."

"What about kissing. How often did you kiss her?"

"Well, thinking back on it, we really didn't kiss that often. I don't think she liked the way I kissed, so we just stopped doing that."

"Did you and Nancy argue often?"

"No, almost never."

Dr. Van DeMere made a few more notes. "So how did the divorce make you feel?"

"Shitty. I was devastated. Confused. Hurt. Angry. The sense of betrayal was overwhelming. Someone with whom I had spent almost half of my life suddenly turns out be a stranger and leaves me, for another woman no less. It was humiliating."

"Why humiliating?"

I exploded: "Beth didn't even have a dick and she apparently could fuck better than I could."

Dr. Van DeMere nodded his head. "Did you have any desire to get revenge for Nancy's unfaithfulness?"

"I don't know what you mean."

"Well, did you think about hurting Nancy or Beth?"

"You mean physically? Like hitting them or something?"

"Yes."

"No. I'm not a violent person by nature."

Again Dr. Van DeMere arched his eyebrows. "Perhaps not normally, but recent events seem to indicate that you can be quite violent."

I sat there for a minute, actually angry. How dare he accuse me of being violent? But in the next moment, I had to admit Dr. Van DeMere had a point. A man who shoots twenty people is pretty damn violent. I tried to think back to the shooting. Did I shoot those students because I was angry at Nancy? I wasn't thinking of Nancy that morning, at least I don't remember specifically thinking of her. But it was true that I thought about her a lot, wondering what she and Beth were doing in France, and wondering if there was anything I could have done differently to have avoided losing her. Still, it makes no sense that I would lash out at my students because I was mad at Nancy. She was in Paris with Beth. Nothing I did here could affect any revenge on her there.

"I'm sorry Dr. Van DeMere, but it doesn't seem likely to me that I killed those students to get even with Nancy."

"I agree with you, Professor. I am not suggesting that your divorce caused you to shoot those students; just that the divorce was emotionally traumatizing enough to cause a depersonalization disorder that essentially detached your conscious self from your body. Your body carried out the crime, directed in some part by your unconscious or subconscious mind. But your true self — the rational person who is Professor Jackson — was merely along for the ride, powerless to either understand why your body was behaving as such, or able to stop it. I am relatively satisfied that is, in fact, the case."

"So if I understand you correctly, Dr. Van DeMere, that would suggest that I had some unconscious or subconscious reason for shooting my students, right?"

"Probably."

"That's the part that I want to find out. What was that reason that compelled me to kill my students? How do I find that out?"

"Well, Professor. That is beyond the assignment that Mr. Stanton has given me. If we are successful in this defense, you can explore that later with the prison doctors. But let's move on, because there is another area I want to explore with you to remove it as an impediment to my diagnosis. Mr. Stanton has obtained copies of the reviews of your courses completed by your students for the last two years. I have reviewed them, and I suspect that the State will argue that you killed those students because you were angry about the mediocre student reviews you received. What do you say to that?"

"I think that is nonsense. I wasn't mad at my students or any of my former students either. I was teaching a required freshman English course. The entire freshman class has to take it. They had never been in a class with me before, so they had never had the chance to give me any kind of review — good, bad or indifferent."

"But you were aware, weren't you, that your prior students had not given you high marks on your teaching?"

"Yes, I had read the student reviews each year when they came out. But there were plenty of professors who got worse comments than I did. For the most part, my students acknowledged that they learned the material and that the course was worth taking. They just didn't like my teaching style — not flamboyant or entertaining enough — and in some instances, they didn't like the fact that I did not grade on the curve."

"How did that make you feel?"

"That didn't bother me. If I had wanted to be a stand-up comic, I would have not chosen teaching and scholarship as a profession. And as far as I was concerned, I gave students the grades they earned"

"Had you received similar student reviews at the other colleges you taught at?"

"Basically. The comments were pretty consistent: smart, well-prepared, boring, tough grader."

"Don't most colleges take such reviews into account when making tenure decisions?"

"They count for something. But at most schools, research and scholarship count for more. Teaching is less and less important these days, as professors and schools fight for grant money based upon research proposals."

Mr. Stanton interjected: "So is it fair to say that you did not, even on an unconscious level, make a connection between the prior student reviews and your current students?"

"That's right. As I have explained, there is no connection."

Mr. Stanton looked at Dr. Van DeMere and smiled. "Anything else you need to cover, Doctor?"

Dr. Van DeMere sat there looking at me intently, rubbing his chin. "One more thing, Professor. Do you feel remorse for the shootings?"

"Of course I do. It was a terrible thing."

"Do you feel in your heart that you are the one who did the shooting?"

That was an interesting question. On the one hand, I clearly did the shooting. But on the other hand, I had great difficulty believing that I had actually done it. "I guess the best answer I have is that I know that I did the shooting, but because I can't understand why, I don't really accept that I did it."

Dr. Van DeMere smiled broadly. "Exactly my point. Mr. Stanton, we have taken up enough of the professor's time. Let's get going so that I can prepare my report."

Mr. Stanton turned to Dr. Van DeMere: "Doctor, you go on ahead. I need a few more minutes here with Professor Jackson." Dr. Van DeMere pounded on the door, and a guard came and let him out.

Chapter 6

After Dr. Van DeMere left the room, Mr. Stanton asked: "What do you think of Dr. Van DeMere?"

"His credentials are less than sterling, and his examination didn't seem very thorough. Is he really the best we can do?"

"Look, Professor. We're pushing the envelope here. The theory we're presenting is, well, let's just say it is novel. There aren't a lot of shrinks out there willing to think outside the box. They are afraid in a high-profile case like this, they will get torn apart on the witness stand if they go out on a limb, and their reputation will be hurt. So there are fewer to choose from. Also, I don't want to bankrupt you with some guy who will say anything but charges one thousand dollars an hour. I think Dr. Van DeMere will do what we want to give the jury something to think about, which is all I need him to do."

"Isn't Dr. Van DeMere worried about his reputation?"

Mr. Stanton ruefully smiled. "When a man gets to a certain age, reputation becomes less important. Don't worry about Dr. Van DeMere, he'll do fine. The prosecution and its shrink may disagree with Dr. Van DeMere's opinion, but they really can't definitively prove it wrong. That's the beauty of a psychiatric defense: it is one shrink's word against the other. As long as the jury hears it and I can argue it, it's a horse race, which is all we can really ask for."

"When will Dr. Van DeMere issue his report?"

"Soon. I expect that he will finish it this week."

"Then what happens?"

"We will file it with the Court, and serve it on the prosecutor. Then their shrink will go over it, and when the State is ready, we will schedule a time for their shrink to examine you. I will be in the room with you, along with the prosecutor."

"Will the State's psychiatrist be allowed to ask any questions that he wants?"

"Yes, within reason. If there is a question that I think is unclear, I will ask him to re-phrase it. If he asks a question that I don't want you to answer, I'll tell you not to answer. We don't have to answer all their questions, but if we don't, they can use that refusal to argue to the jury that we're trying to hide something. So unless there is something really egregious, I am intending to let you answer all their questions."

"I'm okay with that. I have nothing to hide."

"There is one exception: you should never disclose our conversations. If answering one of the shrink's questions would require you to tell them something that you and I discussed, you should refuse to answer. That's the attorney-client privilege. No one can make you talk about what you and your attorney discuss."

"Will the prosecutor be allowed to ask me questions, too?"

"No. He's there just as an observer, and to represent the State in case legal issues come up."

"What do you know about the prosecutor?"

"He's been with the state's attorney's office for six years. He's tried several murder cases, and won all of them. In fact, I had a murder case against him a few years ago. It got pretty nasty."

"What do you mean?"

"Well, my client was a nurse in a hospital in Manchester, New Hampshire, who had been accused of mercy-killing some of her patients with terminal illnesses. Because of some pretty compelling finger print and DNA evidence that implicated my client, Johnson thought he had a lay down. But I came up with some witnesses that almost swamped his case by suggesting that several other nurses could have committed the crimes. However, it came out on Johnson's cross-examination that some of these witnesses were under the mistaken impression that they would be paid for their testimony. I had never made any such promise to them. But I later learned that Johnson had some investigators interview these witnesses before the trial and the investigators had planted that idea in their minds. In any event, once the jury heard that the witnesses thought that they would be paid for their testimony, those witnesses' credibility was shot. Johnson won the case. I have been looking forward to the opportunity to even the score with Mr. Johnson."

"Anything else I should know about Mr. Johnson?"

"Supposedly, he has ambitions to be the state Attorney General. A win in the largest mass murder case in state history sure wouldn't hurt his chances."

I thought about this for a moment. "Could you do some research on his other cases? I mean like find newspaper clippings about them, maybe some descriptions of his style so that I can have a better feel for what I'm in for?"

"I guess I could. I could have my paralegal bring it to you with a cover memo from me, saying that I had specially picked out some information to help prepare you for the trial. That would make it privileged subject to the attorney work-product. Although all your other mail will be read and screened by the warden, even he isn't allowed to read materials designated as attorney-client privileged, only to check to make sure there is no contraband included."

"Okay, then please do that. Also, do you have any idea who the state will choose to buy its psychiatry expert?"

Mr. Stanton thought for a few seconds. "No, not really. I suspect that the state does not have a large budget for expert witnesses, so they would like to keep it in-house if they could. I know that there are some psychiatrists on the State Police staff, I just don't know if any of them will be qualified to respond on this depersonalization disorder defense. We'll just have to wait and see."

"Will the state disclose the name of their psychiatrist before my examination?"

"Yes, I think that I can insist on that."

"Then I would like you to do the same sort of research on their psychiatrist — educational background, articles he's published, prior testifying experience, that sort of thing, and send it to me at least a week before the examination."

"Professor, have you been watching old Perry Mason reruns? You're beginning to sound like a lawyer. But yes, I can get whatever information I can find on the shrink before the examination. I would need to do that anyhow to prepare myself to cross-examine the shrink at trial"

"Good. Thank you. Is there anything else I need to know?"

Mr. Stanton rose to leave. "We'll talk again before the examination. Just remember: the state's psychiatrist is not on your side. His job is to make you look sane, and rebut Dr. Van DeMere's depersonalization disorder theory."

I nodded my head, acknowledging my understanding, and shook Mr. Stanton's hand. But I secretly hoped that these words of warning meant that the state's psychiatrist would want to uncover why I had committed the crime, which is exactly what I wanted.

Chapter 7

I was looking forward to this afternoon because Mr. Stanton's paralegal was supposed to deliver to me a package with the background information on the prosecutor and the State's psychiatrist. I was anxious to learn a little more about my adversaries, and it would be a modification of the almost unchanging rhythm of life in a penal institution. Like the breathing of a living organism, prison life ebbed and flowed in response to a regular, often monotonous schedule that nonetheless was strangely comforting.

I got up every morning at the same time — 6:00 a.m. — when the lights in all the cells were turned on. I had developed the habit of doing some calisthenics immediately upon rising to get my blood flowing, and maintain some semblance of body tone. At six thirty every morning, a guard took me to the bathroom facilities to shower, shave and take care of other personal needs; unlike the other inmates, I got to shower alone, for my supposed protection. Then it was back to my cell for breakfast at 7:00 a.m. Breakfast alternated between tasteless, dried out scrambled eggs with soggy toast, or oatmeal that was the consistency of drying cement. A cup of liquid sludge, which was called coffee, accompanied all breakfasts.

The rest of the morning, I would spend reading books from the prison library, or magazines sent courtesy of Mr. Stanton. At 11:00 a.m. sharp every day, a guard escorted me to a small courtyard for exercise, which consisted of walking around the perimeter of the yard. At noon, lunch was delivered to my cell. Lunch consisted of some sort of sandwich on stale bread and a glass of lukewarm milk. In the afternoon, I either worked on a scholarly paper I had started writing before the shooting, or napped. Dinner was served promptly at 6:00 p.m., and consisted of either rubbery chicken and rice, or mystery meat stew over rigid mash potatoes. After dinner, I usually read some more until lights out at 10:00 p.m.

Other than the miserable food, I felt reasonably comfortable with the routine of prison life. I was a private person by nature, and didn't really feel the need for a great deal of social interaction. I loved books and reading, and now I had all the time I could possibly want to indulge that passion. And I got time to work on my scholarly article. So all in all, life was not so bad.

At the appointed time, a guard appeared and led me to a visitation room where Linda Denton, Mr. Stanton's paralegal, was waiting. She was a thin, gum-chewing young woman in her twenties, with long hair and an over-abundance of eye shadow, making her face look raccoon-like. We shook hands and she gave me a package containing more than two inches of documents. She asked me if I had anything I wanted her to tell Mr. Stanton before our weekly meeting tomorrow afternoon. I told her no, and sent her on her way. I took the package and the guard escorted me back to my cell.

I deliberately did not begin reviewing the material Mr. Stanton had sent until after dinner, so that I would have a solid three to four hours to spend looking at it. I took the envelope over to the small desk in my cell and opened it. On top was a short memo from Mr. Stanton that read:

"SUBJECT TO THE ATTORNEY-CLIENT AND ATTORNEY WORK PRODUCT DOCTRINES—CLIENT'S EYES ONLY!"

To: Dan Jackson
From: Gus Stanton, Esq.

At your request, for the purpose of providing you legal advice, and as part of my preparation for your upcoming trial, enclosed please find articles and other information I have gathered, based upon my mental impressions and analysis, regarding Carl Johnson that could be pertinent to your defense. I am also enclosing a copy of Dr. Van DeMere's expert report that was filed with the Court and served upon the prosecution this week.

The prosecutor has disclosed to me the identity of its psychiatric expert. It is Dr. Paige Wells, a psychiatrist who works for the State Police. I have also enclosed some information that I was able to find about her background and experience.

I will be back in touch when I hear from the prosecution regarding the scheduling of your examination by Dr. Wells.

Sincerely,
Gus Stanton, Esq."

Below the memo, there was a black, three-ring note book with tab dividers separating several different categories of documents. The first page inside the notebook was a table of contents. It indicated that documents concerning Carl Johnson's educational and professional background were behind tab one, so I flipped to that section.

I first looked over a short biography of the man. Johnson was a true son of New Hampshire. He had grown up and gone to high school in Manchester. He did his undergraduate studies at the University of New Hampshire, majoring in something called "Justice Studies," which I assumed was the equivalent of a criminal justice major offered at other schools. In fact, I had taken a course in criminal justice, which focused upon criminal procedure, in a summer course at the University of Wisconsin at Madison after my sophomore year. It had been a fascinating course, and was my first introduction to the insanity defense. Johnson apparently did not graduate with any particular honors or distinctions, like Phi Beta Kappa or *cum laude.* He then went on to law school at the University of New Hampshire, graduating again without any honors or

distinctions. There was no indication that he was on the
law review or any other law school publication.

Johnson was, however, on the law school mock trial
team. His team had placed third in the regional mock trial
contest that was held among the New England law school
mock trial teams that would have included teams from
Harvard and Yale. My conclusion from this biography was
that Carl Johnson may not have been the greatest student or
writer, but he was probably pretty good on his feet, and at
questioning witnesses. Murder trials were not essay exams,
so his modest academic record was no reason to believe
that Johnson would be anything less than a formidable
courtroom adversary.

After graduating from law school, Johnson went to
work for a small law firm in Manchester, Howry &
Hampton, where he did civil litigation, everything from
landlord-tenant suits to litigation concerning the
interpretation of contracts. He worked there for about five
years, but apparently never was made a partner in the firm.
From there he went to the New Hampshire Attorney
General's office, initially as an Assistant Attorney General.
Johnson held that position for five years, principally trying
high-profile murder and political corruption cases. Two
years ago, he was appointed by the Attorney General to the
position of Senior Assistant Attorney General, signifying
that his accomplishments had been noticed by the upper
echelon of government.

I turned to tab two of the notebook, which the table
of contents stated contained information on Johnson's
experience in murder trials. This was what I really wanted
to see. Mr. Stanton had provided a list of about ten murder
trials that Johnson had handled, with a brief description of
each case and the length of the trial. Most of the trials were
three to four day affairs, apparently open and shut cases.
Two of the cases, however, had received substantial
notoriety, were lengthy, had expert witnesses, and involved

insanity defenses. As to these cases, Mr. Stanton had included a more detailed description and some newspaper articles reporting on the trials and Mr. Johnson's performance in particular. Reference to a third murder case involving an insanity defense had an asterisk next to it; a notation at the bottom of the page indicated that a more fulsome description of that case could be found in tab four's materials on Dr. Wells' testimonial experience.

In the first case, which occurred five years ago, Johnson had tried a murder case involving Richard DeForest, who was accused of killing his father, mother, two brothers and two sisters as they slept in their beds in their Nashua, New Hampshire home. The twenty-six year old defendant had stumbled into the Nashua police station at 5:30 a.m. one morning, claiming that his family had been attacked by two men in dark ski masks brandishing pistols. The men had supposedly broken into the house and confronted DeForest's parents in their bedroom. Deforest told police that he had heard the break-in, and listened to what transpired from his bedroom down the hall. He told the police that the men seemed anxious and irrational, and they kept asking for the location of "the meth lab." He told the police that when his father denied the existence of any meth lab, the intruders became upset and started shouting "liar, liar" at his parents. Suddenly, DeForest said he heard multiple gun shots, at which point he ran from his room and out the front door, and hid in the garage. He heard several more gun shots from the house as he hid. After about a half hour had passed, he supposedly went back into the house to find his entire family had been shot dead in their beds.

From the newspaper accounts included in the notebook, several parts of DeForest's story aroused police suspicion. First, why hadn't DeForest's brothers and sisters heard the break-in or the men yelling in the parents' bedroom and fled as he had? Certainly, they would have heard the initial gunshots. Second, why were the bodies all

found in bed, with no sign of struggle, and with a single
bullet wound in the head? It seemed unlikely that crazed
meth addicts would be so precise; DeForest's description of
the shootings had made it sound as if the killers had
sprayed a hail of bullets around the rooms.   Third, the
ballistics report indicated that the bullets that killed each
family member had been fired from a single gun —a .35
Marlin rifle, not a pistol.   Nashua gun store records
indicated that DeForest had purchased a .35 Marlin rifle
less than two years earlier.

Once the factual predicate of DeForest's story
evaporated, his criminal defense lawyer came up with a
new theory: DeForest had killed his family because he
heard "voices" telling him that his family was plotting to
kill him.   Both the prosecution and defense presented
competing psychiatric expert testimony on the question of
DeForest's sanity.   According to one of the newspaper
accounts, Johnson's cross-examination of the defense
expert had sealed the case for the prosecution:

"DeForest Found Guilty After Prosecutor Gets Defense Expert to Admit Defendant Was Sane At Time of Killings.

Nashua, New Hampshire. In a surprising turn of
events at the trial of accused mass slayer Richard DeForest,
prosecutor Carl Johnson startled the courtroom when he
succeeded in getting Dr. Irving Schwartz, the defense
expert psychiatrist, to admit that DeForest was sane when
he killed his two sisters, two brothers and parents.   On
direct examination by DeForest's attorney, Dr. Schwartz
had asserted that DeForest was a heroine and LSD abuser,
and suffered from antisocial personality disorder, a form of
mental illness that made him not responsible for his actions.
However, on cross-examination, Mr. Johnson carefully led
Dr. Schwartz through the medical literature on the

condition, ultimately getting Dr. Schwartz to admit that persons with antisocial disorder do understand right from wrong, and the nature and gravity of their actions. After Dr. Schwartz left the stand, the defense rested, as did the prosecution. The jury returned a verdict of guilty of six counts of second degree murder in less than an hour of deliberation. Sentencing is set for March 15th."

So Mr. Johnson did his homework before he got to the courtroom. I wondered what literature was out there regarding Dr. Van DeMere's depersonalization disorder theory. I wrote myself a note to bring this up with Mr. Stanton.

The second case involved a grisly home invasion and machete attack by Jackie Quinlan, which left one woman dead, and her young daughter seriously wounded. The newspaper articles indicated that at trial the defense had offered two experts who testified that the Quinlan had antisocial personality disorder, but again on cross examination, Johnson had been able to get both experts to admit that the defendant knew what he was doing at the time of the murder. In what the reporters called a highly unusual turn of events, Quinlan took the stand himself to try to convince the jury that he was insane. He claimed that he had been beaten, tortured and starved as a child by his mother. He testified that he had fantasized about taking his mother into the woods and cutting off little pieces of her, hoping to hear her scream in pain and for mercy. He also testified that he dreamed of pouring boiling water over "sensitive" parts of her body, pulling her limbs from their sockets and sprinkling her with sugar so that the birds would come and pick at her body. When asked about the murders in question, he said that he thought the woman was his mother, and that she got what she deserved. Quinlan's testimony had lasted an entire afternoon, and was largely rambling and incoherent. As the court went into recess until the next morning, veteran courtroom observers predicted to the press that Quinlan had succeeded in establishing that he truly was crazy.

But the next morning, according to the newspaper accounts, the worm turned when Mr. Johnson strode to the podium and began his cross examination. He methodically marched Quinlan through the day before the murder, tracing his every step, from the clothes he chose to put on in the morning to the selection of the machete from an army surplus store in town the night before the murder. As to every choice or decision that Quinlan had made during that day, Johnson asked: "why did you do that?" Quinlan invariably had a reason for each of his actions. And when Quinlan described in gory detail plunging the machete into the victim's body twenty-seven times, Johnson led Quinlan through each strike of the machete, asking after each one: "And why did you do that?" To which Quinlan responded twenty-seven times: "Because I wanted to kill her, of course." The jury convicted Quinlan of first degree murder in less than thirty minutes of deliberation.

I set down the notebook on the desk and thought a bit about what I had just read. Even people who are pretty damn crazy can't pull off an insanity defense — even if they go on the stand and sound completely loony. I hadn't even considered whether I would testify at the trial. I wrote myself a note to discuss that, too, with Mr. Stanton.

I picked up the notebook again and found the tab for the background information on the State's psychiatric expert, Dr. Paige Wells. First I found her resume. She attended Brown University as an undergraduate, majoring in biology, and graduated summa *cum laude*. Then she attended a combined MD/PHD program at Harvard, specializing in psychiatry. Before coming to the New Hampshire State Police, she had taught abnormal psychology at Amherst College. I had taken a similar course at Dartmouth the fall of my junior year — we called it "Nuts and Sluts."

Dr. Wells had testified as an expert only once before in a murder trial about three years ago while she was still teaching. The case was State of New Hampshire versus Connors. I turned to the next tab which contained some of the newspaper accounts of that trial. That case involved Jason Connors, who was accused of murdering his wife after discovering that she had been having an affair with his best friend. According to the newspaper articles, the Connors' cleaning lady had come to work on a Thursday morning to find Mrs. Connors naked, tied spread eagle to their bed, and essentially skinned with a boning knife that lay on the bed beside her. The police were immediately called to the house, and found Jason Connors drunk and huddling in the basement. The newspapers indicated that Jason's fingerprints had been found on the boning knife. Dr. Wells had been retained as an expert witness for the defense, and testified that the shock of discovering his wife's infidelity with his best friend had pushed Jason into a psychotic state in which he did not know right from wrong. She was on the witness stand for one day of direct examination and three days of cross-examination by the prosecutor — who was none other than Carl Johnson. After over a week of deliberation, the jury found Jason Connors guilty, but only of murder in the second degree, which resulted in a sentence of only twenty years instead of life in prison.

So that's how Johnson had selected Dr. Wells as his expert. He has seen her in action as an adversary, and apparently liked what he saw. She hadn't succeeded in convincing the jury that Jason was crazy, but she'd done the next best thing: convinced the jury that it was a crime of passion. I then flipped back to her resume to see if she had written any articles. She had written several articles in various scholarly publications. I scanned them to see if any looked relevant to my situation. Most did not seem pertinent to my case, but one did catch my eye.

About three years ago, Dr. Wells had published an article entitled "Re-thinking Diagnosis and Treatment of Dissociative Disorders," in the New England Psychiatric Journal. Mr. Stanton had included a copy of the article behind tab 5 of the notebook, so I turned to that tab to review the article. The article was filled with psychiatric jargon and mind-numbing, five-dollar words, and I wasn't sure that I was really understanding all of what Dr. Wells was saying. But what I did understand from the article was that Dr. Wells was attacking the conventional wisdom that dissociation was a coping device that resulted from exposure to "stressors," more commonly known as emotional trauma. Dr. Wells characterized the prevailing view as associating dissociation disorders with "intense objective stressors," usually involving some childhood trauma; this was characterized as the "Post-traumatic Model." Proponents of the Post-traumatic Model believe that dissociation disorders are associated with very high rates of childhood trauma, especially sexual abuse. Apparently Dr. Van DeMere was not completely in sync with this "Post-traumatic Model," because he had stated that he didn't need to delve into my childhood experiences in arriving at his opinion; he had stated that the most recent trauma of my divorce was sufficient to trigger the depersonalization disorder.

In any event, in her article, Dr. Wells criticized the studies that supposedly support the "Post-traumatic Model" as lacking objective corroboration of the abuse. Instead such studies relied primarily on the subjects' own descriptions of abuse with no further investigation to see if such reports could be independently verified. The article pointed out that diagnosing a person as having a dissociative disorder and then asking them if they remember having been abused in childhood is what is known as a retrospective study. In contrast, prospective studies that follow people who have had a documented childhood trauma have failed to demonstrate that childhood trauma leads to dissociative disorders. In fact, the article posited that prospective studies of persons who had suffered emotionally traumatic events in adulthood did not support the notion that emotional trauma is a trigger for dissociative orders.

The article concluded by noting that more recent findings of both clinical and nonclinical studies have suggested a link between sleep-related disorders and dissociation. When patients were deprived of sleep under experimental conditions, they exhibited dissociative symptoms, including waking dreams, nightmares, hallucinations, and loss of memory. An increasing number of studies suggest that when patients diagnosed with dissociative disorders are treated for sleep problems, their dissociative problems show significant improvement. While emotional trauma cannot, and should not be ruled out as a possible trigger for dissociative disorders, other factors, including sleep-related problems should also be explored in any diagnosis and treatment program.

This article, combined with Johnson's prior experience with Dr. Wells, made it crystal clear why Dr. Wells had been selected as the State's expert. She was going to challenge Dr. Van DeMere's "Post-traumatic Model" approach, and argue that it could not be used to establish that I had a depersonalization disorder. I assume that Mr. Stanton, having compiled the information in the notebook, must have arrived at the same conclusion. This is something that I needed to discuss in further detail with Mr. Stanton tomorrow afternoon during our weekly visit.

My thoughts were interrupted by the signal for "lights out," followed by a sudden plunge into darkness. I got ready for bed, and a troubled sleep. I couldn't get out of my mind the various questions that the materials I had reviewed had raised. I would have lots of issues to discuss with Mr. Stanton during his next weekly visit.

Chapter 8

The next morning, a guard came to my cell and informed me that I had a visitor. I was led to a small interview room, where I found Tim waiting for me. He was again dressed in his priest's black suit and white collar. We embraced and took seats on opposite sides of a steel table. Tim began:

"Dan, it's good to see you. We didn't get a chance to talk much at the arraignment, but I wanted to let you know that I understand why you didn't plead guilty. So don't worry; I am not mad at you or anything. Confronted with that split-second decision, I think that I would have probably done the same thing, if for no other reason, to buy some time."

"Thanks, Tim. I was worried that you wouldn't understand."

"I have had some extended discussions with some of my colleagues at the Boston Diocese, and I've learned quite a bit about your Mr. Stanton. I've also talked with some of the Diocese lawyers, and may have a way to get you out of this death penalty box and back into a position where you can plead guilty and accept a life sentence."

"Okay. But before we start, Mr. Stanton advised me that you need to be my spiritual advisor, so that our discussions are privileged. Otherwise, the prosecution could make you testify about what we talk about. Are you okay with that?"

"Dan, I have felt like your spiritual advisor since we were freshman. I have no problem in formally assuming that role."

"Good, but what about our first discussion? Are you comfortable with saying that you were my spiritual advisor for that meeting?"

"Sure. We talked about saving your soul, didn't we? Look, seriously, I have no trouble saying that you are my spiritual advisee, period."

"All right. Tell me about what you found out about Mr. Stanton."

Tim pulled a file folder full of documents from his briefcase. He opened the file and looked at the first few pages of notes before beginning.

"Well, Mr. Stanton definitely is a Dartmouth grad. He was a government major and graduated summa *cum laude*, Phi Beta Kappa. He was a member of the lacrosse team and played long-stick middie. His nickname on the team was "Howitzer," because his favorite thing was to hit the opposition players so hard that they lost their sticks and their gloves flew off their hands. He was also a member of Theta Delta fraternity, which, at the time, was one of the rowdier houses on campus. I found a picture of him in an old Daily Dartmouth skiing down the Theta Delta staircase during Winter Carnival."

We both chuckled for a moment. So Mr. Stanton had been a bit of a wild man in his day. Yet, he had graduated near the top of his class. Impressive.

"He went on to Harvard for law school, and did well there, too. He was number three in his class, editor of the law review and won the moot court competition. Upon graduation, he was hired by Grey, Thurgood and Hollins, one of the most prestigious Boston firms. He started in their civil litigation department and was viewed as a rising star. He second chaired some important cases early in his career, and tried his first cases on his own when he was just a third year associate — something that had been unheard of in the history of his firm. He made partner after only five and one-half years at the firm — another first at the firm. By the time he had been a partner for five years, he was made the head of the firm's litigation department. His meteoric rise in the firm had not only attracted the attention

of the firm elders, but also the daughter of the firm's
chairman, Sarah Hollins, who met Stanton at one of the
firm's summer parties. After a whirlwind courtship,
Stanton and Sarah were married and purchased a penthouse
apartment in the city."

"Then how did he end up in a solo criminal defense
practice?"

"Well, that's where it gets interesting. The rest of
the story comes from what the Diocese lawyers were able
to piece together from old legal gossip magazines and some
inside sources at the Grey, Thurgood and Hollins firm.
One of the firm's biggest clients was Milford People
Movers, a manufacturer of escalators and moving
walkways used at most of the airports, department stores
and shopping malls around the country. There had been
several accidents around the country involving children's
clothing getting caught in the escalator's mechanism
causing serious injury. One of the company's engineers
had written a memo containing an analysis of the accidents
and the escalator mechanism in question. The memo
concluded that the mechanism was improperly designed. It
also concluded that a relatively small fix was possible, but
would cost three hundred and fifty dollars per escalator.
Because there were literally thousands of escalators in
place, the memo concluded that it was not 'practical' for
the manufacturer to offer the fix to its customers free of
charge."

"The manufacturer retained Grey, Thurgood and
Hollins when it was sued in Boston federal court by the
parents of Jamie McAndrews, a child injured at a
downtown department store. Jamie's pant leg had gotten
caught in the escalator mechanism, mangling his leg so
badly that it was amputated below the knee. The case was
assigned to Stanton, as the head of the litigation
department. Stanton had successfully handled a prior
accident case a few years back involving the escalator

model in question, was basically familiar with the product, and had a game plan for defending the case."

"Milford People Movers had its own internal legal department, and the case had been assigned internally to be supervised by Peter Letterbalm. Mr. Letterbalm started at the company in the accounting department, got his law degree at night and then was promoted into the legal department. He had never tried a case, but one of his job functions was to supervise litigation filed against the company. In the first meeting between Letterbalm and Stanton, he expressed the view that Stanton's hourly rate was excessive, and therefore he wanted him to assign a first or second year associate to the case to do most of the work. Letterbalm made it clear that he expected to see more of the associate's time on the file than Stanton's. Stanton thought that Mr. Letterbaum's attitude was penny-wise and pound foolish because Letterbalm was essentially eliminating Stanton's experience and knowledge from the case. But Letterbalm was the client representative on the case, so Stanton acquiesced to his directive and assigned a young associate to the file."

"Did something go wrong in the handling of the case that caused Stanton to leave the firm?"

"Well, yes, but the story is somewhat complicated. As a normal part of the discovery process in a civil suit, the parties exchange requests that ask the other side to produce certain categories of documents. In keeping with Mr. Letterbalm's instructions, Stanton had the young associate assigned to the case review client documents to determine which ones were responsive to the plaintiff's requests. Somehow, the Milford People Movers' engineer's memo regarding the design defect was among the documents being reviewed by the associate. Although the memo was not directly responsive to any of the plaintiff's requests, someone from the client had handwritten 'Jamie McAndrews' on the top of the memo with a bright red pen, with a large red arrow pointing down to the section of the memo that described the design defect. It was never entirely clear whether the associate actually reviewed the memo and decided it was responsive because it had the plaintiff's name scrawled on the top, or simply failed to notice that the memo was among the client documents. In any event, the memo got produced to the plaintiff's lawyer, without Stanton's knowledge. In keeping with Mr. Letterbalm's instructions, Stanton had not reviewed any of the documents himself prior to their production to the plaintiff's counsel to keep the bill down."

"Two days later, Stanton received a new document request from the plaintiff's lawyer asking for documents concerning other accidents. Plaintiff's lawyer also sent along a formal request that attached the memo and asked for the identity of the memo's author, as well as the identity of the scribner of 'Jamie McAndrews' on the top of the memo. Stanton was flabbergasted. He had never seen the memo before, and as he read it, his heart sank, knowing that it doomed the defense of the case: it not only identified numerous other similar accidents, but ascribed the cause of those accidents as a defect in the escalator. The handwritten 'Jamie McAndrews' with the bright red arrow pointing to the defect paragraph was a devastating admission. His first instinct was that the plaintiff's lawyer must have stolen the memo from the company somehow, because there was no way that his young associate would have produced a document like this to the plaintiff without showing it to him first. But when he examined the document more closely, he saw numbering on the bottom of the document that had been placed there by his paralegal to identify the document as one produced by the defense in the case."

"Stanton supposedly summoned the young associate into his office, showed her the plaintiff's lawyer's requests, which included the memo, and demanded an explanation.

The young associate had none, and sat, head down and whimpering, as Stanton proceeded to berate her and then fired her on the spot. As she ran from his office in tears, Stanton asked his secretary to bring him a copy of the document request in response to which the memo had been produced, to see if its production had been clearly required. The only request to which the memo was arguably responsive was a request calling for 'all documents that refer or relate to Jamie McAndrews.' His handwritten name on the memo arguably made the document responsive to the request. Stanton decided that would have to be the explanation to the client: the memo had to be produced because it was responsive one of the requests. That certainly wasn't his fault."

"But when he called Mr. Letterbalm to inform him of the plaintiff's new requests, Letterbalm was furious. Letterbalm asked Stanton why he hadn't objected to the request as overbroad, or at a minimum, why the memo had been produced without bringing it to his attention. Stanton acknowledged that it was a mistake, and that the young associate who had failed to bring the memo to his attention had been fired. That did not mollify Letterbalm one bit. He shouted at Stanton that he was the partner on the file, and he should have reviewed the documents before they were produced. Letterbalm blurted out that Stanton better put his firm's malpractice insurance carrier on notice, because Milford People Movers was going to have a substantial malpractice claim arising from Stanton's negligence."

"According to insiders at the firm, Stanton was taken aback by Letterbalm's assault, but quickly regained his equilibrium and calmly responded that he had been handling the case exactly as Letterbalm instructed, with more associate time and less of his time on the file. Moreover, it was curious that the memo had been among the documents shipped over from the client for review, and that someone at the client had apparently linked the memo to the case by writing Jamie McAndrews name on it. Did Mr. Letterbaum have any idea how that had happened, Stanton had asked. That infuriated Letterbalm even more, and he slammed down the phone, ending the conversation."

"The next morning, Stanton was summoned to Mr. Hollins's office. Stanton was informed that Milford People Mover's general counsel had called Hollins to announce that not only was the firm being fired from the McAndrew's case, but that Milford was removing all of its corporate and real estate work from the firm, which would cost the firm millions of dollars in lost fees. In addition, Milford had put the firm on notice that it would be submitting a malpractice claim against both Stanton and the firm for the costs associated with any settlement or verdict in the McAndrews case, as well as any settlements of future suits that were filed as a result of the memo becoming public. Hollins also told Stanton that Milford had filed a formal complaint with the Massachusetts bar against Stanton for his alleged incompetence in handling the McAndrews case. The story goes that at that point, Hollins told Stanton that under these circumstances, it would be best if Stanton took a leave of absence from the firm until the furor blew over."

"Did Stanton resign? Is that how he ended up as a solo?"

"Not exactly. Stanton tried to explain to his father-in-law that both he and the firm had a very good defense to any charges of malpractice: he had followed Mr. Lettebalm's directives on how to handle the case, someone at the client had included the memo in the documents to be reviewed for production to the plaintiff's counsel, and someone at the client had written Jamie McAndrews' name on the memo, making it almost impossible not to provide the document to the other side. Stanton insisted that a joint call to Milford's general counsel would clear up this whole unfortunate misunderstanding by placing the blame where it belonged: on Mr. Letterbalm, and his decision to keep the fees low, at the cost of the quality of representation afforded."

"Did his father-in-law agree to call the general counsel?"

"No. He supposedly asked Stanton if the directive from Mr. Letterbalm was in writing. When Stanton replied that it was a verbal instruction, Hollins shook his head sadly and said that he was sure that Mr. Letterbalm would deny it, and that it would just be Stanton's word against Letterbalm's. The chairman said that perhaps the relationship with the client could be ultimately repaired, but it would require some gesture of atonement from the firm, not engaging in a pissing contest. Stanton's leave of absence would have to be that gesture."

"So then did Stanton resign?"

"According to insiders at the firm, Stanton's reaction to the leave of absence suggestion was to get up from his chair, reach over to shake his father-in-law's hand, and proceed to punch him in the face with a round-house left hook, breaking the poor fellow's nose. Stanton said he quit, and would sue the firm, if necessary, to get all the money that he was entitled to under the partnership agreement. He stomped out of the chairman's office, went to his own office, grabbed his briefcase and left the firm, never to return."

"That couldn't have gone over to well with his wife."

"It didn't. Again, according to firm insiders, Stanton left the office and went immediately to a bar across from Fenway Park, and proceeded to get exceedingly drunk, even for a Dartmouth guy. When he got home, the other shoe dropped. His wife's father had called her from the emergency room where his nose was being treated, and told her everything that had transpired. Sarah was furious and began screaming at Stanton as soon as he crossed the threshold of the apartment. Stanton, of course, was in no mood to put up with anymore abuse. Instead of responding to his wife's belligerence, he marched into the bedroom, packed up a suitcase and stormed out of the apartment. The divorce was final in lightning speed, with Sarah ending up with most of the assets."

"So is that when Mr. Stanton began his solo practice?"

"Not immediately. He tried, for a while, to get another position at a large firm, but once word got out of the particulars of his departure from Grey, Thurgood and Hollins, nobody would touch him. So, after about six months of drinking and wallowing in his own despair, Stanton opened his own solo practice. Word on the street was that after his experience with the inadvertent production of the memo, Stanton refused to hire any younger lawyers to work with him, and became a lone wolf. Word on the street also was that Stanton became obsessed with winning at any cost to show the legal world the mistake that Grey, Thurgood and Hollins had made by forcing him out."

"What do you mean by 'win at any cost'?"

"Well, according to the Diocese lawyers, Stanton got the reputation as a guy willing to cut corners, if you will, to get his clients off. Not necessarily unethical, but willing to sail pretty close to the wind, as they say. When Stanton was on the other side of a case, the opposing lawyer knew he was in for a knock-down, drag out fight. No quarter asked, none given."

"What ever happened to the complaint that Milford made to the state bar against Mr. Stanton?"

Tim smiled. "Well, to give Mr. Stanton his due, he represented himself in the bar proceeding, and when he got his chance to cross-examine Mr. Letterbalm, he drilled Letterbalm a new asshole. He got Letterbalm to admit that it was his handwriting on the engineer's memo, and that he had mistakenly included the memo in the documents sent over to be reviewed by the firm. The bar complaint was dismissed, and Mr. Stanton vindicated."

"So did Mr. Letterbalm lose his job after that?"

"To the contrary, consistent with the Peter Principle, he was ultimately promoted to Assistant General Counsel. Go figure."

I thought for a moment about Mr. Stanton's story. It didn't seem like he had really done anything wrong in the McAndrews' case, other than do what Mr. Letterbalm had told him to do. Letterbalm was the one who had made the mistake. However, clearly Mr. Stanton had not reacted appropriately by slugging his father-in-law. If one was going to be represented in a desperate murder case, though, I think I would want a lawyer with a chip on his shoulder and a reputation as a tough fighter for his clients. That sure sounded like Mr. Stanton.

Tim saw me pondering what he had told me, and then asked:

"So, what do you think of your Mr. Stanton now?"

"He's not perfect, but as you like to say, none of us are. However, he's smart and tough, so I'm glad that he's on my side."

"Really? No second thoughts?"

"Look, Tim. I already told you that I called a bunch of lawyers and no one wanted to touch me with a ten foot pole. I'll stick with Mr. Stanton."

Tim shook his head slightly and sighed. "Okay, but let me tell you about my discussions with the Diocese's lawyers about a way around the death penalty and a possible plea deal."

"Okay, shoot."

"You need to tell Mr. Stanton to approach the prosecutor and offer to plead guilty and accept a life sentence, with no possibility of parole, in return for an agreement by the prosecutor not to seek the death penalty."

I sat silently for a moment, just staring at Tim. "That's it? That's the brilliant strategy from the Diocese lawyers?"

"Well, yes. It gets you back to where we were the other day when we spoke at the Hanover police station. You accept responsibility for the crimes and accept the punishment."

"Things have changed since then, Tim. First, there is no guarantee that the prosecutor would even agree to such a proposal. Mr. Stanton tells me that Mr. Johnson has political aspirations to run for New Hampshire Attorney General, and a conviction and death sentence in a high profile case like this would be a huge feather in his cap. Second, I met with Dr. Van DeMere, the psychiatric expert Mr. Stanton retained, and he thinks that I do have a mental illness. He said that although my body carried out the crime, my conscious self wasn't in control. That's how I feel about it, too."

Tim's lips turned down and pressed together tightly. "I thought we were in agreement. You shot those students, and in order to get redemption, you need to acknowledge what you did and seek forgiveness."

"Tim, what I'm saying is that it may be that I am not responsible for killing those students. It was the result of a mental illness. I shouldn't have to accept responsibility for that."

"Tell me about this Dr. Van DeMere. What makes him think that you have a mental illness?"

"Well, I have to admit that his academic credentials aren't impressive. But he practiced psychiatry in Boston for almost forty years, and says that he has made a study of what he calls dissociative disorders. He says that my divorce was a traumatic event that caused me to develop a 'depersonalization disorder,' which is why I don't know why I shot my students."

Tim was silent for a moment, but I could tell from the look on his face that he was not happy about this new development. "You will have to be examined by the prosecutor's psychiatrist as well, right?"

"That's what Mr. Stanton said."

"Will you at least agree to keep an open mind on this whole insanity defense until after the prosecutor's psychiatrist examines you? When you see that report you may feel differently. And it may not be too late, at that point, to try the plea deal I just outlined."

I shook my head affirmatively. "Of course I will keep an open mind. Look, Tim, I appreciate everything you're trying to do for me, and your continued friendship. Don't give up on me. I just don't want to accept responsibility for something for which I am really not responsible."

Tim smiled slightly. "Don't worry. I won't give up on you. But I am going to continue to ask the hard questions and make you think about them carefully."

"I will. I promise."

With that, Tim stood and we shook hands. As he turned to leave, Tim said: "Just remember. This insanity defense is a dance with the devil. And if you wait until the music stops, it may be too late to find another dance partner."

Chapter 9

The time for Mr. Stanton's weekly visit arrived, and the guard came and led me from my cell to the interview room where Mr. Stanton was waiting. We shook hands and I took a seat across the table from him. Mr. Stanton pulled a legal pad from his tattered briefcase, along with a black three-ring notebook that looked identical to the one he had sent me. Mr. Stanton started:

"Professor, we have a lot to do today, so I want to get right to it. Did you get a chance to review the materials I sent to you yesterday?"

"Yes. And I have a few questions that I would like to ask you concerning the material."

"Okay, but then I want to concentrate on getting you ready for the examination by Dr. Wells. What's up?"

"Well, first of all, I noticed that Mr. Johnson had successfully undermined an expert witness in one of those murder trials by resorting to medical literature that undercut the expert's opinion. I was curious: have you looked to see what the medical literature has to say about Dr. Van DeMere's depersonalization disorder theory?"

"I haven't had time myself yet, but I have asked Dr. Van DeMere to collect all the articles he can find. That's fairly routine for the expert to do, so you don't have to worry about that."

"But if that is so routine, why didn't that other expert do it?"

"I don't know. Maybe the defense attorney didn't ask the expert to do it. Or maybe the defense attorney knew that there was bad stuff out there and didn't want the expert to collect it and consider it. All I know is that I don't practice that way. We'll be ready — Dr. Van DeMere will be ready."

"That's good. Another reason I'm bringing it up is that I read Dr. Wells' article that you included in the notebook. Although I didn't understand all of it, she seems to think that there are studies out there that undercut Dr. Van DeMere's theory that my divorce triggered a depersonalization disorder, and I wanted to make sure you and Dr. Van DeMere were aware of them."

"As I said, we will cover the waterfront to make sure that we are ready. Anything else?"

"I noticed in one of Mr. Johnson's trials, the defendant raising the insanity defense took the stand himself. I was aware that I couldn't be forced to testify, but I hadn't really given any thought to whether I should testify. Do you think that's something that would help our insanity defense?"

Mr. Stanton sat quietly for a moment, apparently thinking carefully about his response.

"As a general rule, I advise my clients in criminal cases not to take the stand, unless the case has gone so badly that their testimony can't make it any worse, and then only if they insist. Lots of bad things can happen to you when you take the stand. First of all, the prosecutors love it. Although very few defendants ever actually testify, every prosecutor I know spends at least one day of preparation in anticipation that the defendant will take the stand. As a result, the prosecutor is loaded for bear in terms of cross-examination questions designed to expose every little inconsistency in the defendant's story. Second, the defendant's testimony can open the door to the introduction of evidence that the prosecutor otherwise could never get in, like the defendant's past criminal record. Finally, there is the significant risk that because of the cross-examination, the defendant will come off as a villain and fiend, whom the jury will come to loathe. An angry jury is almost always bad for a criminal defendant. So, as of right now, I think that I would stick with my normal advice: don't take the stand."

"But wouldn't my taking the stand, looking the jury in the eye, and explaining how I don't know why this happened, but want desperately to understand it, make me a more sympathetic person? I mean, I would think that it is harder to sentence someone to death when you realize that he is a troubled human being."

"Look, Professor, I don't know how to say this politely — no one who shoots fifteen students is going to get much sympathy from a jury unless you can credibly assert you were threatened or beaten by them, which we know is not the case. I think we win or lose this case on the experts. But as we get closer to the trial date, I will devote an afternoon to preparing you just in case we decide to put you on the stand. Does that make you feel better?"

"Yes, actually it does. You may be right that it wouldn't be a good idea for me to testify, but I want to be ready so that we have a choice to make, if we need to make one."

"Okay. Anything else?"

"No, I think that covers what I had wanted to talk about."

"Good.   Now let's focus on the upcoming examination by Dr. Wells, which is scheduled for next Tuesday at 10:00 a.m."

"Where will it take place?"

"Here at the prison, although apparently the prosecution has arranged for it to occur in the Warden's office, which is a lot more comfortable than this damn interview room."

"How long will it go on?"

"There's no official time limit, but if I think it is getting too long, I will stop it and go see the judge. Here are the things that I want you to remember. First, you will not be under oath, but that doesn't mean that you are free to lie. Although the prosecution is not allowed to use what you say to Dr. Wells itself in evidence, it can use it to impeach you if you were to take the stand and testify to something different. So you want to be careful in how you answer the questions."

"I understand."

"Second, you are only obliged to answer the question that Dr. Wells asks. So listen carefully to her questions, and answer only the question that she asks. That doesn't mean just answer yes or no. That will be impossible, because Dr. Wells will do her best to ask open-ended questions to get you talking. But what it does mean is, for example, if she asks you where you went for summer vacation, do not answer with where you went in the fall, winter or spring—or why you went where you went for summer vacation. Understand?"

"Yes."

"Also, it's okay to tell her that you don't know the answer to a question, or can't remember what the answer is. In fact, it's vitally important that you admit that you don't know why you shot those students. She will be trying to get you to figure out a reason for that, and don't fall into that trap. Remember, the fact that you don't know why you did it is the heart of Dr. Van DeMere's depersonalization disorder diagnosis. Don't let her shame you into coming up with some explanation for that."

Although I knew what Mr. Stanton was talking about, I still secretly hoped that Dr. Wells would uncover why I had committed the crime. But there was no reason to cause Mr. Stanton undue worry at this point, so I simply said "I understand."

"Okay, there is one more thing I tell my clients before they testify, and it applies to this examination as well. You need to take your time. I want you to follow a process in response to every one of Dr. Wells' questions. Here it is. First, listen to the question — the whole question — very carefully and make sure you understand it. If you don't understand it, don't try to figure out on your own what she means. Tell her you don't understand and then wait for her to ask another question or re-phrase it. Second, if you have heard and understood the question, then I want you to think quietly to yourself about what your answer is going to be. People get themselves in trouble when they start answering a question with no clear idea where the answer ends. Know where the answer ends before you start talking. Third, once you've listened and thought about your answer, pause for a moment to gather yourself before you start talking. Fourth, give the answer to the question. Fifth, stop talking, re-load and get ready for the next question. Is that clear?"

"Won't I look conniving, taking so much time between the question and the answer, like I'm trying to make stuff up?"

"Not if you approach each question the same way from the very beginning. You will establish a rhythm that will soon seem natural. At worst, you will seem to be like a deliberate responder."

"Won't such a process and deliberateness make me seem less insane?"

"I don't think so. The type of insanity defense we've staked out for you doesn't depend upon you being irrational and drooling. So there is no need to try to affect some demeanor that is foreign to you. Do you think you can follow this advice?"

"Yes, I think so."

"All right then. I will be back here next Tuesday morning at about 9:30 a.m. to go over this briefly once more, and answer any more questions you may have. Then we will go to the Warden's office and let Dr. Wells conduct her examination."

Mr. Stanton rose from his chair, shook my hand, and left. I was escorted back to my cell to ponder what Dr. Wells' examination would reveal about the shootings, and myself.

Chapter 10

I could not believe how quickly Tuesday morning arrived. It seemed like my session with Mr. Stanton had ended, I had gone back to my cell, went to bed, and suddenly four days had passed. I really couldn't remember how I had spent the time in those intervening four days, but no matter. The big day of the meeting with Dr. Wells was finally here.

I met with Mr. Stanton at 9:30 a.m. as we had discussed. He led me back through the basic rules he wanted me to follow in answering Dr. Wells' questions and the process of answering he wanted me to adopt. I nodded my head and indicated I remembered and understood his instructions. I was getting a little nervous, and felt a thin sheen of sweat at my brow and under my arms. I think Mr. Stanton could feel my anxiety, and said:

"Okay Professor, do you have any other questions or concerns that I can help you with before we go up to the Warden's office?"

"I do have one question. What happens if I convince Dr. Wells that I have a depersonalization disorder and therefore suffer some form of insanity?"

"That's hard to say. If Dr. Wells and the prosecutor are convinced that you are mentally ill, then they could file a motion with court saying that they agreed with the defense and ask that the court enter an order confining you to the state mental hospital for treatment until you are cured. But because New Hampshire's insanity rule really doesn't require a true, medically recognized mental defect, it's also possible that even if they think you have a depersonalization disorder, they won't agree that it should excuse you from responsibility for the crime, and push on to trial. So don't concern yourself with trying to win over Dr. Wells. Just answer her questions and let Dr. Van

DeMere and me figure out what to do with your answers. Anything else?"

I shook my head no. Mr. Stanton called for the guard, and we were led to the Warden's office.

I had never been to the Warden's office, or met the Warden, for that matter. I was led through a dark wooden door into a large, carpeted office that had a fireplace at one end of the room, and a large mahogany desk at the other. Two over-stuffed chairs sat on either side of the fireplace. Seated in one of those chairs was a strikingly beautiful woman, with long blonde hair and crystal blue eyes. She wore a white suit with a blue blouse that was buttoned so as to just provide a suggestion of her ample cleavage. That must be Dr. Wells. Two full-size couches faced each other perpendicular to the fireplace and about eight feet from it. Carl Johnson, dressed in a conservative gray suit, white button-down shirt and solid navy tie, sat on the couch on the same side of the room as Dr. Wells. The wall above the fireplace was adorned with a painting of an old-fashioned sailing ship being tossed about in a violent sea. A valiant crew member encased in full foul-weather gear bravely straddled the bow sprint of the vessel, attempting to bring down the foresail. I recognized that painting from an art history class I took at Dartmouth. It was entitled "The Widow Maker."

In front of the large mahogany desk were two wooden chairs. A medium-sized man with thinning dark hair and glasses sat behind the desk in a crisp blue suit and red power tie. That must be the Warden, I thought. He rose, introduced himself to Mr. Stanton, and shook his hand. He nodded to me, but said nothing. I was then led to the far end of the room. Mr. Johnson and Mr. Stanton simply glared at each other, without exchanging any pleasantries or handshakes. Mr. Johnson did not even acknowledge my presence. Then Mr. Johnson said:

"Mr. Stanton and Mr. Jackson, I would like to introduce you to Dr. Paige Wells. As you know, Mr. Stanton, Dr. Wells is with the New Hampshire State Police and has been designated as the State's expert in this case." Dr. Wells rose from her chair and gracefully strolled over and shook Mr. Stanton's hand. Then she turned towards me:

"You must be Professor Jackson. I am Dr. Paige Wells, and I will be asking you some questions today." She looked directly into my eyes as she spoke and held my gaze in hers like a vise. She held out her hand towards me. I shook it without speaking.

"Would it be all right if Professor Jackson sat in that chair by the fireplace and I sat in this chair, with Mr. Stanton sitting on this couch?" She pointed to the couch that was on the same side as my chair, where Mr. Stanton would essentially be facing Mr. Johnson.

Mr. Stanton spoke up: "That would be fine. We are ready to begin whenever you are."

We all settled in to our respective places. I took a few deep breaths to calm myself, and then looked over at Dr. Wells, who was staring at me intently. Dr. Wells broke the silence:

"Before we get started, I wanted to introduce myself a little bit more and tell you what I hope to accomplish here today. I am a psychiatrist by training. I have spent a substantial amount of time studying abnormalities of the mind, and I have also spent a great deal of time studying the psychosis of mass murderers. I have been trying to gain an understanding of why some people commit such crimes, so that I can develop a way to identify those who might be at risk for such behavior and get them treatment before they can injure anyone. By pleading not guilty by reason of insanity, you have admitted to shooting your students. I know that Dr. Van DeMere believes that you are suffering from a depersonalization disorder causing you not to know why you committed the crimes, but I want to ask you some questions to see if I can find out why this happened. I don't really care if my conclusions are favorable to the prosecution or the defense. I want to learn as much as I can about you to see if I can prevent this from happening to someone else. Do you understand?"

I sat there for a moment, both to follow Mr. Stanton's answering process and to ponder Dr. Wells' statement. Dr. Wells somehow looked familiar to me; I strongly felt that I had seen her somewhere before, but that was impossible. Also, something about her voice seemed familiar. That, too, was impossible. So I let that initial impression pass and concentrated on answering her question. Ironically, she wanted what I wanted: to understand why I shot my students.

"I do understand."

"Also, before we begin, I wanted to know how I should address you. You have a Ph.D., and are thus entitled to be called 'Doctor' just as much as I am. Or, would you be more comfortable with me addressing you as 'Professor?'" Dr. Wells smiled.

I sat stone-faced looking at her. I recognized that smile. Women used it as a way to disarm and manipulate men. My ex-wife had used that same smile just before telling me that she wanted another pair of shoes or an expensive purse, or to purchase the BMW convertible that she ended up driving away in after the divorce was final. No, I wasn't falling for that. And I wasn't falling for this "Doctor" crap either.   I knew what she was doing: attempting to break the ice by flattering me and suggesting that we were really on the same footing and could be buddies. Well, two could play this game.

"'Doctor' seems a bit too formal, don't you think? Why don't I just call you 'Dr. Wells' and you can call me 'Dan.'" There, I had turned the tables on her. I controlled the "naming" function, not her.

She smiled even more broadly. "Great, Dan. I think your suggestion is a good one. I have some questions I would like to ask you. Shall we get started?"

"Sure."

"I would like to get an understanding of your background. Where did you grow up?"

"River Falls, Wisconsin."

"Tell me a little about your family growing up."

"There's not much to tell. My father was a plumbing contractor, and my mother a secretary for a small local accounting firm."

"How was your relationship with your father?"

Here it goes. The shrinks inevitably want to know about your parents. Did they beat you? Humiliate you? Was your mother domineering? Did she dress you in girls' clothes? God, I had gone through all these types of questions during the marriage counseling that preceded my separation and divorce. This wasn't going to get me anywhere in understanding why I had taken those guns to class. I suppose there was no way to avoid it. But what should I tell her about my father?

Dad was a quiet man. He came from a large family that had scrapped by during the Great Depression by depending upon each family member to pull his own weight. His father, my grandfather, used to tell stories of how the family would go for days with little food, living on what game they could hunt or fish they could catch. I knew the stories were true because my Dad was about the best hunter and fisherman in western Wisconsin. Every hunting season, Dad bagged a deer, using only one shot to bring it down. Every summer, Dad could coax large walleyes onto his lure with seemingly effortless ease. But Dad never spoke of the Great Depression or his upbringing. It was something that had obviously molded his determination to work hard and put food on the table, but he either couldn't or wouldn't share what that experience had been like with his own family.

Dad was equally silent about his service in World War II. He had served in the Army as an infantry soldier in North Africa and Italy. When he would take off his shirt in the summers to swim or do yard work, I could see a few scars on his back and arms, souvenirs of his Army days. One of the scars was a long, jagged one that sliced along his back and side; a few smaller round-shaped blemishes marked his upper shoulder and bicep. When I was 10 years old, I had asked him about the scars. He said simply that he had gotten them in the war and turned away.

After Dad died, I was helping my mother go through his belongings and found old photos of Dad with his unit in Italy. And I found letters he had kept from soldiers in his unit, thanking him for saving their lives, not just once, but several times. From the letters I learned that Dad was considered the bravest man in his platoon, and that he often put himself in mortal danger to save his buddies. One letter from a member of his platoon recounted the story of how my Dad got the scar on his back: it was a knife wound suffered in hand-to-hand combat with Nazi soldiers in Sicily that had almost killed him. From other letters I learned that Dad had been shot on several occasions in battles; that explained the round-shaped blemishes on his shoulders and upper arms. Among Dad's belongings was a long rectangular wooden box. I opened it to discover that he had been awarded the Silver Star for valor, along with a Purple Heart. Other men might well have bragged about such exploits and proudly displayed such medals. There seemed to always be some blowhards down at the local barbershop recounting supposed adventures from the war. But Dad never said a word about winning these prestigious awards, or his conduct that had merited such recognition.

Dad just wasn't an open person. He kept his feelings and his thoughts pretty much to himself. I don't ever remember seeing my mother and father hugging or kissing. Dad never hugged or kissed me. As I entered my teenage years, we sometimes shook hands. But there was never a physical or emotional bond between us. Yet, he taught me to hunt and fish and to take responsibility for myself, and I admired and loved him. I knew that he loved me, in his own way. So how do I answer her question?

"My father was a reserved guy. He worked hard, kept his nose clean, and provided for his family."

"Did you and your father share any common interests?"

"A couple, but not many. We would hunt and fish together, when he had the time. But he never went to college, and was kind of anti-intellectual, whereas I loved school and was a good student. He was good with his hands. I wasn't."

"How was your relationship with your mother?"

My mother never went to college, but was the best read person I have ever known. She encouraged me to read Shakespeare and the great Renaissance philosophers. After dinner, she and I would sit at the table discussing different observations about these great writers and their works, while my father went to his chair in the living room to supposedly watch television, but in reality, fall asleep. Mom was also a keen follower of current affairs, and lively dinner time discussions would often erupt concerning gun control, civil rights and other topical issues. Her arguments were always well-reasoned and articulate. She was never condescending or shrill. She listened to what I said and asked insightful questions to expose the weaknesses in my reasoning. I always felt that she was my intellectual soul mate.

That being said, there was not a strong physical or emotional bond between us. I don't really know if I was breast fed or not (the marriage counselor had asked me that question, suggesting the answer might explain my breast fetish), but I know that despite our close intellectual connection, I do not remember Mom hugging or kissing me, aside from an occasional peck on the cheek. Like my father, Mom, too, was a quiet, private person, not prone to displays of affection. But I worshiped her, and did everything I could to make her proud of me.

"I had a good relationship with my mother. We were a lot alike in terms of our intellectual interests and had a lot of good discussions."

"Did your parents have a good relationship with each other?"

That was a difficult question to answer, and one I had wondered about growing up. Although both Mom and Dad were normally reserved individuals who expressed little emotion, they did quarrel from time to time. The quarrels were usually over something that seemed to me to be relatively minor, like Dad leaving the garbage by the back door instead of taking it out to the garbage cans, or leaving his dishes in the sink instead of rinsing them and putting them in the dishwasher. But I sensed that no matter what purportedly sparked the argument, there was some unstated, underlying controversy that almost always led to an escalation of full emotional fury. In a matter of minutes in these episodes, both Mom and Dad would be yelling and swearing a blue streak at each other. There would be slamming of doors and threats of divorce. But just as quickly as the emotional tide had rolled in, it would roll back out again, and things went back to normal. I came to accept these episodic outbursts as just part of the normal ebb and flow of married life, and assumed that all marriages experienced something similar.

"I think so. I mean, they were married for over 35 years."

"Did they ever fight in your presence?"

"What do you mean by 'fight'? They argued from time to time, but nothing serious. There was never any physical violence involved, if that's what you mean."

"What did they argue about?"

"Everyday stuff — chores, schedules, spending too much money on fishing rods."

"Were you ever aware of any accusations of infidelity by either of your parents?"

"No. That would never have happened. Although they were not terribly religious people, they took their marriage vows seriously. In my family, your word was your bond. You didn't go back on your word because of disagreements over chores or fishing rods."

"Did you feel loved by your parents?"

This was getting silly. "Of course. They sacrificed a lot to send me to Dartmouth to school. I knew that they loved me."

"What type of discipline did your parents use when you misbehaved?"

"Are you asking whether my parents beat me?"

"Did they?"

"Of course not. My parents never even spanked me."

"How did you parents discipline you?"

"My mother was the disciplinarian. Dad never seemed to be around when discipline needed to be administered, so my mother made most of the rules and enforced them. She either used a 'time out,' or just gave me a look that let me know that I better straighten up. That was all it took to get the message across."

"All right. Did you have any aunts, uncles, and cousins?"

"My father came from a pretty large family, and had three brothers and two sisters. I had twelve cousins. My mother was an only child, so I didn't have any aunts, uncles, or cousins from her side."

"Did your aunts and uncles live close to you growing up?"

"Yes, relatively speaking. Some of them still lived in River Falls, and a couple had moved to Minnesota near St. Paul, about forty-five minutes or so away. "

"Did you see them often?"

"Every holiday, important birthday and important anniversary there were family gatherings and the whole clan would assemble, usually at my grandparents' house."

"That was your father's father?"

"Yes."

"Did you enjoy those family gatherings?"

"Yes, those are some of my happiest childhood memories. My grandparents were larger than life to me. My grandfather was a small, balding man who always had a sparkle in his eye and a grin on his face. He walked with a cane that he used to hit the grandchildren in the rear end when he wanted our attention. We would all squeal with delight when he did so. He used to 'hire' the grandchildren to perform errands for him, like running to the drug store to pick up the type of chewing gum he liked, and paid us a quarter when we returned. Back in those days, that seemed like a lot of money to us. Grandma was also a stitch. She had grown up in a wealthy Iowa farming family, and had developed a love for gambling. Every Christmas, Grandma would pull out a roulette wheel and chips and play roulette with the grandchildren. We always had a great time. The uncles and aunts all got along pretty well, and would drink and laugh and tell family stories from their youth."

"Were you close with your grandparents?"

"I was close with my father's parents, but not my mother's. Her father had died when she was sixteen, and her mother lived pretty far away in Milwaukee, so I didn't see her much."

"Now I have to ask you what may seem like an insulting question, but it's necessary to eliminate certain possible causes for your behavior. Did anyone in your family — mother, father, aunts, uncles, cousins — ever touch you in a way that made you feel uncomfortable?"

"Are you asking me if I was ever molested by someone in my family?"

"Well, yes."

"Absolutely not. Nothing like that ever happened."

"All right. You said that you were a good student in school. Did you have many friends growing up?"

The truth was that I was a little too nerdy for a lot of the boys in River Falls, most of whom loved to play touch football and pond hockey, and were pretty good at it. I, on the other hand, was not much of a physical specimen, and would rather have curled up with a good book instead of banging my brains out playing sports. Still, I found some kindred spirits.

"I had a fairly small group of friends who were very loyal, but I was not the most popular guy in school, if that's what you're asking."

"Did you have any serious illnesses as a child?"

"Just the normal stuff: chicken pox, measles, mumps, bouts with the flu. Nothing too serious."

"What would you say was the most traumatic thing you remember happening to you in your childhood?"

I thought for a moment, not because it was difficult to provide an answer, but rather to consider how much of the story to reveal. I decided that if I had any hope of finding out why the shootings had happened, it would be by providing some information to Dr. Wells so that she would have something to work with.

"I think the most traumatic thing I can remember from my childhood is the one time when my father lost his temper with me, and hit me."

"I thought you told me that your parents never spanked you?"

"They didn't. And this wasn't a spanking. It was a single, hard slap at my head. But it was the only time that my father or mother ever hit me. I guess that is why it sticks out in my mind."

"Can you tell me about how it occurred?"

"My father and I used to go to a barber shop in town to get haircuts together. During one visit when I was about six years old, the barber started asking me questions, just to pass the time as he was snipping away. He asked me how things were going at home. For some reason, I blurted out that things were going okay, except when Mom and Dad got in arguments and started swearing at each other. The men in the shop all laughed. Dad, sitting in the next barber chair, was mortified. He tried to laugh it off and switch the topic, but for some reason I continued on detailing the precise swear words that flew back and forth and the loudness of the shouting. As we left the barber shop, I remember Dad grabbing my arm and harshly whispering in my ear: 'Wait until we get home and tell your mother how you have embarrassed the family.'"

"When we got home, Dad marched me into the kitchen where Mom was making dinner and told her the whole story. I will never forget the look of anguish on my mother's face. I blushed with embarrassment and stared at the floor. My Dad grabbed me by the arm and shook me hard, and kept repeating: 'Why would you do such a thing?' But I didn't have an answer, and began crying as he shouted the same thing, over and over. Finally, out of frustration, he gave the back of my head a vicious slap. I saw stars and gulped for air. My mother screamed 'Stop!' and rushed to my side, glaring up at Dad. Dad let go of my arm and stamped out of the kitchen."

"Later that night, as I was getting ready for bed, there was a knock on my bedroom door. 'Can I come in for a minute?' my father asked. 'Sure,' I responded. I don't remember being afraid that I was going to get hit again, but if I had any such reservations, they quickly evaporated when I saw my father's demeanor upon entering my room. Dad came in slowly, his hands slack by his side, and shoulders slumped. He stared nervously at the floor for a moment. He spoke softly: 'Danny, I am sorry that I hit you in the kitchen. I lost my temper. It made me mad that you would talk about family matters to outsiders. You have every right to be worried when Mom and I argue, but you need to come talk to us about it, not blurt it out in front of strangers. Your mother and I love each other, and we love you. Don't ever doubt that. It was wrong of me to hit you. I will never do it again. Do you believe me?'"

"Dad looked so sad. His eyes were red, like he had been crying. I felt sorry for him. And I was also in amazement, because Dad had never opened up to me in this way, showing vulnerability and sharing his feelings. I knew how hard that must be for him. I told him, 'it's okay, Dad. I know you were angry with me, and I'm sorry that I said those things in the barbershop. I don't really know why I did it. But I promise you that I will never do anything like that again.'"

"Dad breathed a heavy sigh, I think of relief, and said "Thanks, Danny." He turned and left my bedroom."

"Dad was as good as his word. He never struck me again. We never spoke of the barbershop incident again. It was also, perhaps, the last time that my father said out loud that he loved me. It was not, however, the last time that my parents argued. But I think, after the barbershop incident, the arguments bothered me less, for some reason."

The room fell silent, save for the crackling of the fire in the fireplace. I looked over at Mr. Stanton, assuming that I would see a scowl on his face, indicating that I was talking too much, but he seemed lost in thought himself. Mr. Johnson also seemed in a private spot in his mind. Dr. Wells continued:

"Let's talk for a moment about your high school years. Did you like high school?"

"I always liked school and learning. River Falls High School wasn't necessarily the most academically rigorous, but I think I got a good education there."

"Did you participate in any extra-curricular activities?"

"I was on the debate team. No sports or anything."

"Did you do much dating in high school?"

"Some."

"Did you have a special girlfriend?"

"I started dating Nancy, my ex-wife, in my freshman year in high school. We dated pretty much exclusively during high school, and really through college. We got married after my first year in grad school. But I assume you know all that from Dr. Van DeMere's report."

"Did you have sexual relations with Nancy during high school?"

"Just the normal 'petting' type of thing. We didn't sleep together until we were sophomores in college."

"How many girls had you kissed in high school?"

"I think just Nancy."

"How many girls have you slept with, other than Nancy?"

"One. A one-night stand during my freshman year while I was on a road trip to Green Mountain Junior College, a girls' school near Dartmouth. I can't even remember her name."

"What is the most traumatic event you remember from your high school years?"

"Actually, I don't remember anything as being particularly traumatic about high school. I had a pretty good time, and was able to get into the college I wanted, so I had nothing to complain about."

"How did you pick Dartmouth as a place to go to school?"

"As you might imagine, there weren't too many Ivy League graduates living in River Falls, and there were no Dartmouth Alums there. But there was a LaCrosse, Wisconsin Dartmouth Alumni Club that gave out a book award every year to the high school junior in Western Wisconsin who was deemed to be the most outstanding and promising student in their high school. My junior year, I received a letter in the mail informing me that I had been selected to receive the Dartmouth Book Award. I didn't even know where Dartmouth was. I was invited to attend a luncheon down in LaCrosse to receive the award, and was introduced to several Dartmouth alums of various ages, each of whom encouraged me to apply."

"When I went back to River Falls and talked about it with my high school adviser, he told me not to bother because no one from River Falls had ever been accepted at an Ivy League school. Despite his advice, I applied and got in. We couldn't afford to have me go look at the school before deciding whether to accept or not, so I just decided that I'd be the first River Falls graduate to go to Dartmouth. And I loved every minute of it."

"Even though you loved every minute of it, was there anything that you can recall happening to you during your college years that was traumatic or upsetting?"

That was easy enough to answer, but I really didn't want to get into it. I should have known that it would come up sooner or later. I took a deep breath, held it for a moment, and then exhaled.

"I was involved in a terrible car accident in the winter of my junior year. My twin brother, David, was killed in the accident. I was seriously injured and spent several weeks in the hospital recovering, most of it in a coma."

Dr. Wells stopped, put down her pen and pad in her lap and looked at me. I could feel great empathy and sadness in her gaze. She did not speak for several minutes, and when she did, her voice cracked ever so slightly:

"I am very sorry for your loss, Dan. You hadn't mentioned that you had a brother, much less a twin."

"You hadn't asked whether I had any siblings. I wasn't trying to hide anything."

"Of course you weren't. I neglected to ask you. I guess I should ask now whether you have any other brothers or sisters."

"No, it was just David and me."

"I realize that this may be a painful memory to dredge up, but I am going to need to explore this part of your personal history in some detail. We've been going at it for over two hours. I suggest that we take a lunch break, and start up again at two o'clock, if that is satisfactory with everyone."

Mr. Stanton and Mr. Johnson nodded their heads. I nodded mine. Mr. Stanton came over to me and whispered in my ear that we would meet in the interview room at 1:45 to get ready for the afternoon. The guard came and escorted me back to my cell for my stale sandwich and lukewarm milk. I knew in my heart that the next session of Dr. Wells' questioning would be the most difficult. But I didn't believe that it would shed any light on why I had shot my students.

Chapter 11

I couldn't really eat my lunch. I was too pre-occupied with thinking about the upcoming discussion of the accident that killed David. It was a topic that I normally assiduously avoided thinking about. Now Dr. Wells would drag the whole sordid tale out of me, dredging up all the bad memories. But there was no avoiding it now. The cat was out of the bag.

I met with Mr. Stanton at 1:45 in the interview room. Mr. Stanton started out the conversation: "You never mentioned that you had a twin brother before."

"No. It never came up."

"Well you can be sure that Dr. Wells is going to go into it in depth this afternoon. Are you ready for that?"

"I think so. It happened a long time ago. I don't see that it really has anything to do with this."

"I hope you're right. I did speak with Dr. Van DeMere over the lunch break to bring him up to date on what had transpired during the morning and your revelation about your twin brother. He didn't seem to think any of that would alter his diagnosis."

"So I haven't screwed up yet?" I smiled weakly.

"No you're doing fine. Just go back in there and remember the rules we discussed about how to answer questions. You'll be fine."

The guard escorted us back to the Warden's office, and we resumed our respective positions. Dr. Wells and Mr. Johnson were already there, waiting for us. Dr. Wells started the afternoon session:

"I hope you had a good lunch, Dan. I now need to ask you some questions about your deceased twin brother. I know that this must be a very difficult topic for you, but I feel that it is an important part of who you are, and may provide insight into the current situation. First, were you and David identical or fraternal twins?"

"David was my twin, but far from an identical one. He was handsome. I was more of a plain-Jane. He had twenty-twenty vision. I wore thick glasses. He was captain of the high school football, hockey and baseball teams. I was captain of the debate team and president of the student council, because nobody else ran for the job. Everybody in school was, or wanted to be, David's friend. I had a small circle of nerdy friends. He had a series of girlfriends and sexual conquests throughout high school. I was a virgin until my sophomore year in college. He could help my father repair things around the house. I couldn't drive a nail straight to save my life. I was the smart one, the one who brought home straight "A's" on every report card, while David stumbled along with "B's" and "C+'s." I got into Dartmouth, with a scholarship. David barely got into University of Wisconsin at River Falls."

Dr. Wells broke into my narrative: "How did your parents treat the two of you? I mean, did your mother prod David to do better in school? Did your father prod you to try athletics? How did they praise each of you? Or did they?"

"David's academic short-comings never caused my parents any consternation. Mom never really got on David's case about his grades. She would simply smile and say that God gives to each of his children their own gifts, and left it at that. Dad never said anything to me about playing football or any other sport. I think he knew that would be folly. The only praise I got for my academic prowess was a 'nicely done' from my mother. My father never said a word about my grades, or David's, for that matter. But he was at all of David's football, hockey and baseball games."

"Were you jealous of David?"

"I know that it sounds like I was, but not really. Maybe envious, wishing that I could be a little more like him. But I loved him. And I think that he loved me, at least most of the time."

"What do you mean he loved you most of the time?"

"Well, sometimes he went out of his way to protect and help me. For example, when we were smaller, and the kids in the neighborhood got together for pick up football or baseball games, he always made sure that I got picked for his team; otherwise there was a pretty good chance that neither team captain would have picked me at all. He looked out for me at school, never letting anybody bully or tease me. And I mean anybody. I remember one time when we were in first grade and in the same class, our teacher punished me for talking out of turn, and David ran up and kicked her in the shins. That was the last time that we were allowed to be in the same classroom together."

"Can you think of other examples of David protecting or helping you?"

"To make me feel good, when we were by ourselves, he nicknamed me 'Batman,' while he took the nickname 'Robin.' Of course, in reality, we both knew that our positions were exactly reversed."

"How did David act towards you at other times?"

"As we got older, he would call me "Professor" when we were with the other guys, sort of making fun of my academic prowess, which he knew I didn't like. I suppose to get even, I wouldn't let him copy my homework, which made him furious. His retaliation for that was to make me look like a fool at the pickup football games by deliberately throwing the football at me so hard that it was impossible to catch, and then turning, shrugging his shoulders and rolling his eyes at the other guys when I dropped the ball. He could be charming or annoying, depending upon his mood and who the audience was. It did sort of piss me off that when others were around, he had the tendency to put me down."

"Did you ever tell David that you loved him, and did he ever tell you that he loved you?"

"Not in so many words. You'll remember that we were brought up in a family that didn't go for open demonstrations of affection or emotion. But he knew. I would never have done anything to hurt David."

"That's a curious thing to say, Dan. Did someone accuse you of trying to hurt David?"

"Well, David did die in the car accident. And I was driving. Mom and Dad never said anything out loud, but I could feel their extraordinary sadness, and who else was there to blame? Like the captain of a ship, as the driver, I had to accept responsibility."

"Tell me about the accident."

I paused to gather myself. "David had come up to visit me at Dartmouth for Winter Carnival weekend — a four-day span of drunken debauchery. The whole campus really gets into it. There was a huge ice sculpture of a castle on the center of the campus Green. Each of the fraternity houses also had their own miniature ice sculptures, some quite elaborate. Several of the frat houses had bands and parties. Girls from all over the Northeast travelled to Hanover to see their boyfriends, or in the hopes of meeting a guy to shack-up with for the weekend. The Daily Dartmouth, the college newspaper, had once sardonically declared that if all the women who came to Hanover for Winter Carnival were laid end to end, no one would be surprised."

Dr. Wells chuckled for a moment, and I had to smile myself. I continued:

"David had heard about Winter Carnival and what a great party weekend it was, and basically invited himself to come up for the event. He flew to Boston on Thursday morning, took the Vermont Transit bus up to White River Junction, and grabbed a cab over to Hanover. I had told him that I would meet him in front of the Hop, the student activities center, and I don't think I will ever forget the look on David's face as he got out of the cab: he had this big shit eating grin and literally bound up to me with his duffel bag in one hand and skis in the other. We shook hands, and David's first words were 'where's the beer?' It was only 11:00 a.m., and I had a big English mid-term exam on Monday to study for, so I told him that would have to wait for a while."

"My then girlfriend, Nancy, was coming up from Holy Cross for the weekend, so my dorm room, which was a single, would be fully occupied. I had managed to save a spot at my fraternity house for David to sleep on the couch, which was a three block walk from my dorm. So I led David to the frat house where he could dump his stuff, introduced him to some of my fraternity brothers, gave him the extra key to my room in case of emergency and went off to get a couple of hours of study in for my exam."

Dr. Wells broke in. "You belonged to a fraternity? I thought you said that you were the nerdy one."

"Well, once I got to Dartmouth, I discovered that there were a lot of very smart guys there, and it wasn't thought to be "nerdy" to be interested in intellectual pursuits. The Dartmouth debate team was one of the best in the country, and one of the fraternities was made up largely of debaters, and guys from the college radio station and the Daily Dartmouth, the school newspaper. That's the one I joined."

"Okay. Sorry to interrupt. Go on."

"Well, the funny thing about that weekend was that I didn't actually spend much time with David from Thursday through Saturday, and when I did see him, he made an ass of himself. First, on Friday afternoon while I was trying to study, David kept coming by the room, on his way to being plastered, to ask me questions about where certain things were on campus. Then, after Nancy arrived early Friday evening, he shadowed our every move, from dinner to the frat dances around campus, making snide remarks in front of Nancy about what a waste it was for me to be at a place where one could ski and hike when I was such a pansy. For the rest of the weekend, David, being David, made himself right at home and had a great time skiing during the day and drinking and partying at night. We always had an open keg at the fraternity house, and David took full advantage. Naturally, all I heard from my frat brothers was what a great guy David was, and how funny it was how different twin brothers could be."

"Because of my English exam on Monday, I had told Nancy that Saturday afternoon would have to be devoted to studying, so she brought some of her books up with her and we dutifully went to Baker Library to hide in the stacks. When we returned to my dorm room just before dinner, I was shocked to discover David completely naked in my dorm room with two partially clothed girls, who I later learned had come over for Winter Carnival weekend from Middlebury College in search of a good time. Nancy was mortified at the scene, and I sternly ordered David to get dressed and get his groupies the hell out of my room. He and the girls sheepishly complied, although under his breath I heard David apologize to the girls for his 'limp dick' brother. Saturday night Nancy and I ran into David again at the dance my fraternity had sponsored for Winter Carnival. David was playing pool with some of the frat brothers, completely hammered. When he saw Nancy and me, he called out "hey Professor," in a slurred voice. My frat brothers hadn't heard that nickname for me before, and several of them who were around the pool table broke out in laughter. I turned, gave David the finger, and tried to disappear with Nancy on the dance floor. We didn't see David again for the rest of the night, and that was okay with me at that point."

"After the dance, though, David and I got into an argument. I didn't see him again until late afternoon on

Sunday, and told him I wanted him to leave. To accomplish that goal, I ended up borrowing a car and driving him down to Boston." I took in a deep breath and let it out. "Could I get a glass of water, please, before we continue?"

Dr. Wells smiled and said "Sure."

While I waited for some water, I pondered the part of the story that I had left out. On that Saturday night, after the dance had ended, I left with Nancy to go back to my room. Once in my room, Nancy and I quickly undressed each other and began kissing and fondling each other. We'd both had a fair amount to drink, so our inhibitions were extremely low. Although we normally just made love in the traditional missionary position, I grabbed both of Nancy's hips, pulled her to her knees, and straddled her from behind. She let out a loud, excited cry as I entered her. As I began pounding away, she began moaning "oh Dan, oh Dan," until she was virtually shrieking it. I was enjoying myself, too, and was more or less lost in the moment.

I didn't initially hear the door to my room being unlocked. Suddenly, David came bursting into the room, beer bottle in hand, accompanied by three of my other frat brothers, and flipped on the light. Nancy screamed, tried to disengage and cover herself with the bed sheets. I was left hanging there, my private parts in plain view, while David and the brothers laughed hysterically.

I jumped up from the bed and took a wild swing at David, missing him badly. I pushed and shoved David and his accomplices out of the door, yelling at the top of my voice that I was going to fucking kill them all for this. As I slammed the door, I could hear their drunken laughter as they literally bounced off the walls of the hallway.

I was fuming mad, and turned back to Nancy, who with the sheets up to her chin, was sobbing uncontrollable. She screamed at me to leave the room, and leave her alone.

I pulled on some sweat pants and a tee shirt and dutifully slept in a friend's room down the hall. The next morning, I awoke to find that Nancy had left to return to Holy Cross. The note she left said that she knew it wasn't my fault, but she just couldn't face David after he had seen her in such a compromising position. She said that she would call me during the week once David was gone.

I spent the rest of the morning and afternoon hunting for David. I was seething with anger. If I got my hands on David, I was going to beat his head in with any implement I could find. This time, he'd gone too far. I wasn't going to let him get away with it. But David was nowhere to be found. Not at the frat house, not at the student center, nor in any of the restaurants on Main Street. By late Sunday afternoon, I finally caught up with David in the basement of the frat house at the bar. By then, my anger had subsided somewhat, although I was still furious.

However, before I could even get started, David was apologizing profusely, saying that he was totally drunk and didn't realize what he was doing. He said that he had arranged to have a dozen roses sent to Nancy at Holy Cross with my name on them, and mailed a written apology to her, in which he assured her that neither he nor the frat brothers had seen her naked. This was typical David. Screw something up big-time, and then apologize big-time as well. He wasn't going to get off that easy this time. I remember telling him:

"Listen, David. You are a complete asshole. You come to my school and act like a jerk. You've embarrassed me in front of my friends. You really made a mess of things for me with Nancy. I don't know if she'll ever really forgive me. So I want you off this campus pronto. Like, right now. Not tomorrow."

David starred down at his feet for a moment, and then looked me in the eye. "Okay. I get it. But look, there are no more buses today down to Boston. So unless you can borrow a car to drive me there, I'm stuck here until tomorrow."

And that was how we had ended up on the road out of Hanover on the way to Boston that fateful evening. Although I loathed the thought of spending two hours in the car with David, at that point I was willing to do anything just to get him out of my hair.

A guard handed me a glass of water which I chugged down. I set the glass down on the end table next to the chair, ready to answer further questions. "Where were we?"

Dr. Wells looked down at her notes. "You were telling me about how you and David had gotten into a fight on Saturday night, and that on Sunday afternoon, you told him he had to leave, and ended up driving him to Boston. Can I ask what you fought with David about?"

No way was I going to answer that honestly. "It was just one of those drunken fights that guys get into. I'm not sure I even remember now what it was about. But I do remember being very angry at him and wanting him off campus. So I talked my buddy Kevin into loaning us his car to drive down to Boston. It took a little convincing, which occurred over a few beers in the basement of the frat. Finally, Kevin agreed, gave me the keys and off we went."

"We had to walk all the way down to the remote student parking lot that was out past the gym and football stadium. It had started snowing earlier in the day, and as we started walking to the car, it was snowing heavily. As we were trudging along, I began thinking that maybe driving down to Boston tonight was not such a good idea. The weather was bad, I had drunk a couple beers, and under normal circumstances I had a strict rule against drinking and driving. But I was still angry at David, and wanted him off this campus and out of my affairs. So we pilled in Kevin's green Ford and took off."

"I decided to drive down Main Street out of Hanover towards the Lebanon regional airport, and catch Highway 89 down to Boston there. Main Street turns into state highway 10, a two lane road that meanders along the Connecticut River on the New Hampshire side. Once away from Hanover, there were few road lights along the dark, winding road. Peering out through the windshield, the glare of the headlights on the snow was blinding, making it almost impossible to even see where the right side of the road was. I slowed down, but visibility did not improve much."

"After about ten minutes on the road, we were approaching a sweeping left hand curve. David had been yapping at me for the entire ride thus far, recounting all the adventures he had at Winter Carnival. All the beers he drunk and the girls he fucked. It was just becoming too much for me to handle. I glanced over at him, while he was blathering away looking out the window, took my right hand off the wheel, and reached over and slapped him hard in the face. He instinctively reached out and grabbed my arm. My left hand on the wheel pulled the opposite direction to resist, sending our car over the center line and into on-coming traffic."

"I suddenly saw headlights in front of me, coming right at us. An eighteen-wheeler, seeing our car veer into its lane, had apparently braked and begun sliding on the snow. Through the snow pelting our windshield I could see a blurred image skidding right towards us, with the trailer jack-knifed across the entire road. It was twenty yards away. Then fifteen yards. Then ten. And still the truck with its trailer continued on its path, blocking the entire road. There was nowhere to go. No place to hide. I stamped on the breaks and cried out 'Shit.' David shouted 'Holly fuck,' and I could see out of the corner of my eye David instinctively reach out with his hand for the front of the dashboard to brace for impact."

"Of course, in retrospect, stamping on the brakes was precisely the wrong thing to do. That just caused the car to fish-tail in a violent manner. But in some ways, it was fortunate that our car started skidding when it did. Ultimately, in my desperate attempt to counter-steer to fight the fish-tail skid, I over-corrected and caused the car to spin completely around. It sounded like a cannon going off as the truck's trailer hit the back and side of the car. Our car was slapped like hockey puck over the embankment of the road, and it rolled over several times. We weren't wearing seat belts, so we got tossed around like clothing in a washing machine. I hit my head hard on the steering wheel and was then slammed back into my seat and against the roof of the car. I could vaguely hear David screaming. I blacked out."

"The next thing I remember is feeling someone pulling me from car. I tried opening my eyes, and the world around me was spinning wildly. There were flashing lights from emergency vehicles, and firemen and paramedics rushing about. Out of the corner of my eye, I saw David. He had been thrown through the windshield of the car, with his head and torso lying on the hood of the car, and his lower body stuck inside the car. His coat had been ripped open, and his shirt was covered with blood. His eyes stared blankly into the snowy sky. I tried to cry out to him, but felt my field of vision diminishing as everything eventually turned into blackness."

"When I next opened my eyes, I was in the emergency room of some hospital. Doctors and nurses rushed between patients. Again I saw David in the next bed over. A doctor was holding his wrist taking his pulse. I saw the doctor shake his head and turn away. I felt an overwhelming desire to cry and squeezed my eyes closed, whimpering quietly as I drifted out of consciousness once again. I knew that David was dead."

I paused and stared down at my hands. Even after all these years, remembering the accident brought tears to my eyes. After a moment, Dr. Wells responded quietly:

"Dan, I am so sorry for your loss. That is a tragic story. But it was an accident. Surely you understand that, at least at an intellectual level."

"I have re-played and re-played the whole thing in my mind thousands of times, wondering if there was anything I could have done differently. I could have not insisted on driving to Boston, once it started snowing so hard. I could have refused to drive because I had been drinking. And if I hadn't reached over to slap David, well I just don't know. We were young and stupid, and David paid the price."

"You say that maybe you shouldn't have driven because you had been drinking. Did the police test you for your blood alcohol level?"

"No. The public attitude towards drunken driving in New Hampshire at that time was fairly lenient; I think it was 'there but for the grace of God go I.' So I wasn't tested. As far as the police knew, I was perfectly sober. But I wasn't."

"How many beers had you drunk before starting the trip to Boston?"

"I can't remember now, but David and I had started drinking at about 5:00 pm, and we started down for Boston at about 7:00 p.m. So too many to have my full facilities."

"What about the truck driver? It seems to me that he was equally to blame. Did he get ticketed?"

"I don't remember the police giving out any tickets for the accident. So the designation of fault was left ambiguous from that perspective."

"How did your parents react to David's death?"

"I could tell that they were crushed, although I don't recall ever speaking directly with them about David's death. I was in the hospital for about a month after the accident with broken ribs, a crushed shoulder, and head lacerations. I guess they took David's body back home to Wisconsin for the burial, which I could not attend. When I woke up from the coma, I spoke with Mom every day by phone, but she seemed deflated and beaten. I once tried to apologize to her for the accident, but she stopped me and told me that no more need be said about it. My father died of a heart attack six months later. I had never spoken to him after the accident. I think he must have hated me for it. Mom died the following year of cancer. I think her body just invited the nearest virus in and refused to fight. David's death destroyed her will to live."

"Dan, I know how hard this must be for you. But I want to make sure I understood what you just told me. You didn't attend your brother's funeral?"

"No."

"Did you attend your mother's or father's funeral?"

I thought about that for a moment. Strange, I wasn't sure. "I don't remember whether I did or not. I must have, but I do not have a clear recollection of doing so."

"You were a junior at the time of the accident. Did your mother get to see you graduate?"

That was odd. As I sat there, I couldn't remember whether she came to my graduation or not. "I'm not sure. The sequence of events — Dad's heart attack, Mom's death and graduation — is a little fuzzy in my mind. I think she attended my graduation, but I don't have a specific recollection of it."

"Did you ever receive any grief counseling to help you deal with the death of your family members?"

"No."

"Why not?"

"I wasn't comfortable talking about such private matters with a stranger. I wasn't going to make the 'barber shop' mistake again. I had promised my father I wouldn't."

Dr. Wells scribbled on her pad, put her pen down and looked at me intently for a moment. Then she continued:

"I have a few more brief areas to cover, but we've covered a lot of ground, and I think it would be a good idea for us to take a short break before continuing. Would that be alright with you, Dan?"

I nodded my head. I felt emotionally drained and welcomed the suggestion. The guard escorted Mr. Stanton and me to the interview room for our fifteen minute break, as I tried to push the memories of David and the accident back into the recesses of my mind, and re-focus on whatever topics remained to be covered.

Chapter 12

We re-assembled in the Warden's office at the appointed time. Dr. Wells was reviewing her notes as we entered, and did not look up. As I sat down in my chair, she glanced up and smiled briefly at me, before continuing:

"After you recovered from the accident, what did you do?"

"Well, I continued on at Dartmouth for my senior year. I had been thinking of going to law school, but I decided to apply for graduate programs in comparative literature instead."

"Can you tell me why you decided to switch career paths so late in your college career?"

"I had an intellectual interest in the law, but I was also attracted by the lure of the large salaries they were paying young lawyers. But somehow, after the accident, the money part didn't seem so important. I wanted to be in a field where I could be more by myself, with my own thoughts, and not necessarily have to share those thoughts with other people. I wanted some time to just think and figure things out, without the pressure of performing for others."

"But the ultimate career path for a comparative literature Ph.D. was to teach, right?"

"Yes, but that would be five or more years away, and allow me some time to gain some perspective."

"I should know this, but where did you go to graduate school?"

"I went to Harvard. So did my then girlfriend, Nancy, who got her MBA there. We got married after she graduated. She took a job with a Boston investment banking group."

"Where did you honeymoon?"

I had to think for a minute. "As I recall, we really didn't have a honeymoon. We were supposed to go down to Cape Cod for four or five days after the wedding, but there was a transit strike so we couldn't take the bus as we had planned. I tried to rent a car, but Massachusetts had this rule that you had to be twenty-five years old to rent a car, and I was only twenty-three. So we just stayed home in our apartment."

"When you graduated from Harvard, were you able to get a teaching position?"

"Not right away. But eventually, I got a teaching spot at the University of New Hampshire. It meant that I had to commute pretty far for work, and normally stayed one night in Durham, but teaching jobs were tight and I was lucky to get one."

"How long were you at the University of New Hampshire?"

"About six years."

"Why did you leave?"

"They made it clear that I was not going to be given tenure. So I had to go somewhere else."

"Did they tell you why you were not going to get tenure?"

"Well, I had yet to publish anything noteworthy in my field, and the student reviews of my classes were mixed."

"Where did you go?"

"I got a visiting professor position at Holy Cross that lasted about three years. That, too, involved a pretty hefty commute from Boston, but Nancy was pretty adamant that she was not moving from Boston. She liked her job and was getting good promotions. Since she was the primary bread-winner, she told me that she got a veto over where we lived."

"What was your reaction to that?"

"It was hard to argue with. She was making a six-figure income; I was making less than half of what she made."

"How long were you at Holy Cross?"

"I only lasted for one three-year contract. Then I was told to move along."

"Was the lack of publication and mixed student reviews the issue again?"

"Pretty much."

"Where did you go next?"

"I got a temporary position at Haverford down in Philadelphia. That lasted about four years. I rented an apartment in Philadelphia and would drive home to Boston on the weekends. Then I went to Bowden up in Maine. I thought that might blossom into a tenured position because I had finally managed to get something significant published. Bowden renewed my visiting professor status twice. But after about nine years there, it became clear that no tenure position would be available. That's when I came to Dartmouth as a visiting professor."

"Do you like teaching?"

"Yes and no. There is something intellectually satisfying about helping students understand some of the greatest literature ever written. At the schools where I taught, there were some very bright and engaged students who were a joy to teach. But a lot of the students just don't care. They don't do the reading. They don't put much effort in their essays — they don't even proof-read them for spelling and grammatical errors. They are going through the motions. But they expect that their mediocre effort will be rewarded with the "gentleman's B" at a minimum. That kind of performance didn't cut it with me. Although my students seemed to enjoy my lectures well enough, I became pretty unpopular once the grades came out. I didn't grade on the curve. I gave out a lot of C's, because that's what the performance warranted."

"Did your students fill out evaluations on your courses?"

"Some did."

"Were they favorable?"

"As you might guess from what I have just told you, I was not popular once the grades came out, at least for those students who were expecting an easy B."

"What about the good students? Did they give you good evaluations?"

"There were some favorable evaluations, which I always assumed came from those students who performed well and were rewarded with a good grade."

"Do you think that the student evaluations hurt your chances for tenure?"

"Could be one reason. Also, I think I jangled some nerves within the college department structure by trying to teach classes that 'belonged' to other departments. For example, I taught a Shakespeare class that 'belonged' to the English department, and a class on Nietzsche that 'belonged' to the philosophy department. As a comparative literature teacher, I didn't really recognize such boundaries. I guess that made me threatening to some of my colleagues. Tenure was awarded by department, and I didn't really fit into any one department."

"How was your teaching experience at Dartmouth?"

"About the same. The overall quality of the student body at Dartmouth is maybe a little higher, and thus I would get more students in my classes who were interested in the subject and willing to do the work. But the students who turn in the evaluations, more often than not, seem to be the malcontents."

"How did you feel about the students you were teaching this term?"

"I'm not sure what you're asking."

"Well, did they irritate you or make you feel resentful?"

"No. They were freshman, just starting out their academic careers and trying to figure it out. I didn't expect them to be polished scholars."

"So you didn't feel any anger towards them?"

"No."

Dr. Wells paused for a moment, looking over her notes.

"Dan, there's just one more topic I want to cover with you. I've read Dr. Van DeMere's report about your divorce, and I want to ask you a few questions about that. I know that, too, is a painful topic, but there are a few things I need to understand, if that's okay?"

"Fine."

"Dr. Van DeMere's report indicates that it was your wife who wanted the divorce; is that correct?"

"Yes."

"Your wife wanted to leave you for a woman lover?"

"That's what she told me."

"Had you had any inclination before then that your wife was a lesbian?"

"I don't think she is a lesbian. I think she apparently is bi-sexual."

"All right. Did you ever suspect that your wife was bi-sexual?"

"No."

"Have you ever had a sexual relationship with a man?"

"No. I am heterosexual. Period."

"Dr. Van DeMere's report indicates that the marriage counselor you worked with told you that you were emotionally closed and couldn't provide your wife with the emotional intimacy she required. What was your reaction to that?"

"I guess it was probably true. I resented the suggestion that it was my parents' fault for not being emotionally open, because I always knew that they loved me. They didn't do anything wrong."

"But did you *feel* loved by them? It's one thing to know, at an intellectual level, that one is loved, but quite another to *feel* that love at an emotional level."

"I'm not sure, because I am not really sure I understand the distinction you are making."

"All right. Since the divorce have you found yourself unable to sleep at night?

"No."

"Have your eating habits changed? Have you lost or gained a lot of weight?"

"No."

"How about drinking habits. Are you drinking more alcohol than before the divorce?"

"No."

"Were you thinking about your ex-wife the morning of the shooting?"

"No. I don't think so."

"I have only two more questions for you Dan, and then we'll stop. First, did you realize at the time that you were doing the shooting that what you were doing was wrong?"

"I honestly don't recall thinking about that at the time I was doing the shooting. Obviously, I know that shooting people is wrong."

"Okay. Second, do you feel any remorse for having shot those students?"

"Of course I do. They didn't deserve to die, and I am tormented by the fact that I don't know why I did it. It just doesn't make any sense to me. I wish I could undo it, but I can't."

Dr. Wells stood up from her chair and came over to me. I rose from my chair. Our eyes met, and somehow I felt that Dr. Wells had a better understanding of me than I did. She held out her hand, and I shook it. She said,

"Thank you, Dan, for your candid answers to my questions. I wish that we could have met under different circumstances." I mumbled a "thank you."

The guard grabbed my arm to escort me back to my cell. I looked back over my shoulder at Dr. Wells as I left the Warden's office, knowing that the next time I would see her was at the trial. It would be her job to undermine my insanity defense, possibly leading to my execution. Based upon her questioning, it did not seem likely that she would be able to help me answer the question of why I had done the shootings.

Chapter 13

Two days after Dr. Wells' interrogation, Tim came to visit me again. I was escorted to the interview room where Tim and I embraced and then took our respective seats at the table.

"So how did the interview with the prosecution's shrink go? Does she think that you are sane?" Tim asked.

"Hard to say. I mean, she asked me a lot of questions about my relationship with my mother and father, my employment history, and my relationship with Nancy. But I guess the hardest part of the whole thing was discussing David's death, and reliving the car accident."

Tim nodded. "I'm sure even now that has to be a subject that is not easy for you to talk about. I remember that whole, tragic scenario like it was yesterday. I know that you have always blamed yourself, but it was just a terrible, terrible accident. I remember going to the hospital every day and sitting by your bedside, talking to you even though I knew you couldn't hear me. I even said a few prayers for you, which apparently worked, because you eventually did come out of that coma." Tim paused for a moment. "So you told her the whole story?"

"Well, most of it. I mean, I didn't go into detail about why David and I fought on that Saturday night, which lead to my ultimatum that he leave campus on Sunday. But I did tell her that we had fought and I told David that he had to leave."

"Didn't you tell her about how you sometimes hated David because of how he treated you? How can she possibly come to a valid conclusion if you don't give her all the facts?"

"Listen, Tim. She heard enough. She didn't need to hear how he embarrassed me with Nancy, or all the little asshole moves he made that weekend. And I didn't hate David; he just annoyed me from time to time. I shared that stuff with you at the time because you were my best friend. But that all happened over twenty-five years ago. It really doesn't have anything to do with what we're dealing with here."

"Is that what she said?"

"She didn't share any conclusions with me. She just asked questions. Her report isn't due for another week, so I don't know what her opinion will be. I did feel that she was sympathetic to my situation, and understood what I was saying. Funny though, she never did ask me why I shot my students. In fact, we never really discussed the shooting at all."

"She is probably looking for other things in your past that would account for this uncharacteristic violence."

"I guess. There were some questions that threw me for a loop, though."

"Like what?"

"Well, for example, I know that I didn't attend David's funeral back in Wisconsin, because I was still in the hospital after the accident. But I couldn't remember whether I attended my mother or father's funeral. Do you remember that?"

Tim stroked his beard and stared at the ceiling. "Hmm. That's funny. I remember your parents dying shortly after David's accident, but I can't remember whether you attended their funerals or not. But you must have. How could you not have gone to your own parents' funerals?"

"I agree. I must have gone, but I have no memory of it at all. Just like I have no memory of purchasing any guns before the shootings. There's something wrong, I guess, with my memory, but it seems odd that I would forget things like that. Maybe I am insane."

"Any other questions trouble you?"

"Well, one thing occurred to me as a result of Dr. Wells' questions about Nancy. She asked about our honeymoon, which I recalled got cancelled because of a transit strike in Boston."

Tim shook his head affirmatively. "I remember that, too."

"But in thinking about it since the interview, I don't remember where we got married. We should have gotten married back in River Falls, where we grew up and both of our families lived. But I don't remember that happening. Do you remember attending our wedding?"

Again Tim stroked his beard and stared at the ceiling. "Hmm.   Now that you mention it, I don't remember attending your wedding. Maybe it was back in Wisconsin, and only the family was invited."

"I can't envision a scenario in which I would get married and you would not be my best man."

"Oh, I don't know about that. I was never one of Nancy's favorites, you know. I thought she was a driven, ball-busting bitch, and I think that she knew that. Maybe she wouldn't let you invite me. If she had put her foot down, you would have acquiesced in a second."

"That's not true at all. Nancy and I treated each other as equals. She didn't try to order me around. It could never have happened that way."

"Sorry to say it, my friend, but you were pussy-whipped at the time, and never recovered. If you'll remember, I warned you not to marry her. And after you did, she led you around by the nose, always insisting that her career come first and you do all the commuting."

"But she was the one with high paying job. It made sense that her job take precedence."

"Look, Dan. Marriage is more than a financial partnership. It's an emotional partnership. Other than sex, can you honestly say that Nancy ever provided you with the emotional support you needed?"

I pondered that for a moment.   "I think we supported each other emotionally."

"Oh really? Did Nancy ever take an interest in what you were trying to get published to advance your career? Did you ever discuss it?"

"Well, no. But it wasn't in her field. She really wouldn't have known anything about it."

"Did she ever even ask what subjects you were teaching?"

"I can't remember that ever happening. But she was a numbers person. Literature wasn't her thing."

"For people who are truly committed to each other, that wouldn't matter. It isn't about whether she would have known anything about it, or even understood it. She would have understood it was important to you. That's why she would have made it her business to take an interest in it – if she really loved you."

Surprisingly, I found myself getting a little angry with Tim. It was not his place to criticize Nancy. But it was difficult to disagree that, in retrospect, Nancy had not been the right match for me. Yet, part of me still loved her. "Let's forget about Nancy for the moment and focus on what is bothering me: why can't I remember things that should stand out in my memory like monuments? Something is going on here, and I want to find out what it is."

"I have read somewhere that stress can cause memory loss. After what you've been through the last few weeks, it's a miracle that you can remember your own name. Let's not lose focus on the bigger picture here. Are you still intent on pursuing this insanity defense, or can we try to explore a plea bargain that would allow you to accept responsibility and punishment for your actions?"

"I already told you. Based upon what Mr. Stanton has told me, I don't think that this prosecutor will agree to any deal. And in any event, we still don't have Dr. Wells' report. What if she concludes that I do have some form of mental illness? And what if she concludes that with treatment, I can be cured? It doesn't seem right that I should have to spend the rest of my life in jail under those circumstances."

"Look Dan, even if Dr. Wells reaches those conclusions, you are still avoiding the indisputable fact that you killed fifteen people, and need to accept responsibility for that. Has your Mr. Stanton even asked the prosecutor if some kind of plea deal is possible? Trials are expensive endeavors, and my friends at the Diocese say that prosecutors normally only go to trial if it is absolutely necessary."

"I'm not sure if Mr. Stanton has actually broached the subject or not. Once it was clear that the prosecutor was seeking the death penalty, I just assumed that the plea deal was a non-starter."

"I think your Mr. Stanton has avoided bringing up the plea deal with the prosecutor because he is so obsessed with winning. At the very least, you should tell Mr. Stanton to approach the prosecutor about a plea deal. How else will you know whether or not that is a viable option, in the event that Dr. Wells' report concludes that you are sane?"

What Tim was saying actually made some sense, although I did not relish the thought of spending life in prison. "You make some legitimate points, Tim. Let me bring that up with Mr. Stanton in our next meeting and see what he has to say."

"Good. That's all that I am asking, at the moment. But don't put this off. Once Dr. Wells' report comes back, if she concludes that you are sane, it will make it harder to reach a plea deal."

I nodded my head in agreement. Tim and I embraced again, and we went our separate ways. Tim, back to his parish, and me back to my cell, to continue puzzling the mystery of why I was on trial for my life for the murder of my students.

Chapter 14

It seemed like my discussion with Tim had been only a few days ago, but in reality, weeks had flown by and the trial date was almost here. A meeting with Mr. Stanton was scheduled for this morning to go over final preparations for trial. At the appointed time, a guard appeared at my cell to escort me to the interview room. Mr. Stanton, in his usual crumpled gray suit, was sitting behind the table in the interview room waiting for me. He rose, shook my hand, and then settled back into his chair.

"Before we get started, Mr. Stanton, can I ask you a question that has been on my mind?"

"Sure, Professor. Shoot."

"I have been talking with my friend Tim . . ."

"You mean the priest?"

"Yes, that's right. He's a priest. Anyway, he has talked with some lawyers who work for the Episcopal Diocese in Boston, and based on those discussions, he thinks that the prosecutor might still take a plea deal for a sentence of life imprisonment. I promised Tim that I'd ask you about that. Do you think that might be possible?"

The corners of Mr. Stanton's mouth turned down and his eyes narrowed. "Look Professor. I know that your priest friend probably means well, but we really don't need an amateur trying to micro-manage our defense strategy. The whole reason that the prosecution trumped up that kidnapping charge was to get a shot at the death penalty; if Mr. Johnson would have been satisfied with a life sentence, then he never would have gone to that trouble."

"But would it hurt to simply ask him if he'd consider a plea deal to avoid an expensive trial?"

"It would look weak, like we didn't really believe in the insanity defense. Bargaining from weakness is always a mistake. I really don't want a defeatist attitude creeping into your thinking at this point. There will be time later to approach the prosecution about a plea deal, if you want to do that – but after we've scored a few points at trial and have a better bargaining position."

"Mr. Stanton, please don't misunderstand. I wasn't questioning your handling of the case. I just had a question, that's all. I trust your judgment. That's why I wanted to find out what you thought."

Mr. Stanton sighed. "All right, Professor. I didn't mean to get up on my high horse. It's just that I think we can win this, if you give me a chance. And if the case goes well, the time to explore a plea deal will be when the jury is out deliberating. That's when both sides have the most to lose. If you're still interested in a plea deal then, I will approach Mr. Johnson. Okay?"

I shook my head and smiled. "That's fine. Thanks, Mr. Stanton."

"I know that you're probably getting nervous as we get closer to the trial, but we'll see if we can't alleviate some of that concern today. Have you ever seen a trial before?"

"I've seen a few of the lawyer shows on television, but they don't really show a trial from beginning to end. And I did take a criminal justice course one summer while I was in college, so I sort of have an idea how a trial proceeds."

"Those television shows really don't give you a feel for either the tedium or the excitement of a trial. A trial is an organic thing. By that I mean it changes and develops as it goes on. And although you try to prepare for all contingencies, inevitably something comes up that you didn't expect. Let me give you a thumb nail sketch of at least how the trial will proceed. First, the judge will hear and decide any motions in limine. Those are motions that deal with evidentiary matters or address how the trial will proceed. The State hasn't filed any motions; we have filed one. It's a novel one, and not something that I've seen made before, but if it works, it could really throw a curve ball into the proceedings."

"What is it?"

"Well, the motion asks the court to alter the normal order of the presentation of evidence to allow us to put on our defense of insanity first."

"But I thought you told me that the insanity defense had never been successful in New Hampshire, in part, because by the time the defendant gets to put his case on, the jury is already prejudiced against him."

"Exactly. I went back and reviewed everything I could find on cases involving the insanity defense in New Hampshire, and in every single case, the prosecution put on its case first, including, in some cases, taking the jury on a visit to the crime scene, showing graphic photographs of the victims, and generally laying out the facts of the murders in the most gruesome manner possible. The key to our motion is the burden of proof, under New Hampshire law, with regard to the insanity defense."

"Normally, the party with the burden of proof on an issue presents its case first, and also has the right to a rebuttal case. Under federal law, the government has the burden of proof to establish that a defendant is sane, once the insanity defense is raised. But under New Hampshire law, the defense has the burden to prove that the defendant is insane, if an insanity defense is presented. And it occurred to me that the insanity defense admits the commission of the crime. So my motion asks that the defense get to put on its case first, after stipulating to the commission of the murders. We'll keep the stipulation short and sweet, and the State will have limited ability to inflame the jury before they hear our evidence on insanity."

"What about the kidnapping charge? Will you have to stipulate to that as well?" The thought of that worried me, because that was the charge that allowed the state to seek the death penalty.

Mr. Stanton shifted in his chair slightly before answering. "Yes, we'll have to stipulate to that charge as well to get to go first. I have to tell you that, based upon the facts of the shooting, I am very confident that the State would win on that charge anyhow, so we're not giving up much."

"But I don't understand. I didn't kidnap anyone, or tell anyone that they couldn't leave the room."

"To prove kidnapping, all the prosecution has to prove is that the students felt restrained in their freedom to leave. I'm pretty sure that the ten survivors would testify that they were convinced that they would have been shot down if they attempted to leave. I just don't think that we'll be able to overcome that type of testimony. So I think stipulating to the kidnapping charge is clearly justified by the advantage of going first and last. But if you disagree, I will withdraw the motion."

I thought about it for a minute. What Mr. Stanton said made sense. It was a roll of the dice, but I had to agree it seemed worth the gamble. "I'm on board. After the motion is decided, what happens next?"

"Next is jury selection — what's called voir dire. During voir dire, first the judge will ask the prospective jurors a series of general questions to see if there are any obvious reasons why some jurors may not serve on this jury. Then the prosecution and I get to ask the potential jurors questions, supposedly to determine that each one can be a fair and impartial juror. In reality, both sides are trying to figure out which jurors are predisposed to be for, or against, the prosecution or defense."

"Both sides have what are called 'preemptory challenges,' which means that we can reject a juror without explaining why. We also can challenge a juror for cause, if we can show that the juror is biased or unable to perform the duties of a juror. Once twelve jurors and some alternates are selected, we move on to the next phase of the trial."

"Which is?"

"Opening statements, where the prosecution and defense both get a chance to give "the jury a preview of what the case is all about. Again, going first is an advantage, so I hope I will be telling our story first. After that, comes the calling of witnesses."

"Can I ask what witnesses you intend to call?"

"If we get to go first, I think that I am going to call two witnesses: Katie Smith, your department chair, and Dr. Van DeMere. Then we would rest our case. The prosecution would then present its case."

"Who do you think the prosecution will call as witnesses?"

"It will probably call one or more policemen to testify about the crime scene, and Dr. Wells to testify that she believes that you were sane at the time of the murders. I assume that the prosecution would then rest. I then have the right to put on a rebuttal case, maybe by re-calling Dr. Van DeMere to respond to Dr. Wells' testimony. After that, both sides give closing arguments, the judge instructs the jury on the law that is to be applied to the case, and the jury deliberates until it reaches a verdict. Any questions?"

"If the jury convicts me, do I get the death penalty automatically?"

"No. If you are convicted, both sides will get another chance to present any additional evidence relating to the death penalty issue. The jury then decides if the death penalty is warranted. Anything else?"

"I take it from your description of our case that you don't want me to testify?"

Mr. Stanton sat up straighter in his chair and looked me right in the eyes. "As I have told you before, a criminal defendant who testifies generally makes a big mistake, as it allows the prosecution to get out evidence on cross-examination that it otherwise could not have introduced any other way. I say generally because ordinarily, the State has the burden of proof, and the defendant technically doesn't have to prove anything. Here, we have the burden of proof. But I would rather not call you as a witness, unless it becomes absolutely necessary because the case hasn't gone as well as we hope it will. That is a decision that can wait for later, particularly if the judge grants our motion to let us go first and last. We'll get to see if the prosecution's case is strong or weak, and then decide."

"But haven't you already seen Dr. Wells' report?"

"Yes."

"That's really the State's case. Can't you tell if it is strong or weak?"

"Dr. Wells basically says that you were sane and not suffering from a depersonalization disorder because of the divorce. But it all depends on how the jury reacts to Dr. Van DeMere and her. It's not just what the two experts say; it's how they connect with the jury, and probably each juror's predisposition to accept or reject an insanity defense that will determine whether the State's case comes in strong or weak."

"So you're saying that how strong the State's case is may be dependent upon the jury that's selected?"

"I think so. I've done some research of my own into the general public's views of the insanity defense. Psychologists have done studies on this, and the basic take away is that while a substantial majority of the public believes that the insanity defense is sometimes justified, about fifty percent also believe that the defense should be abolished because it allows a person who committed a crime to go free. Based on the studies I've read, it seems as though there are two key predictors of persons who are likely to reject an insanity defense: those who view mental illness as irrelevant to criminal responsibility, and those who perceive an injustice in allowing mentally ill persons to escape punishment and be set free to victimize society again. So trying to pick a jury who will be sympathetic to our defense is going to be tricky."

"On top of that, we have the death penalty issue. People tend to have strong feelings — one way or the other — about the death penalty. The studies I've read suggest that minorities tend to be more opposed to the death penalty than white people, and the very religious more opposed than those not so religious. But on the other hand, about 60% of all Catholics still favor the death penalty, so there are subtleties for which I will have to account. I will need to try to figure out who of our prospective jurors harbors reservations about the death penalty without tipping off the prosecution, because if they come to the same conclusion, they'll use preemptory challenges to bump those jurors off."

"What can you do to try to figure out which jurors might be receptive to my defense?"

"Well, as I said, I get to ask the jurors questions during voir dire to get a flavor for how each one is likely to react to our defense. And I have spent a considerable amount of time the last week or so trying to plan out some questions to accomplish that. Of course, the prosecution will be asking questions to try to find out which jurors are likely to reject the insanity defense. So it will be an awkward dance, of sorts, going on between the prosecution, myself and the jurors. In some ways, it's more of an art than a science."

"How do you keep track of which jurors you want to keep, and which ones to challenge?"

"What I do, and most trial lawyers do, is make two rows of seven boxes on a legal pad. Then, as the prospective jurors get called to go to the jury box, I fill in the names of each juror in the box that corresponds to the seat in the jury box where that juror will sit. As jurors get excused, I scratch their names and add the names of their replacements. I also jot down a word or two to describe the juror, or maybe just put a plus or minus sign, so I remember which ones I like and which ones I don't like."

"Can you really figure all of that out just by asking questions of the jury?"

"Sometimes. Sometimes it's all just a guess and a gut feeling. But after doing this for almost forty years, I do have some experience to draw upon. Any other questions?"

"No, I guess that's all the questions I have right now."

"I will have my paralegal bring you up a suit and some shirts and ties from your house, along with some dress shoes, to wear for trial. I'll see you the day after tomorrow. Try to get some sleep and don't worry."

"What do you think my chances are?"

Mr. Stanton sat back in his chair and stared silently at the ceiling for a moment. "Professor, it's a tough case. We all know you killed those students. We just don't know why. It may well depend upon the jury that we are able to select — how receptive they are to the notion that not knowing why you did it shows that you are suffering from a mental illness. I think with the right jury, there's a good chance we can make that case."

I thanked Mr. Stanton for his time, shook his hand, and was lead back to my cell. Back in my cell, I kept thinking about the impending trial, and my defense. The truth of the matter was in my heart of hearts, I didn't believe in my insanity defense. I was a rational person. I knew right from wrong. Just because I didn't know why I had committed the crime didn't seem like mental illness, just ignorance. None of the so-called "traumas" that I had supposedly suffered during my life seemed linked to any desire to harm the persons who turned out to be my victims, or my inability to understand why I did it. Tim certainly didn't believe that pursuing the insanity defense was the right thing to do. To the contrary, he wanted me to plead guilty and spend the rest of my life in prison atoning for my crime. But I remembered something that Mr. Stanton had said to me during our initial meeting: by definition, isn't someone who guns down twenty people insane? That seemed logical and true. At some level, I must be insane to have done what I did. So like it or not, the insanity defense was my only hope. And it might well depend on the jury that Mr. Stanton would be able to select.

Chapter 15

The day for the start of the trial arrived. Mr. Stanton's paralegal had brought me my suit, shirts and ties for trial as promised. As I dressed in my cell, I could feel the perspiration dripping from my forehead and underarms. It was January, and my cell was drafty and cool. Yet, I was sweating profusely. I could also feel my breathing accelerate. When I bent over to tie my shoes, for a fleeting moment I was afraid that I would pass out from hyperventilation. I sat on the edge of my bed, eyes shut, tightly gripping the edges of the mattress to steady myself. I wasn't even in the courtroom yet, and already I was a basket case.

A guard came to get me and escort me to the van that would take me to the courthouse. The van was black with a State of New Hampshire Corrections Department seal on both sides. There were no windows in the "passenger" part of the van, which consisted of two long benches facing each other. The guards loaded me into the van, and handcuffed me to a metal bar that ran underneath the bench. A steel web separated the back compartment from the driver and guard who sat in the front seat. The van had no other passengers and departed for the courthouse.

Upon the van's arrival at the courthouse, state troopers ushered me in through a side door. Another officer patted me down to make sure I had not secreted anything on my person that could be used as a weapon. Then still another officer lead me into a holding cell adjacent to the courtroom to wait for the proceedings to commence. At 9:15, a deputy led me into the courtroom through a side door and took me to one of the tables facing the judge's bench at which Mr. Stanton was seated. He got up and, after the deputy took off my handcuffs, shook my hand. I took the seat directly beside Mr. Stanton, with his paralegal sitting to my right.

I looked over at the prosecutor's table. Mr. Johnson was sitting, busily writing some notes on the legal pad in front of him, while several other people scurried about lining up notebooks and documents on the table. He did not even seem to have noticed my entrance into the courtroom. The same was not true of the persons who crowded the gallery of the courtroom. As I had entered the courtroom, I had heard the level of murmuring increase sharply. I looked over my shoulder and saw that every bench on the left hand side of the gallery was full, while the other side was roped off and empty. Each person on the full side had the same scowl on his or her face. Undoubtedly, these were the mothers, fathers, siblings and friends of the deceased, all here hoping for retribution. There was one exception: Tim occupied a seat in the first row on the aisle dressed in his priestly black suit and white collar. He smiled at me, slightly nodding his head.

Mr. Stanton saw me glancing back at the crowd, and leaned over and said softly in my ear:

"Forget about them. Are you ready?"

I whispered back, "I think so. But why are half the benches roped off?"

"That's where the prospective jurors will sit when they are brought in for jury selection."

Mr. Stanton nodded towards the prosecutor's table and said: "I think that our motion has thrown Mr. Johnson for a loop. We'll see how the judge rules, but I think we have a chance to go first. Keep your fingers crossed."

Moments later, the bailiff entered the courtroom from behind the bench and bellowed: "All rise! The District Court in and for the Second District is now in session. The honorable Judge Cyrus Winston presiding. Draw near and you shall be heard. Be seated and come to

order.   Case Number 003578; State of New Hampshire
versus Dan Jackson."

During the bailiff's proclamation, Judge Winston
had entered and climbed up to his chair on the elevated
platform that constituted his bench.   He shuffled some
papers around, and then looked out at the courtroom.   "Is
the prosecution ready?"

Mr. Johnson jumped out of his chair, like a sprinter
taking off at the sound of the starter's pistol.   He stood,
ram-rod straight, with his jaw jutting out: "The State is
ready, Your Honor."

Judge Winston continued: "Is the defense ready?"

Mr. Stanton put both hands on the table in front of
him and pushed himself slowly to his feet.   "The defense is
ready, Your Honor."

"All right gentlemen, please be seated.   The first
order of business is the defense's motion in limine number
one to alter the order of proof at the trial.   I have read both
parties briefs and am ready to rule.   Is there anything else
that either party wants to add before I make my ruling?"

Mr. Stanton rose again to his feet.   "Your Honor,
we believe that our position is fully set forth in our motion
and brief, and it is a simple one: because we have the
burden of proof with regard to the insanity defense, and
because that defense essentially admits the commission of
the offense, the only factual issues to try have to do with
that defense and we should be permitted to proceed first,
with an appropriate stipulation read to the jury that the
defendant admits that he committed the offenses charged
by the prosecution, but asserts that he acted as a result of a
mental illness or defect.   Unless the Court has any
questions about that, I believe that is all we have."

"Mr. Johnson, do you have anything further?"
Judge Winston queried.

Mr. Johnson was again quickly on his feet, as if he
had a spring on the backside of his pants.   "Your Honor,

based upon the authority of U.S. v. Anderson, we believe that the prosecution should proceed first. The jury is entitled to know the particulars about this crime. The heinous nature of it. Its enormous scope. The defendant can then put on whatever defense it wants, but it will be in context for the jury. Otherwise, the jury will not understand how the defendant's defense fits into the case."

Mr. Stanton had remained on his feet during Mr. Johnson's short argument. When Mr. Johnson was finished, Mr. Stanton asked "You Honor may I briefly respond?"

"You may."

"The Anderson case is based upon federal law, not New Hampshire law which governs these proceedings. Under federal law, once the insanity defense is raised, the prosecution has the burden of proving that the defendant is sane as part of its case in chief, and so goes first. Under New Hampshire law, the burden of proving insanity is upon the defendant, and therefore it makes sense for the defense to proceed first, in light of the fact that the defense essentially admits the commission of the offense. The stipulation will provide the context that the jury needs and is appropriate. What Mr. Johnson really wants to do is appeal to the passion and prejudices of the jury before the defendant has a chance to present his defense."

Mr. Johnson's face reddened at Mr. Stanton's last comment, and I could see the muscles in his jaw tighten. He started to speak, but Judge Winston held up his hand.

"No need to respond Mr. Johnson. Mr. Stanton is correct. The authority you rely upon is not relevant to this issue. New Hampshire law is different than federal law on this question. I find that the defense motion is well-founded in law and logic, and it is granted. We will proceed accordingly. Mr. Stanton, do you have a proposed stipulation to be read to the jury?"

"I do, Your Honor."

"Have you shown it to Mr. Johnson?"

"I have, Your Honor."

"Mr. Johnson, any comments on the proposed stipulation?"

Mr. Johnson stood there looking down at Mr. Stanton's stipulation. He looked up at the judge and said: "I don't have any problem with the wording of the stipulation, in light of the Court's ruling on the motion. But I do think that it should be read to the jury venire before the start of jury selection, not at the beginning of the trial. Because I think it will be important in picking a jury that they understand that the defendant admits committing these murders and is pleading insanity."

"Mr. Stanton?"

"Your Honor, I don't think that it is necessary or appropriate to read the stipulation to the venire, and it should only be read to the selected jury immediately before the opening statements. I think a short summary of the case by the Court to the venire should be sufficient."

Judge Winston reflected for a moment. "No, Mr. Stanton, I think I agree with Mr. Johnson. The parties have agreed on the wording of this stipulation, and it places the case in context for the prospective jury. I will read it to the assembled venire before jury selection. Now, is there anything else we need to cover before bringing the prospective jurors into the courtroom?"

Both sides indicated that they had nothing further to address before jury selection. Judge Winston motioned to the bailiff to bring the prospective jurors into the courtroom. Five minutes later, the bailiff lead about fifty people into the courtroom, who were ushered into the formerly roped-off benches. Then Judge Winston pounded his gavel on the bench three times and spoke:

"Order in the courtroom!   Ladies and gentlemen, please come to order. I will address first the members of the public who are seated on the benches to my right. You are here and may observe these proceedings only if you strictly comply with what I am about to tell you. You are not to speak with or make eye contact with any of the prospective jurors. If I, or my bailiff, even think that we see any sort of communication or attempt to intimidate any of the prospective jurors, we will immediately remove the offending party and remand them to the custody of the sheriff."

"Members of the public may remain in this courtroom only if they are totally silent while court is in session. Any talking, or any emotional outbursts will result in the immediate clearing of the courtroom of spectators. If, during the proceedings, people need to leave the courtroom, they will do so as quietly and quickly as possible so as to not disturb the proceedings. Do you understand these rules? Nod your heads if you do."

The spectators all nodded their heads, and Judge Winston continued: "Now, the prospective jurors that are seated to my left, let me address you. I am Judge Cyrus Winston, and I will be presiding over this trial. You have been called to perform one of the greatest civic duties bestowed upon our citizens: the duty to serve as a juror. Our country is built upon the rule of law, and the rule of law only functions properly when citizens, like you, perform their duty to serve as jurors. Indeed, I will tell you that one of the things that distinguishes our country from many others is that citizens determine the fate of other citizens — the government can't just put people away or execute them. So I thank you for appearing here today to perform this solemn and important duty."

"In order to perform this duty, it is necessary that a juror not only be fair and impartial, but also appear to be fair and impartial. For example, we wouldn't feel confident about the result of a trial where the jurors were all relatives of the defendant, or all worked for the prosecutors' office." The prospective jurors chuckled briefly.

Judge Winston smiled proudly at his successful little joke, and continued:

"So I am going to ask all of you some general questions just to make sure that there are no obvious problems with any of you sitting as jurors. Then we will pick twelve of you to come up here and sit in the jury box, and the prosecution and defense lawyers will ask you some additional questions. If I decide that you can't sit as a juror for some reason, you will return to the jury assembly room where you came this morning and be told what to do."

"By the way, if for some reason you can't sit as a juror for this case, you have still performed your civic duty by appearing here and honestly answering any questions you are asked. All right, I am now going to ask all prospective jurors to stand and raise their right hands to take the juror's oath, which will be administered by the bailiff."

The prospective jurors rose en masse, and all raised their right hands. The bailiff droned on about being fair and impartial and answering all questions put to them honestly, to which the jurors responded with a chorus of "I do." They then sat down, waiting for the questions that were to come.

Judge Winston began: "Ladies and gentlemen, I am going to read to you a stipulation that has been agreed upon by the State and the defense regarding what this case is about and how the trial will proceed, to give you a little context: 'The defendant in this case is Dan Jackson. Mr. Jackson is a professor at Dartmouth College. On October 10 of last year, Mr. Jackson shot and killed fifteen students at Dartmouth College, and seriously wounded five others. He prevented any of the students from leaving the class room where the shooting took place, and therefore also kidnapped them. Mr. Jackson has asserted an insanity defense because he states that he does not know why he shot his students.' So that is what this case is generally about."

"Now let me introduce the lawyers who will be conducting this trial. To my right is the prosecutor, Mr. Carl Johnson. To my left is the defense lawyer, Mr. Gus Stanton. Please raise your hand if you know either of these gentlemen."

No hands were raised. The jurors all shook their heads indicating that they did not know either man.

"Mr. Jackson, would you please rise. This is Mr. Dan Jackson, who is the defendant in this case. If you know Mr. Jackson, please raise your hand."

No hands were raised. Again, the jurors all shook their heads, indicating that they did not know me.

"Have any of you, or any of your immediate family members ever been convicted of a crime? If so, please raise your hand."

One hand in the last row went up, slowly. It belonged to a frail, older woman with gray hair tied back in a bun.

"Ma'am, could you please stand up." The woman complied. "What is your name?"

"Ellen Brown, Your Honor."

"Why did you raise your hand, Ma'am?"

"My son, who is 26 years old, was convicted of burglary and is serving time over at Concord State Prison."

Judge Winston responded: "I am sorry to hear that. Did he go through a trial?"

"Yes sir, he did."

"Did you attend that trial?"

"Yes sir, I did."

"Do you feel that your son got a fair trial?"

"Judge, I don't know if you have children, but if you do, you know that a parent loves her child no matter what mistakes he makes. I still love my son. But he was guilty — I didn't need a trial to tell me that. Hell, he piled up all the stuff he stole in my garage, as if I wouldn't notice. I was the one who turned him over to the police. So yeah, he got a fair trial."

"Do you think that there is anything about your experience with your son's situation that would prevent you from being a fair and impartial juror in this case?"

"No."

"All right, thank you, Ms. Brown. You may sit down."

Judge Winston proceeded to ask a series of general questions to see if there were any obvious impediments to service on the jury. None of the prospective jurors knew any of the deceased or wounded students; that was not surprising, because very few students at Dartmouth actually came from New Hampshire. None of the prospective jurors were employed by the college. There were a couple state workers among the prospective jurors, but no one who worked for the court system or prosecutor's office, so they were allowed to remain in the pool. None of the jurors had suffered from any diagnosed mental illness. No one had any visual or auditory problems that would make it difficult for them to see or hear the proceedings. Each of the jurors confirmed that he or she could understand and read English. Then the judge changed the tenor of the questions:

"Now, let me address one more issue. This case we think will take four to five days to try. That is not a particularly long trial, and I wouldn't expect that such a time commitment would present insurmountable problems for any of you. But if you believe that, for some reason, you cannot devote that amount of time and would like to be excused from this jury, please raise your hand."

A dozen hands shot up. The judge frowned, and then motioned to a man sitting in the front row with his hand up. "Would you please stand up and state your name? The rest of you can put your hands down for now"

The man rose. He had on a brown checked sport coat and corduroy slacks. His jet black hair was slicked back tight against his skull, and glistened slightly. "My name is Walter Jones, Your Honor."

"Mr. Jones, tell me why you feel that you cannot spend the next four to five days performing the most important civic duty that your country calls upon you to perform."

The entire courtroom went quiet. I could tell from the startled looks on the faces of the other prospective jurors and the audience that no one had expected that the judge would be so heavy handed. Mr. Jones gulped noticeably, and stammered:

"Well, well, you see, Your Honor, it's like this. I mean I know that this is important and all, but I am a traveling salesman, and I work strictly off commission. So if I have to sit here all week, it means I don't make any money at all. I've got a wife and two kids to take care of, so it's a real problem."

"Since you work on commission, Mr. Jones, have there been any weeks during the last year in which you made no sales?"

"A few. But, Your Honor, even in those weeks I'm out there planting the seeds that may lead to other sales later."

"Do all your 'seeds' bear fruit, Mr. Jones?"

"Not all of them, no."

"Will any of your customers die if you don't make sales or plant seeds this week?"

"Well, no, Your Honor."

"Will your wife and children starve?"

"Well, no, but I mean . . ."

"Will you be unable to meet any of your financial commitments if you don't have any commissions this week?"

"I can't say that, Your Honor."

"You do realize that a man here is on trial for his life, don't you?"

"Well, yes, of course I understand that, but . . ."

Judge Winston growled: "Is there anything more important that you can do this week than participate in the awesome decision that must be made here?"

The courtroom was absolutely silent. Mr. Jones looked down at the floor, and then raised his head slightly and said: "I guess not."

"All right then, Mr. Jones, you can sit down. Now who were the others who thought that they had more important things to do than participate as a juror in this case?"

No hands went up. "I thought I saw some other hands up before? No? Last chance. Good." After a few more general questions, Judge Winston stopped his questioning and asked the bailiff to randomly select twelve juror's names from a box at the clerk's table that sat alongside and below the bench. The bailiff read off twelve names, and, one by one, the twelve marched up to the jury box and took their seats. Both Mr. Johnson and Mr. Stanton were feverishly scribbling down what I assumed were the jurors' names on a legal pad. Mr. Stanton's pad had boxes that replicated the chairs in jury box, just as he had explained to me.

The jury box was not exactly a box. There was a front row of seven chairs behind a waist high wooden panel, and a second row of seven chairs, a step up from the first row. The chairs were all perched on a single pole that was affixed to the floor, so none of them could be moved from side to side. The chairs themselves, however, would go slightly back and forth, and as the jurors got seated, there was some groaning of the chairs as they rocked in response to their occupants movements. Six jurors were directed to sit in the front row, and six in the back, leaving one empty chair in each row. Once the jurors were seated, Judge Winston addressed the jurors again:

"Ladies and gentlemen, we are now at the point that I am going to call a recess for lunch. I will want everyone back from lunch at 1:30 and I will ask that the twelve prospective jurors who are now sitting in the jury box to take their same seats upon returning from lunch. Then I am going to let the prosecutor, Mr. Johnson, and the defense counsel, Mr. Stanton, ask you some more questions. Any questions?"

No one raised their hand.

"All right then. Court will stand in recess until 1:30 p.m." Judge Winston banged his gavel and then got up and marched out of the courtroom. A deputy took me to the holding cell next to the courtroom and brought a sandwich and soft drink to me for lunch. Mr. Stanton told me he needed to work on some things during lunch, but would be back at 1:30 p.m. for the afternoon session.

Chapter 16

At 1:30 sharp, the bailiff sang out his announcement of Judge Winston's arrival back in the courtroom. Everyone stood until the judge took his seat behind the bench, and then we all sat down.

"Court is back in session. Ladies and gentlemen jurors, please give Mr. Johnson and Mr. Stanton your full and complete attention, and answer all of their questions honestly. Mr. Johnson, you may proceed."

Carl Johnson got up from his chair, buttoned his suit jacket and marched to a spot about six feet in front of the jury box. He took a moment to look at the jurors. He then smiled and began:

"Ladies and gentlemen, let me introduce myself. I am Carl Johnson, and I will have the honor to prosecute this case on behalf of the people of the State of New Hampshire. Now is the time in the trial — in fact, it is the only time in the trial — when I get to have a conversation with you. After we finish selecting the jury, neither I nor Mr. Stanton is allowed to talk to any juror individually. So if later, you see me in the hallway and it seems like I am ignoring you, it's because I am supposed to act that way, and so is Mr. Stanton. We aren't being rude. We're just following the rules."

Mr. Johnson cleared his throat slightly, and continued. "But now I do get to ask you some questions. I am not trying to pry into your private lives. But I am trying to find out a little bit about you and whether you can be a juror in this case. First, I'd like to ask a general question of all of the jurors in the box. This case has gotten a lot of media coverage. It's not every day that we have fifteen people killed in New Hampshire. So what I would like to know is how many of you have seen or heard media reports about these killings?"

All twelve jurors raised their hands. I scribbled a note to Mr. Stanton that read: "Why is he doing this? Doesn't this help us argue that we can't get a fair trial?" Mr. Stanton glanced over at the note and quickly wrote out a short reply: "He's going to turn this on its head and make it impossible for us to use the pretrial publicity as an argument. Watch."

Mr. Johnson turned to the juror sitting in the first chair on the right of the first row of the jury box. "Mr. Simpson, is it?"

"Yes, that's right." Mr. Simpson was a bald, heavy-set man who appeared to be in his mid-forties.

"Mr. Simpson, could you please share with us what media reports you have seen or heard about the killings."

"Well, I saw some of the local and national television reporting on the murders."

"Anything else?"

"I may have read a few articles in the local paper about the case."

"Was there anything that you saw, heard or read that sticks out in your mind?"

"Well, some of the pictures were pretty graphic; I mean they showed the classroom with all the seats and tables covered with blood. It was pretty horrible."

"Yes, of course it was. Did you hear Judge Winston read the description of the case to which the prosecution and defense stipulated?"

"Yes."

"I know that you're not a lawyer, but just in layman terms, what did you understand that stipulation to mean?"

"I guess as I understood it, the defendant isn't denying he shot those students. He's claiming that he was mentally ill when he did it. I mean, I guess that is his defense."

"Thank you, Mr. Simpson. Do the rest of you agree with Mr. Simpson's understanding of what the judge told you?"

The remaining eleven jurors all nodded their heads affirmatively.

"Now, Mr. Simpson, even though you have seen or heard things about these killings, and maybe even seen some pretty gruesome pictures, do you have any knowledge at this point concerning whether or not the defendant was mentally ill at the time of the murders?"

"Well, no. I mean I haven't heard any of the evidence on that point yet."

"Exactly. So, despite having seen these horrible pictures, with their blood and their gore, are you able to be a fair and impartial juror and give the defendant a chance to present his defense?"

"Yes, sir, I am."

Mr. Johnson looked at each of the other jurors. "Do the rest of you also agree with Mr. Johnson that you can all be fair and impartial to this defendant and listen to his defense, notwithstanding the fact that you know he committed these terrible murders?"

A chorus of "yes" and "uh-uh" rose up from the jurors collectively.

Mr. Johnson smiled slightly. Mr. Stanton wrote a short note to me on a legal pad and slid it over in front of me, which read: "He's smiling because he just got the jury to confirm that they know you committed the crimes. The 'can you still be fair' is just bullshit. People rarely admit that they can't be fair."

Mr. Johnson proceeded to examine each of the prospective jurors about various topics, including their employment, families, hobbies, feelings about mental health and position on the death penalty. When he was finished, Mr. Stanton got his chance to ask the jurors questions. He began with what seemed to me to be a surprising approach:

"Ladies and gentlemen, my name is Gus Stanton, and I represent the defendant Dan Jackson. Now let's be honest with each other: should we even bother with a trial? How many of you have already decided my client is guilty?"

The prospective jurors' eyes opened wide and most of their mouths dropped open, at least a little. They were clearly taken aback by the directness of Mr. Stanton's question.

"How about it, Mr. Steadman is it?" Mr. Stanton addressed juror number two. "You think Mr. Jackson is guilty already, don't you?"

"Well, no. I mean, I know he shot those students, but he may have been mentally ill at the time."

"Does that really make any difference to you? I mean if you know he shot those students, doesn't he deserve to be punished?"

"Not if he's sick. It wouldn't be fair to punish someone who's sick."

"How about the rest of you? Have the rest of you already decided that my client is guilty?"

The remaining jurors all shook their heads indicating no.

"Do you agree with Mr. Steadman that it wouldn't be fair to punish a person who is mentally ill and needs help?"

Most of the jurors shook their heads in the affirmative.

Mr. Stanton then proceeded to find something to talk about with every one of the twelve jurors, without repeating exactly the ground that Mr. Johnson had covered. I knew that Mr. Stanton was trying to divine which jurors might be more open to the insanity defense or opposed to the death penalty, but it was difficult to figure out the

rhyme or reason to the questions he asked. When Mr.
Stanton had finished his questioning, he came back to
counsel table, sat next to me, and feverishly reviewed his
notes on the questioning. Mr. Johnson appeared to be
doing the same thing at his counsel table. Both men were
interrupted from their analysis by Judge Winston:

"Mr. Johnson, does the State have any challenges
for cause?"

"No, Your Honor."

"Does the defense have any challenges for cause?"

Mr. Stanton rose from his chair. "No Your Honor."

"Does the State wish to excuse any juror from this
panel?"

Mr. Johnson stood and announced: "The State
thanks and excuses juror number four."

"Ms. Calloway, you are excused from further duty.
Please return to the jury selection room," explained Judge
Winston. Ms. Calloway complied with the judge's
direction.

"Mr. Stanton, would the defense like to excuse any
other member of this panel?"

"Your Honor, the defense thanks and excuses juror
number eleven."

Without further instruction from the judge, the man
in seat number eleven got up and strode from the
courtroom. This process was repeated four more times,
resulting in a total of ten jurors being excused. When both
parties indicated that they were satisfied with the remaining
two jurors, the bailiff called ten new names, and ten new
prospective jurors came from the gallery to fill in the seats
that had been vacated. The dance began anew, with first
Mr. Johnson questioning the ten new jurors, followed by
Mr. Stanton questioning the newcomers.

After the questioning was completed, most of the
newcomers met the same fate as their predecessors — a
polite exclusion from service on this jury. More names

were called and more people from the gallery dutifully trudged up and took the seats emptied by the last group, followed by more questioning by the lawyers. Finally, after this had been going on for almost three hours, with ten jurors accepted, Judge Winston called for a fifteen minute recess.

I was taken to the holding room and joined by Mr. Stanton. Mr. Stanton was sweating and his face was drawn. "So how are we doing?" I asked.

"Okay, I guess. Of the ten jurors we have seated, I think that I have a good shot with at least four of them."

"How can you tell?"

"It's more of a gut feeling than anything else. I just feel that I connected with four of them, and not so much with the other six. There's nothing in their answers that I can point to that would make me think the four are favorable to us — if there was, Johnson would have used one of his challenges to get rid of them. The next two will really tell the story. How many challenges have I used?"

"Nineteen."

"That means that we only have one more. How many has the prosecution used?"

"By my count, nine."

"That means that Johnson only has one challenge left. Good."

"How much longer will this take?"

"Probably only about another hour or so. Let's get back to the courtroom." Mr. Stanton knocked on the door, and the deputy came to escort me back to counsel table.

The judge called the court to order, and the audience dutifully complied. The bailiff called two more prospective jurors up to take seats number four and nine. Mr. Johnson stood to begin his questioning of these two new jurors:

"Let me ask you, Mr. Alford in seat number four, what do you do for a living?" Mr. Alford had a neatly trimmed mustache and wore a short, almost military-style haircut. He was dressed in a checked shirt and bright red sweater.

"I work for Carl's Toyota as a car salesman."

"Are you married?"

"Yes, for fifteen years."

"Children?"

"Two, a boy and a girl."

"Mr. Alford, were you surprised to learn that the defendant was raising an insanity defense?"

Mr. Alford's brow creased slightly. "I guess I was sort of surprised, now that you mention it."

"Why?"

"Well, from what I had read and heard, he was a college professor and had no history of mental illness. So I didn't expect that he'd claim that he was insane."

"Do you have any feelings about the insanity defense?"

"Not really. I mean, it seems to me that it's awfully easy after the fact to claim that you were mentally ill. But I don't know. I really don't have much experience with it."

Mr. Johnson scribbled a few notes on his legal pad. "Mr. Alford, do you have any feelings, pro or con, about the death penalty?"

"Not really. I don't really know what makes the death penalty apply to one case and not another."

"If Judge Winston instructs you that you may find the death penalty applicable to this case involving kidnapping and the killing of fifteen students, do you think that you would be able to vote in favor of the death penalty?"

"I suppose so, if the law says it applies."

"Thank you, Mr. Alford, that's all the questions I have for you at this time. Now, Ms. Reedy in chair number nine, may I ask you a few questions."

"Yes, sir." Ms. Reedy was a young woman in her twenties, with long blond hair and fetching green eyes.

"Ms. Reedy, could I ask you what you do for a living?"

"I am a bank teller in Hanover."

"How long have you held that job?"

"About four years."

"Did you go to college before that?"

"Yes."

"Where?"

"Green Mountain Junior College."

"While you were in college, did you visit Hanover often?"

"I dated a couple Dartmouth guys, so yes, I visited Hanover."

Mr. Johnson scribbled a short note on his legal pad and continued:

"Have you ever known anyone who has seen a psychiatrist for treatment of some mental or emotional disorder?"

"No."

"Do you know any psychiatrists?"

"No."

"Do you have any opinion about the field of psychiatry? Do you think they're real doctors or just quacks?"

"Oh, they're real doctors. I mean, I took a psychology class in college, and there were all sorts of studies mentioned that had been done by psychiatrists."

"So you believe they're real scientists?"

"I think so."

"Do you have any opinion about the insanity defense generally?"

"Not really."

"You have an open mind, then, and will listen to the testimony of the psychiatric experts to help you understand it?"

"Yes, sure."

"Thank you, Ms. Reedy. That's all the questions that I have."

Mr. Stanton slowly got up from his chair and approached the jury box. Looking at Mr. Alford, he asked:

"If I understood one of your answers to Mr. Johnson's question, it was that you could vote for the death penalty if the law says it applies, is that right?"

"Yes, that's right."

"What if the law says that the death penalty could apply, but didn't necessarily have to apply — what would you do then?"

"Well, you mean if it was totally up to me as to whether or not to vote for the death penalty?"

"Yes — if the law said it could apply, but wasn't required. What would you do?"

Mr. Alford sat quietly for a moment, looking straight ahead, but with a faraway look in his eyes. "It would be awfully hard to sentence a man to death. If there was any good reason not to, I guess I'd be inclined not to do it."

"Thank you, Mr. Alford. Now Ms. Reedy, I only have a couple questions for you. You've sat here patiently all day listening to the questions that Mr. Johnson has asked of prospective jurors, and the questions that I've asked of prospective jurors. Have any of those questions raised any doubt in your mind about your ability to be a fair and impartial juror in this case?"

"I don't think so."

"Can you think of any reason that you could not be a fair and impartial juror in this case?"

"Only that I already know the outcome of the trial."

Mr. Stanton did a double take and stood there with his mouth slightly ajar, head cocked. I looked over at Mr. Johnson. Ms. Reedy's answer had caused him to look up suddenly from his notes and stare at her. His mouth was slightly agape as well. And when I looked up at the judge, his mouth was set in a stern scowl.

Mr. Stanton stammered: "Excuse, me, Ms. Reedy. What did you just say?"

"I already know the outcome. I'm clairvoyant, you see. Everybody in town knows that. I have courtroom staff call me all the time when juries are out to find out what the result will be. I've had to promise not to tell who they are, because they could get in trouble, I guess. But I've known how this case is going to turn out for several weeks now — ever since I first read about it in the newspaper."

Judge Winston broke in: "Young lady, don't say another word. I'm afraid that in this courtroom, we wait for the jury to return its verdict to find out how the case comes out. I am excusing you for cause, and ordering you not to discuss this case — or your belief as to its outcome — with anyone until the jury comes back with a verdict. Do you understand my order, Ms. Reedy?"

Ms. Reedy blushed noticeably and squeaked "Yes, Your Honor."

The bailiff then read off yet another name, and a new prospective juror, a middle-aged woman with a slightly chunky build, took seat number 9. Mr. Johnson turned his attention to the newest addition.

"Ms. O'Connor, can you tell us what you do for a living?"

"I'm a full-time mother of six."

"That sounds more like overtime, than full-time," Mr. Johnson said with a light-hearted laugh. The entire jury box joined in laughing, and Ms. O'Connor beamed with pride. "Tell me, Ms. O'Connor, what does Mr. O'Connor do for a living?"

"He's a policeman here in West Lebanon."

"How long has he been on the force?"

"Twenty-three years."

"I would like to ask you a question about the death penalty, which is potentially an issue in this case. How do you feel about whether it's a good thing or a bad thing that murderers can be executed, if the evidence and the law permit?"

"Well, in my religion — I am a Catholic — we believe that all human life is sacred. So, on the one hand, any taking of life is wrong. But, on the other hand, the Bible also talks about an eye for an eye. So even God apparently believes that there are some circumstances in which the death penalty might be justified, I suppose."

"So there are some circumstances in which the death penalty is justified?"

"Yes, I suppose, in especially egregious cases."

"Okay. Thank you. That's all the questions I have."

Mr. Stanton stood up and from counsel table said: "Ms. O'Connor, with six children to take care of, will it be a burden for you to sit as a juror in this case for four to five days?"

"No, not really. I mean the kids are school all day, and they all have after school activities to keep them occupied until I get home."

"That's fine. Just wanted to make sure the kids would be okay."

"Well, thank you. It was nice of you to ask."

"That's all the questions I have. Thank you."

I was surprised that Mr. Stanton didn't ask more questions of Ms. O'Connor, but assumed he must have his reasons. Judge Winston asked: "Mr. Johnson, does the State have any challenges for cause for these last two jurors?"

"No Your Honor."

"Mr. Stanton?"

"No challenges for cause, Your Honor."

"Mr. Johnson, does the State wish to exercise any further preemptory challenges?"

"No Your Honor."

"Mr. Stanton?"

"No, Your Honor."

Two alternate jurors were selected, questioned and accepted quickly, and the jury selection process was complete. It was almost 5:30 p.m. Judge Winston pounded his gavel and addressed the courtroom. "Ladies and gentlemen, that concludes the jury selection process. Would the jurors and alternates please stand, raise your right hands, and take the juror's oath that will be administered by the bailiff."

The bailiff read the jurors' oath, with the jurors reciting his words in a monotone drone. When that was completed, Judge Winston continued: "The Court will stand in recess until tomorrow morning, when we will begin the trial with opening statements from the lawyers. I instruct and order each juror to refrain from talking about this case with anyone — either with other jurors or with your family members or friends. We will begin again tomorrow at 9:00 a.m. sharp. Court is adjourned." Everyone in the courtroom stood as Judge Winston exited the courtroom. The audience then began filing out.

I turned to Mr. Stanton as he was packing up his papers. "So how did we do? Do I have a chance with this jury?" Mr. Stanton looked up at me smiling. "Yes. I'm very happy with what we got. I think that if the evidence comes in as I hope it will, we have a fighting chance. Keep your chin up. The fun begins tomorrow."

Chapter 17

When I was led to counsel table the next morning, Mr. Stanton's appearance had dramatically changed. His gray suit looked cleaned and pressed, and he wore a white button-down collar shirt with a subtle maroon tie. His hair was cut relatively short, making it appear less gray and browner, and the pony-tail was gone. I stood there with my mouth wide-open, just staring at him. I leaned over and whispered in his ear:

"Why did you cut your hair?"

"You saw the jury we picked yesterday. Did you see anyone with a pony-tail or long hair? No. This is New Hampshire, not Boston, and I figured that I better start looking like the natives."

"But they all saw you yesterday with the long hair and pony tail. Won't they think this make-over is a bit contrived?"

"Not in my experience. Jurors have short memories. What is most important is what they have seen or heard most recently. And from here on in, they're going to see Gus Stanton sans pony-tail. Trust me. I know what I am doing."

"Okay. So are we ready to go?"

"Yes, I think so. We'll do the opening statements first, and then I will call two witnesses: Ms. Smith, your department head, and one of your students, Lilly Simpson. Then I'll put on Dr. Van DeMere and rest."

"Wait a minute. You never said anything about calling Lilly as a witness. How can she possibly help?"

"I interviewed her, and she'll help us. Just watch."

At that moment, the bailiff announced the arrival of the judge and everyone jumped to their feet. As the judge took his seat, and organized the papers on the bench in front of him, the courtroom settled back into silence, and I turned to scan the crowd before the proceedings commenced. I saw Tim in his usual aisle seat in full priestly regalia. Our eyes met, and we both smiled slightly. I turned back to face the judge, ready to begin the ordeal.

"The State of New Hampshire v. Jackson. On trial," the bailiff boomed out. Judge Winston looked over at the jurors, and then the assembled crowd in the peanut gallery.

"Ladies and Gentlemen of the jury. We are now at the point in the trial where we will hear the opening statements of counsel. The opening statements are not evidence in the case. They are simply an explanation — a road map, if you will — of what each counsel believes the evidence that will be introduced during the trial will show. Please give each counsel your complete attention. Mr. Stanton, are you ready to proceed?"

"Yes Your Honor." Mr. Stanton slowly arose from his chair, and walked to a spot directly in front of the jury box. He purposefully made eye contact with each of the jurors, and then began, "May it please the Court, Counsel," Mr. Stanton said, nodding his head first in the direction of Judge Winston, and then in the direction of Mr. Johnson.

"Ladies and Gentlemen of the jury. Good morning. As you know, my name is Gus Stanton, and I represent the defendant Dan Jackson. This trial is about a tragedy that occurred on the Dartmouth College campus on October 10 of last year. Fifteen students were killed. Five others were seriously wounded. My client, Dan Jackson, acknowledges that he fired the pistols that caused this terrible carnage. But the evidence is going to show that although his fingers may have pulled the trigger, his mind never intended for this horrific crime to occur. He had no intent to kill or injure. He did not plan this crime, and he was as surprised as anyone when he found the pistols in his briefcase and began firing. He was suffering from a mental defect or illness at the time these crimes occurred that legally excuses him from responsibility for these mind-numbing acts."

"The evidence is going to show that Mr. Jackson has no history of violence. He has been a law-abiding citizen all of his life, and for the past twenty-five years has dedicated his life to teaching young people. He is well-respected by his colleagues. He didn't have any motive for the killings. In fact, he is the last person that anyone who knew him would have thought would have been involved in a mass killing."

"But he was. So the question arises, 'why?' Why would a seemingly law-abiding college professor suddenly commit this act of violence? We will present evidence from Dr. Albert Van DeMere, an experienced psychiatrist, who will tell you why he believes Mr. Jackson shot these students. Dr. Van DeMere will testify that based upon his examination of Mr. Jackson during the last month, and based upon his years of study and experience, it is his opinion that Mr. Jackson suffers from a depersonalization disorder. It is a form of mental illness that causes an individual to be disassociated from reality and even his own physical being. It is like watching oneself in a dream, unable to control what one's own body is doing. It is caused by great emotional trauma, and Dr. Van DeMere will testify that Mr. Jackson has recently suffered such an emotional trauma: the discovery of his ex-wife's infidelity and his subsequent divorce after 25 years of marriage. This cataclysmic event in Mr. Jackson's life caused this depersonalization disorder, as his mind withdrew from the real world to escape the devastating emotional injury that had been inflicted upon him."

"But Mr. Jackson does not want or expect sympathy for his situation. He realizes that he has inflicted a great injury upon these students and their families. If he could undo it, he would. But he can't. He needs psychiatric treatment, perhaps for years, to overcome this mental illness. That's all he asks for: a chance to become normal again, to contribute to society again, and in some small way, try to make up for the sorrow that his mental illness has caused. We think that after you have heard the evidence, you will agree that Mr. Jackson needs treatment, not punishment. Thank you for your attention."

Mr. Stanton walked back to the jury table, clapped his hand on my back, and then took his seat. The courtroom was absolutely silent.

"Mr. Johnson, is the State ready to give its opening statement?" asked Judge Winston.

Mr. Johnson quickly rose, and standing ram-rod straight, responded: "With the Court's permission, the State would like to reserve its opening statement until after the defense has rested, and give that statement immediately before the State begins its case."

A murmur went through the courtroom. I leaned over and whispered to Mr. Stanton, "What's going on? I thought that you said that both sides would give their opening statements."

Mr. Stanton seemed lost in thought momentarily. He stroked his chin briefly, and responded: "This is unusual. Johnson must have some surprise in store for us that he doesn't want to reveal until the last moment, so we won't have much time to respond to it. Not much we can do, however."

Judge Winston pounded his gavel and croaked "Order in the Court! I won't warn those of you observing this trial again: no outbursts or I will clear the courtroom. Now, Mr. Stanton, does the defense have any objection to Mr. Johnson's request?"

Mr. Stanton got up on his feet and turned slightly towards the jury. "Well, it is surprising that the State doesn't want the jury to hear what it thinks the evidence will show, but I guess I don't have an objection, other than it inconveniences the jury."

"Your Honor. . ." Mr. Johnson began to respond, but was cut off by Judge Winston:

"Mr. Johnson, there is no need for further commentary. Your request is granted. Mr. Stanton, please call your first witness."

"The defense calls Katie Smith to the stand."

Katie Smith rose from the peanut gallery and strode towards the witness stand. Katie was about forty-five, wore horn-rimmed glasses and had closely cropped, reddish hair — a shade of red that was not known to appear in nature. She had on a dark gray skirt and jacket over a white blouse, open slightly at the neck. She took the witness stand, placed her hand on the Bible and swore to tell the truth. Mr. Stanton, stood, leaning slightly on the counsel table and began his examination:

"Would you please state your name for the record?"

"Katie Smith."

"You are the head of the English Department at Dartmouth College?"

"That's right."

"How long have you had that position?"

"About four years."

"You know Dan Jackson, don't you?"

"Yes, he's a professor in my department."

"How long have you known him?"

"About two, two and a half years."

"Were you involved in the decision to hire Professor Jackson?"

"Yes."

"As part of that process, did you contact other colleges where he taught?"

"A few."

"Why did you do that?"

"Well, to make sure there was no history of poor teaching performance, or poor personal habits, which would disqualify him from teaching at Dartmouth."

"When you say 'poor personal habits,' what do you mean?"

"Well, like rowdiness, drunkenness, troubles with the law, that sort of thing."

"Did you learn anything from those calls that was of a disqualifying nature?"

Mr. Johnson jumped up from his chair: "Objection! Hearsay."

Mr. Stanton turned to the judge, and responded: "Your Honor, I am not asking what was said in those conversations, just whether it was of a disqualifying nature."

Mr. Johnson quickly replied: "Your Honor, that is a ridiculous distinction. He is seeking to elicit from this witness conclusory testimony based upon what third parties said to her. That is hearsay."

Judge Winston pondered the question for a moment, and said: "The objection is sustained. Ask your next question, Mr. Stanton."

"Ms. Smith, did you have a standard practice regarding what you did if you learned anything of a disqualifying nature in your reference calls?"

"Yes, if anything of a disqualifying nature was learned in reference calls, the candidate was not pursued further."

"After speaking with Professor Jackson's former employers, did you decide to hire him?"

"Yes."

I had to smile slightly. Mr. Stanton had cleverly gotten around Mr. Johnson's objection. The jury now knew that Ms. Smith had not been told of anything disqualifying about my background. I was impressed.

"Did you have an opportunity to observe Professor Jackson in the class room?"

"Occasionally."

"What did you observe about Professor Jackson's interaction with his students?"

"It was extremely professional and courteous. He treated his students with respect, and tried to make them better."

"Any hint of a foul temper?"

"No."

"Any yelling or screaming at the students?"

"No."

"Any suggestion of inappropriate physical contact with the students."

"Absolutely not."

"Now let me ask you this: did you know that Professor Jackson recently got divorced?"

"Yes, I was aware of that."

"Did you notice any change in Professor Jackson's behavior or demeanor after the divorce."

"Well, he just seemed to stay a little bit more to himself. I mean, he was never a tremendously outgoing person, but he seemed to be more of an island unto himself, if you know what I mean."

"Were you surprised to learn that Professor Jackson had shot some of his students?"

"Shocked. That is not the Dan Jackson that I know. It's unthinkable."

Mr. Stanton smiled slightly, and said "I have no further questions at this time for Ms. Smith."

Mr. Johnson jumped to his feet to begin his cross-examination:

"Ms. Smith, did you ever think that Professor Jackson was insane?"

"Well, no."

"That's all the questions I have. Thank you."

Mr. Stanton rose slowly and sauntered over towards the jury box, before turning slightly towards Ms. Smith to begin his re-direct examination.

"Ms. Smith, do you know whether Professor Jackson was suffering from a mental illness when he shot those students?"

"No."

"So when you were answering Mr. Johnson's question, you were referring to Professor Jackson's mental state over the last couple of years?"

"That's right."

"Do you think that killing fifteen students and wounding five others are the acts of a sane person?"

Mr. Johnson flew out of his chair: "Objection! No foundation. This witness is not an expert who can offer such an opinion."

Mr. Stanton turned gruffly towards Mr. Johnson, pointing his finger: "It seems, Your Honor, Mr. Johnson thought Ms. Smith was competent to answer his question as to whether Professor Jackson seemed insane, but I'll withdraw the question, because the answer is self-evident. Ms. Smith, I have no further questions. Thank you."

As Mr. Stanton sat down he leaned over to me and said: "Doesn't matter that I didn't get an answer. The jury heard the question and it will resonate with them: sane people don't kill fifteen people."

I stared at Mr. Stanton and said nothing. I realized for the first time that he thought I might really be crazy.

Judge Winston squeaked: "Counsel, call your next witness."

Mr. Stanton rose: "The defense calls Lilly Simpson to the stand."

Lilly, a fairly tall, young sandy-haired woman, came forward from the audience. She climbed up to the witness stand, took the oath, and was seated. I could see pearls of sweat at the top of her bangs, and she licked her lips several times while looking around the courtroom. Mr. Stanton began:

"Would you state your name, please?"

"Lilly Simpson."

"How old are you?"

"Nineteen."

"Are you a freshman at Dartmouth College?"

"Yes."

"You were one of the students in Professor Jackson's class room on October 10 of last year when the shooting occurred?"

"Yes I was."

"Were you injured?"

"Miraculously not. I was sitting towards the side of the room, and dove for the floor as soon as the shooting began. So I was very lucky."

"Could you see Professor Jackson immediately before and during the shooting?"

"Yes. I could see him clearly just before the shooting. During the shooting, I wasn't looking directly at him. But after the shooting stopped, I did look up and watch Professor Jackson, and see him finally leave the class room."

"Please tell the jury what you saw immediately before the shooting."

"Well, it was kind of weird. Professor Jackson came in the class room and set his briefcase down on top of the desk in the front of the room. And then he opened it, and just stood there staring into it."

"Did he look like he was surprised by what was in the briefcase?"

Mr. Johnson jumped to his feet: "Objection! Calls for speculation — Ms. Simpson is not a mind reader."

Mr. Stanton shot a stern glance towards Mr. Johnson. "Your Honor, let me re-phase the question to satisfy Mr. Johnson. Lilly, have you ever been to a birthday party?"

Mr. Johnson exploded: "Objection! Your Honor this is wholly irrelevant to these proceedings."

Mr. Stanton smiled broadly. "Your Honor, I'm just laying a foundation to satisfy Mr. Johnson's mind reader objection." Several jurors smiled, too, and a few even chuckled.

"Proceed, Mr. Stanton."

"Lilly, can you answer my question?"

"Sure, I've been to birthday parties."

"Have you ever seen the birthday boy open a present that he wasn't expecting?"

"Yes."

"Tell us how his face looked."

"Well, his jaw dropped a little, and his mouths made like a small 'o.'"

"Is that how Professor Jackson looked when he opened his briefcase and stood there staring into it?"

"Yes, that's what it looked like. Someone opening a present and seeing something he didn't expect."

Mr. Stanton looked over his shoulder at Mr. Johnson, who sat jaw clenched, slightly blushing. Mr. Stanton continued:

"Tell us what happened next."

"Well, after several minutes of just standing there staring into the open briefcase, Professor Jackson reached into the briefcase and pulled out two guns, and began shooting."

"Did you get a look at Professor Jackson's face at that moment?"

"Yes, for a few seconds, before I dove for the floor."

"Can you describe how his face looked?"

"Well, he had sort of a blank look on his face. His eyes were glazed over and staring straight ahead, like he wasn't really seeing anything."

"And at that point, I take it, you dove for the floor?"

"Yes."

"Now you also told us that you looked up after the shooting had stopped and observed Professor Jackson, is that right?"

"That's right."

"Tell us what you saw"

"Professor Jackson stood there, looking down at the guns in his hands, and then he sort of grimaced and dropped the pistols, shaking his hands. He then turned and walked out of the class room and closed the door."

"Did you hear Professor Jackson say anything before he left the class room?"

"He spoke very softly, but I thought I heard him say, 'My God. How did this happen?'"

Mr. Stanton stood very still and dipped his chin to his chest, as if lost in thought. A dramatic pause for the jury, I supposed. After a moment, he looked up and said: "Thank you, Lilly. That's all the questions I have."

Lilly's testimony surprised me. I didn't remember grimacing, shaking my hands or saying anything after the shooting. But clearly her testimony had been helpful to my insanity defense. I looked over at the prosecutor's table and saw Mr. Johnson and his team in a huddled conference. Judge Winston broke the silence: "Mr. Johnson, do you have any questions for Ms. Simpson? Mr. Johnson?"

Mr. Johnson half-rose from his chair and responded: "No Your Honor. I want to spare Ms. Simpson from reliving that horrific day any further." Judge Winston turned to Lilly and said that she was excused, and she exited the courtroom.

"Your Honor, as its next and last witness, the defense calls Dr. Albert Van DeMere to the stand."

Dr. Van DeMere appeared at the back of the courtroom, and strode purposefully to the witness stand. He was sworn and seated, and Mr. Stanton began his examination:

"Please state your name and home address."

"Dr. Albert P. Van DeMere. 736 Boylston Street, Boston."

"How old are you, sir?"

"82 years old."

"Are you currently employed?"

"Not full time anymore. I do some consulting work from time to time."

"You hold a medical degree and license, is that correct?"

"Yes. I hold a medical degree from the American Caribbean Medical School. I am licensed to practice medicine in the State of Massachusetts."

"Did you have a specialty area of your practice?"

"I specialized in psychiatric medicine."

"Were you formerly engaged in the practice of psychiatric medicine?"

"Yes for more than forty years in the Boston area."

"Have you ever testified as an expert witness in psychiatry before?"

"Several times, in both state and federal courts in Boston."

"Did I retain you to provide expert services in this case?"

"Yes, you did."

"Pursuant to that retention, have you reached an opinion to a reasonable medical certainty regarding whether Professor Jackson was suffering from a mental defect or illness at the time of the October 10 shooting?"

"Yes I have.

"Before you tell us what that opinion is, Dr. Van DeMere, would you please tell the jury what you did to arrive at that conclusion?"

"I first read all of the police reports concerning the incident. Then I met with Professor Jackson and examined him. I then went back and consulted various treatises and scholarly articles on the subject of depersonalization disorders."

"Anything else?"

"Of course I also relied upon my over forty years of experience as a practicing psychiatrist as well."

"Of course. Now, based upon everything that you did, can you please tell the jury your opinion concerning Professor Jackson's mental state on October 10 of last year, at the time of the shootings?"

"Certainly. It is my opinion that Professor Jackson was suffering from a depersonalization disorder at the time of the shootings, which is a form of dissociative order, and therefore really did not understand what was happening or why it was happening, or have the ability to stop it."

"Doctor, what do you mean by a 'depersonalization disorder'?"

"A patient with a depersonalization disorder has persistent or recurring feelings of being disconnected from his physicality, feeling as though he is not completely occupying his body, or detached from his own thoughts or emotions. Some patients describe it like being in a dream and watching their bodies carry out activities with no ability to control them."

"Is this a recognized form of mental illness in the field of psychiatry?"

"Indeed it is."

"Doctor, what causes someone to develop this depersonalization disorder?"

"Medical science is not entirely certain as to what causes depersonalization disorders, but most medical scholars agree that its onset is related to severe emotional trauma."

"What kind of emotional trauma, Doctor?"

"Well, let's take Professor Jackson's case as an example. During my examination of Professor Jackson, I learned that he was married, happily he thought, for twenty-five years to his high school sweetheart. Last year, his wife confronted him and told him that she had been having an affair with someone else for a number of years, that the "someone else" was a woman, and that she wanted a divorce. That was extremely traumatic for Professor Jackson. His mind and his psyche could not successfully process that stress. So he developed a depersonalization disorder that provided an escape mechanism for his mind."

"Is that like the movie 'Sybil,' where the woman had multiple personalities?"

"No, that is another kind of dissociative disorder, but it is believed to be caused by severe trauma as well."

"In your opinion, did Professor Jackson have the ability to control his actions on the day of the shootings?"

"Probably not. Again, medical science is still learning about the boundaries of this disorder, but it is generally believed that when a person is in a dissociative state, he really has no ability to control his body. It's as if he was sleep walking. He may be aware of what his body is doing, but he lacked the ability to control it."

"Does that mean that Dr. Jackson is currently dangerous? Is it likely that he will have another episode where he might shoot people?"

"He is still suffering from the depersonalization disorder, but how and when it will manifest itself is really unknown. But he definitely requires psychiatric treatment to address his condition."

"Can he be cured?"

"In the realm of mental illness, we do not often use the word cure. We say, instead, that a patient can learn to manage his disorder. And yes, I believe with the proper treatment, Dr. Jackson can learn to manage his condition."

"Thank you Dr. Van DeMere. I have no further questions at this time."

Mr. Stanton marched back to counsel table, and sat back in his chair. Mr. Johnson got to his feet and strode

over to the far corner of the jury box, where he could get a
good look at both the jury and Dr. Van DeMere.

"Dr. Van DeMere, I am Carl Johnson, and I
represent the State of New Hampshire. You didn't tell the
jury where you went to college. It was at University of
West Virginia, wasn't it?

"Yes, that's right."

"You graduated in 1955, correct?"

"Yes."

"And at that time, were you aware that the
University of West Virginia pre-med program was ranked
45th in the nation?"

"No. It was a relatively new program when I went
there."

"And this American Caribbean Medical School that
you got your degree from, it's located in Jamaica, isn't it?"

"That's right."

"Nothing very American about it, is there Doctor,
other than the fact that it accepted American applicants
who couldn't get into a medical school in the United
States?"

My discomfort with Dr. Van DeMere's credentials
was proving to have been well-founded. Mr. Stanton shot
out of his chair: "Objection! Lacks foundation and is
argumentative."

Judge Winston peered over the bench at Mr.
Johnson: "Mr. Johnson, can you re-phrase your question?"

"Yes, Your Honor. I'll go at it another way."

"Dr. Van DeMere, how many medical schools
located in the United States did you apply to?"

Dr. Van DeMere squirmed slightly in the witness
chair. "I'm not sure that I remember the exact number. It
was a long time ago."

"Yes, Doctor, I know that it was a long time ago.
But did you apply to five medical schools in the United
States? Ten? Twenty? One hundred? Can you at least

give me an estimate of the number of medical schools you applied to in the United States?"

"I'd estimate somewhere between twenty and thirty."

"Somewhere between twenty and thirty. All right. You didn't get admitted into any of those schools, did you?"

"Back in those days, competition was very tight at United States medical schools, and no, I didn't get into any of them."

"In fact, Doctor, you didn't get into any medical school other than the American Caribbean Medical School, did you?"

"That was the only medical school that I got into."

"Do you know whether American Caribbean Medical School is accredited with the American Medical Association?"

"Currently, I don't know. It was when I went there."

"Did you know that it lost its AMA accreditation two years after you graduated, and closed its doors the next year?"

"No, I didn't."

"Looks like you got your degree just in time. Now that we have a better idea of your academic credentials, let's explore your past service as an expert witness. You told this jury that you'd been designated an expert witness in 'several' cases in both state and federal courts in Boston, didn't you?"

"Yes."

"What does the word 'several' mean to you?"

"I don't understand what you are asking."

"Well, does 'several' mean more than five? More than ten? Let me just ask straight out: how many times have you been designated an expert witness?"

"I don't remember the exact number."

"What is your best estimate?"

"Over what period of time?"

This was starting to get bad. Dr. Van DeMere looked like he was trying to be evasive. I glanced over at Mr. Stanton and noticed that he had the arms on his chair in a stranglehold, with his hands almost turning purple he was squeezing so hard. Mr. Johnson continued:

"Let's make it easy for you, Doctor. Ever."

Dr. Van DeMere again squirmed in his chair, and averted his eyes for a moment. In a diminished voice, Dr. Van DeMere virtually whispered: "I think my best estimate is three times."

A murmur ran through the audience. I saw a couple of the jurors shake their heads. This was not good. Mr. Johnson smelled blood in the water, and he was circling to complete the kill.

"Only three times. I see. When was the last time you were designated as an expert witness?"

"About ten years ago."

"None of those cases involved a diagnosis of depersonalization disorder, did they?"

"No."

"They were divorce cases where one spouse or the other was seeking an order of protection, correct?"

"That's correct."

"And you were called to give an 'expert' opinion as to whether one or both spouses had violent tendencies, true?"

"Yes."

Mr. Johnson had obviously done his homework. He seemed to know all the answers before Dr. Van DeMere even responded. I looked over again at Mr. Stanton, who looked pale and sweaty.

"All right, Doctor Van DeMere, let's turn to your 'years of experience' in private practice. You never treated a patient who you diagnosed as having a depersonalization disorder, did you?"

"Not that I can remember."

"Well, isn't that something you'd likely remember in preparing to testify in this case and tell this jury that Professor Jackson had this disorder?"

"Not necessarily."

"Very well, Doctor. Let's move on. You are familiar with the American Psychiatric Association?"

"Yes."

"It is the main professional organization of psychiatrists in the United States, correct?"

"Yes."

"Similar to the American Medical Association, except just for psychiatrists?"

"That's right."

"The Association publishes something called the Diagnostic and Statistical Manual of Mental Disorders, right?"

"Correct."

"That's sometimes referred to as the DMS?"

"Yes."

"You would agree that the DMS codifies psychiatric conditions and is used as a key guide for diagnosing disorders?"

"I would."

"You didn't follow the DMS recommendations concerning screening for depersonalization disorder, did you?"

"I believe that what I did was consistent with the DMS."

"Doctor, I didn't ask you if what you did was consistent with the DMS. I asked you to admit that you did not follow the DMS recommendations for screening for depersonalization disorder. You didn't follow the DMS, did you?"

"Not precisely, no."

"Now you are familiar with the Structural Clinical Interview for DMS-IV Dissociative Disorders, aren't you?"

"Yes, I am familiar with that."

"It's a detailed questionnaire designed to help medical professionals identify persons who may be suffering from dissociative disorders, including depersonalization disorders, right?"

"That's my understanding."

"Are you aware that the effectiveness of that interviewing technique has been evaluated favorably by the National Institute of Mental Health?"

"Not specifically, but it wouldn't surprise me."

"Using the structural clinical questionnaire to interview a patient would typically take three to five hours, wouldn't it Doctor?"

"I'm not sure how long it would take. It would probably depend on the patient."

"Well, the questionnaire is more than two hundred and fifty questions, isn't it?"

"It could be about that length."

"The fact is that you don't know how long it would take to follow the structured clinical interview because you've never used it with a patient, have you?"

"I haven't asked all of those questions, no."

"And you didn't follow the structured clinical interview questionnaire in interviewing Professor Jackson, did you?"

"I didn't ask him all of those questions. The structured clinical interview is merely a guide, not a requirement, and based upon my analysis of Professor Jackson, I did not feel it necessary to ask every one of those questions."

"Tell me, Doctor, how long did you take to interview Professor Jackson?"

"It probably took about an hour."

"One hour?"

"That's what I just said."

"Did you meet with Professor Jackson again after your interview?"

"No."

"Do you really expect this jury to believe that although you didn't follow the DMS recommendations regarding screening for depersonalization disorders, you didn't use the structural clinical questionnaire, and you met Professor Jackson exactly once for one hour, you were able to reach your opinion to a reasonable medical certainty?"

"Objection!" roared Mr. Stanton. "Argumentative."

Mr. Johnson smiled slightly. "I'll withdraw the question and move on to something else. Now Dr. Van DeMere, you told this jury that you reviewed scholarly articles and treatises in arriving at your opinion in this case, correct?"

"Yes."

"You turned over to the prosecution all of the materials you reviewed, didn't you?"

"I think that I did."

"I noticed a book that was on the list of materials turned over to the prosecution authored by Professor Thomas Frumm of the University of Illinois. You're familiar with Dr. Frumm's book regarding depersonalization disorders?"

"Indeed I am."

"Professor Frumm is a recognized expert on this subject, is he not?"

"Yes."

"You've read Professor's Frumm book entitled 'Diagnosing Dissociative Disorders'?"

"I have not only read the book, but Professor Frumm actually asked me to look over his draft for the book before it was published. His wife and mine are cousins."

"I take it that you would have pointed out any obvious errors to him that you saw, as a professional courtesy?"

"Certainly."

"Did you find any errors in Professor Frumm's draft?"

"Other than typos and some grammar errors, no."

Mr. Johnson went over to counsel table, retrieved a book, opened it to a particular page, and then asked: "Then would you agree with Professor Frumm's observation, found on page 186 of his book that, quote, Medical research into depersonalization disorders overwhelming demonstrates that depersonalization disorders generally stem from childhood or adolescent stress incidents, including physical or sexual abuse, and other serious emotional trauma, unquote."

Dr. Van DeMere sat still and quiet as a stone, staring out into the courtroom. "May I see the page that you are reading from?'

"Certainly, Dr. Van DeMere. Your Honor, may I approach the witness?" Judge Winston nodded his head. Mr. Johnson strode up to the witness stand and handed over the book. "Take a look, and then please answer my question."

Dr. Van DeMere adjusted his monocle and used his finger to scroll down the page of the book. After a moment, he cleared his throat and said: "Yes, I agree that is quote, generally, unquote, the case. But not always."

Mr. Johnson went back up to the witness stand and retrieved the book from Dr. Van DeMere. "Well let me ask you this, Dr. Van DeMere. Isn't it true that you didn't ask Professor Jackson anything about his childhood or upbringing?"

"In light of the fact that there had been no previous manifestation of a depersonalization disorder episode prior to his divorce, I did not feel it was necessary to delve into the distant past to find the source of the problem."

"So the answer to my question is no, you didn't ask Professor Jackson anything about his childhood or upbringing, correct?"

"That's correct."

"Now, let me get this straight: you relied upon the most recent traumatic event in Professor Jackson's life because there hadn't been any previous depersonalization episodes, correct?"

"Yes. If Professor Jackson had been suffering from a depersonalization disorder caused by something in his childhood, one would have expected to see a manifestation of it long before now."

"Let me read to you another passage from Professor Frumm's book, the draft of which you reviewed prior to its publication: quote, It is common for persons suffering from depersonalization disorders to be a-symptomatic for years after the traumatizing event, or they may experience depersonalization episodes and be unaware of what is occurring, end quote. You agree with that statement, don't you?"

This time, Dr. Van DeMere didn't ask to see the book. "It may be 'common' for that to happen, but it would be quite unusual, in my opinion, for there to be a long latent period between the traumatic event and the symptoms."

"So I guess you disagree with Professor Frumm, an individual you have told this jury is a recognized expert in his field?"

"Yes, I guess I do."

"Who would you think is more recognized as an expert in depersonalization disorders, you or Professor Frumm?"

"I really wouldn't know."

"Okay, Doctor, I have just one more question for you. Did Professor Jackson ever tell you that he knew that shooting those students was wrong?"

"I never asked that question."

"I didn't ask you if you asked him that question. During your interview did he tell you that he knew that shooting those students was wrong?"

Dr. Van DeMere looked away from Mr. Johnson and up at the ceiling. "It may have come up. I can't recall exactly."

Mr. Johnson shook his head slightly. "That's all I have for this witness, Your Honor."

I looked over at Mr. Stanton. He was rifling through the notes on his legal pad. Judge Winston said "Mr. Stanton, any further questions for Dr. Van DeMere?"

Ultimately, Mr. Stanton stood. Sweat stains now marked the underarms of his suit coat, and his face had a sheen. "No, Your Honor. Nothing further. The defense rests."

Judge Winston addressed the courtroom. "Ladies and gentlemen, we have now finished the case in chief for the defense. Tomorrow morning, at 10:00 o'clock we will begin with the prosecution's case. The jurors are reminded that they are not to talk about the case among themselves or with anyone else. Court is adjourned."

Everyone in the courtroom rose as Judge Winston left the bench and exited the courtroom. Mr. Stanton grabbed his legal pads with notes and stuffed them in his briefcase. I noticed that his hands were shaking. I leaned over and whispered in his ear: "Do we need some time to talk? I mean, this didn't go too well. Do we need to re-think my testifying?"

Mr. Stanton turned and looked me in the eyes: "Dr. Van DeMere didn't hold up as well as I had hoped on cross. But we still got good testimony from the other two witnesses. I need to go back to the office to finish preparing for Dr. Wells' cross-examination, so I don't have time to dwell on this with you right now. But let's meet tomorrow morning before court and we'll hash it out. I'll tell the deputy to bring you to the witness room around 9:00 am."

"One more thing. Can you ask the deputy if I could meet for a few minutes with my friend Tim, who is sitting over there in the courtroom?"

"Oh, you mean the priest. Sure. I'll take care of it." Mr. Stanton motioned the deputy over and whispered in his ear. The deputy nodded his head affirmatively. I was then escorted to the witness room, while the deputy went to get Tim.

Tim came into the witness room and gave me a big hug, but his face was creased with worry lines. I asked:

"So, how do you think it went?"

Tim looked away for a moment, as if searching for the right words. "Look, Dan. I have to be honest. It didn't go that well. Your department chairperson was okay, and your student I think helped humanize you a bit. But that Dr. Van DeMere was a disaster. He came off as a quack, who really didn't examine you thoroughly enough to come to any conclusion. I am genuinely worried."

I shook my head in agreement. "So am I."

"What does your Mr. Stanton think?"

"He didn't say too much. I am under the impression that he still thinks he can win this."

"Did you talk with him about the plea deal, like we discussed?"

"Yes."

"And?"

"Well, he doesn't think that Mr. Johnson would be interested, and that it would have shown weakness to go to him before trial."

"You mean he hasn't even ask Mr. Johnson if he would be interested in a plea deal? I thought we agreed that you were going to insist on that before the trial started."

"Mr. Stanton didn't think that it was a good idea, and I have to rely upon his judgment on these things. He agreed to approach Mr. Johnson about a plea deal once the jury starts its deliberations, if I want."

"The way this is going, that will be way too late. I'm no expert on jury trials, but I'd say that your defense is barely above water at this point. If the prosecution is able to score some points during its case, you'll be sunk. Mr. Johnson won't feel any pressure to do a deal at that point."

I was getting a little annoyed at Tim's pessimism. I mean, wasn't my best friend supposed to help cheer me up? Yet, I knew that Tim had my best interests at heart, and wanted me to have realistic expectations. "Look, Tim. Maybe the prosecution's case won't go so well. And there's another possibility: I could take the stand and testify in our rebuttal case."

Tim's face noticeably brightened. "You testifying could make all the difference. You could admit that you did the shootings, profess real remorse and grief for the victims, and seek forgiveness. You absolutely have to testify. The jury may convict you, but I doubt that they sentence you to death. A life sentence is all we hoped for in a plea deal anyhow. So, by testifying, you get the plea deal, even if Mr. Stanton doesn't want to show 'weakness,' or Mr. Johnson doesn't want to do the deal. That's brilliant." Tim smiled broadly.

"Not so fast, Tim. I've talked to Mr. Stanton about this, and he strongly advises against me testifying. He says that it could open all sorts of doors that Mr. Johnson could exploit on cross-examination, making things even worse. He said that we would revisit the issue after the prosecution finished its case, but was pretty much dead-set against it."

"Whose decision is it? I mean, if you insist on taking the stand, doesn't Mr. Stanton have to honor your directive?"

"Yes, I think he does. But I am going to take Mr. Stanton's advice for now — let's see how the prosecution's case comes in, and then I'll have to decide whether to take the stand or not."

Tim stood, nodding his head affirmatively. "I'm okay with that. But I strongly feel that only by testifying can you convince this jury that you don't deserve to die. Keep that in mind as you think this through."

"I will," I promised. We shook hands, and I was led away for my return trip to prison, where I had all night to ponder what my chances would be after the prosecution began it case tomorrow.

Chapter 18

The next morning the deputy escorted me into the witness room next to the courtroom, and my handcuffs were removed. It was just nine o'clock, and Mr. Stanton was not there yet. I took a seat and waited.

A few minutes later, Mr. Stanton rushed into the room, put his briefcase down on the table and shook my hand. He looked more like his old, disheveled self. His suit was all wrinkled, and looked as if he had slept in it. His shirt top button was undone, and his tie askew. He must have had a long night.

I started the conversation: "It looked to me like Dr. Van DeMere got creamed yesterday. I told you that I was concerned about his credentials and warned you to make sure he'd covered his bases with the scholarly literature. Mr. Johnson really did his homework, and it looks like we didn't. My friend Tim agrees that our case did not come in well. Jesus. Do I even have a prayer at this anymore?"

Mr. Stanton stammered: "Just relax a minute. Look, it's true that Dr. Van DeMere took some hits. I was as surprised as anyone about his wife being cousins with that professor from the University of Illinois, and his having reviewed the draft of that book. But nobody could have seen that coming. I bet even Johnson was surprised by that one, but I have to admit that he certainly made the most out of it. Dr. Van DeMere's opinion is still in evidence, and I can argue to the jury based on it. Nothing that Johnson did to him establishes that your divorce wasn't the precipitating traumatic event triggering this disorder. And don't forget — we still have the un-refuted testimony of Lilly about how oddly you acted the day of the shooting, and what you said. That strongly supports our argument that you didn't really know what you were doing. Johnson was so stunned by that testimony that he didn't even try to cross examine her. Remember, the New Hampshire rule on insanity is different than everywhere else. We don't technically even need to fit within a medically-recognized mental illness to win. We're still in the ball game. I have a few tricks up my sleeve for Dr. Wells, too. They aren't going to be able to prove that you weren't affected by a mental illness or defect at the time of the shooting. I still think that, at the end of the day, the jury is going to accept the argument that sane people don't randomly kill fifteen people."

I found myself being slightly buoyed by Mr. Stanton's optimism and assessment of the case. Maybe he was right, and Tim was wrong. Dr. Van DeMere didn't do great, but he may have done enough, with everything else, to carry the day. But I still had some concerns, so I asked: "Should we start thinking of putting me on the stand to buttress our defense?"

"Not yet. Let's see how the prosecution case comes in. We know what Dr. Wells will say. But I have a feeling that Johnson has a surprise of his own to spring, probably calling some witness we aren't expecting. I went over and over the witness disclosure list last night, and I really can't figure out who it will be. But we'll find out soon enough. Anyways, let's revisit this discussion after the prosecution case comes in. Then we'll see how we feel."

I really wanted this decision to be made, one way or the other, but I had to put my trust in Mr. Stanton. "Okay."

Mr. Stanton looked at his watch. "It's almost nine-thirty. Let's get into the courtroom so I can get my stuff set up, and look over my notes." Mr. Stanton opened the witness room door and motioned to the deputy, who came and put my handcuffs back on for the short walk to counsel table.

I looked over at the prosecution table and saw Mr. Johnson busily reviewing notes on his legal pad. Sitting next to him was Dr. Wells. She looked stunning, dressed in a white suit with a blue blouse. She saw me looking over at

her and I thought I saw a small smile on her face and a nod
of acknowledgement. Intellectually I realized that she was
there to convince the jury that I should be punished by
death, but I still harbored an inexplicable belief that she
also wanted to help me understand why this had all
occurred. I then glanced over and saw Tim in his usual seat
in the peanut gallery. He looked at me with his mouth set,
unsmiling, but nodded his head slightly to acknowledge
me.

The bailiff called the courtroom to order, and we all
stood as Judge Winston ascended the bench. After three
pounds of his gavel, Judge Winston croaked: "Does the
prosecution wish to make its opening statement now?"

Mr. Johnson quickly stood, and announced: "Yes,
Your Honor. May it please the Court. Counsel. Ladies
and Gentlemen of the Jury. Good morning. As you may
remember, my name is Carl Johnson, and I am here today
representing the State of New Hampshire. I want to spend
a few minutes this morning telling you what I think the
evidence in this case will show."

"On October 10 of last year, there was a brutal
massacre of fifteen Dartmouth students in Hanover, New
Hampshire. We know who the perpetrator of this carnage
was — the defendant, Professor Dan Jackson. He admits it.
But he claims that he was insane at the time and therefore
not responsible for his actions. We will show you that is
not true. Professor Jackson acted in a methodical,
calculated manner in executing his students. He purchased
the pistols from Hal's Gun Store in Lebanon just one week
before the killings. The extended magazines that housed
the bullets that tore through the bodies of his students were
purchased just days before the shooting. And you will hear
from one of the survivors of this slaughter who will testify
that Professor Jackson was frustrated and angry with the
class for what he called their slovenly approach to class
work. That is why Professor Jackson committed this crime.

It was a deliberate attempt to punish his students for their supposed failure to live up to his exalted academic standards. Finally, Dr. Paige Wells, a well-respected psychiatrist and teacher, will testify that, based upon her examination of Professor Jackson, he was not suffering from a 'depersonalization disorder' at the time of his attack on his students. To the contrary, she will testify that in her expert opinion, Professor Jackson was sane and understood the nature of his acts. The State believes that after you have heard all of the evidence, you will conclude that Dan Jackson was sane and is guilty of murder in the first degree. Thank you for your attention."

I leaned over and whispered into Mr. Stanton's ear: "What is this bullshit about me threatening my students. That never happened. Do you know which survivor he intends to call?"

Mr. Stanton was scribbling furiously while I talked, and when I had finished, he turned and whispered back in my ear: "I'm not sure which survivor he intends on calling, because he listed them all on his witness list. I had my paralegal interview as many of them as would talk to us, and this is the first I am hearing of any threats. We'll just have to wait and see who they call. I did subpoena the school records on each of the survivors, so when we know who he is calling, I'll look through that student's records to see what we can use."

Judge Winston demanded: "Mr. Johnson, call your first witness."

"The State calls policeman Howard Edwards to the stand."

Howard Edwards strode from the audience dressed in his neatly-pressed police uniform. He had a somewhat boyish appearance about him, and looked as if he had played football at some point in his life. He took the stand and was sworn. Mr. Johnson started:

"State your name and your address for the record, please."

"Howard Edwards. I live at 2714 Concord Street, Hanover, New Hampshire."

"By whom are you employed?"

"The Hanover Police Department."

"How long have you worked there, and what is your rank or title?"

"I've been there six years. I am a sergeant."

"Sergeant Edwards, as part of your duties as a member of the Hanover Police Department, did you participate in the investigation of the killings of fifteen students that occurred on October 10 of last year."

"Yes I did."

"Your Honor may I approach the witness?"

"You may," intoned Judge Winston.

Mr. Johnson walked towards Sergeant Edwards with a series of photographs in his hand. "I ask you to look at what has been marked as State Exhibit 1. Is that a true and correct depiction of how the scene of the crime appeared when you arrived on October 10?"

"Yes, it is."

"Please look at the photos that we have marked as State Exhibits 2 and 3; do they also truly and correctly depict how the scene of the crime appeared when you arrived?"

"Yes, they do."

"Your Honor, the State offers State Exhibits 1-3 into evidence."

"Any objection, Mr. Stanton?"

Mr. Stanton jumped to his feet. "Your Honor, we do have an objection. Could we approach the bench for a side-bar?" Judge Winston nodded, and Mr. Stanton walked quickly towards the bench, where he was joined by Mr. Johnson. Mr. Stanton spoke in a hushed voice, presumably so the jury could not hear, but from counsel table I could.

Mr. Stanton continued: "Your Honor, we do object. The defense has stipulated to the commission of the crime. Pictures of the crime scene are therefore not relevant to any disputed factual issue in this case. And I suspect that if admitted into evidence, Mr. Johnson will next want to publish these photos to the jury — in fact, I think I see some blow-ups of these photos behind counsel table. That would be highly prejudicial. In light of the stipulation, the probative value would be outweighed by the prejudice to the defendant."

Mr. Johnson responded in a slightly less hushed voice: "Your Honor, the jury is entitled to see exactly what transpired on the morning of October 10, and the stipulation does not do that. In addition, the State believes that these photos will help place the testimony of Ms. Simpson, who was called by the defense, and the survivor that the State intends to call, into context."

Mr. Stanton replied: "The locations of the dead bodies and the gory detail of the blood throughout the room is clearly intended to inflame the jury's passions against the defendant. It can't possibly have anything to do with Ms. Simpson's testimony, because she does not even appear in these photos. Allowing these photos to be displayed would be highly prejudicial."

Judge Winston sat chin in hand, and lost in thought. "Mr. Stanton, I am going to over-rule your objection. Committing the crimes was highly prejudicial to your client. Showing the jury what that means is fair game. State Exhibits 1 through 3 are admitted in evidence. Mr. Johnson, you may continue."

Mr. Stanton trudged back to counsel table and plopped down in his chair, his lips pursed. This was going be bad, I was sure. Once the jury saw those pictures, they'd never be able to forget them.

Mr. Johnson continued: "With the Court's permission, I would like to display blow ups of these photos to the jury." Judge Winston nodded: "You may proceed." Blow ups of the three photos were placed on easels in front of the jury box. I watched the faces of the jurors. Deep frowns and grimaces were on the faces of almost every juror. Some jurors covered their mouths and looked away. Even the jurors that Mr. Stanton had thought might be favorable to us looked disgusted. Finally, after a few minutes, the blow-ups were taken down, and the examination of Sergeant Edwards continued:

"Sergeant Edwards, can you please tell the jury what you did to investigate this crime?"

"Well, in the class room, I found the pistols in a briefcase bearing the initials "DJ." I had the guns dusted for fingerprints and later confirmed that the prints on the guns were those of Professor Jackson. I also collected bullet casings, and bullet slugs retrieved from the bodies from the coroner's office. Testing by the New Hampshire State Police ballistics department confirmed that the bullets came from the two guns I found in the class room."

"Sergeant Edwards, were you ever able to confirm where and by whom the pistols were purchased?"

"Yes. We obtained from Hal's Gun Shop in West Lebanon a receipt for the purchase of the two guns, bearing a signature that we were later able to confirm was Professor Jackson's."

"When were the guns purchased?"

"October 1."

"Were you able to determine when the bullet magazines for the pistols were purchased?"

"Yes sir. October 4 from Hal's Gun Shop in West Lebanon, again verified by a signed receipt by Professor Jackson."

"Thank you, Sergeant Edwards. That's all I have for now."

Mr. Stanton got to his feet and approached the witness box. "Sergeant Edwards, you look to be in pretty good shape — did you play a little football in college?"

Sergeant Edwards smiled slightly and said "No, but I do try to keep in shape."

"Ever had to run down a suspect you were pursuing?"

"Yes."

"Has that occurred with some frequency — that you appear at the scene of the crime and the suspect tries to run away?"

"It's not an uncommon occurrence."

I looked over at Mr. Johnson sitting at the prosecution's table. He was squinting, as if he was trying to see where Mr. Stanton was heading with this line of questioning. He was perched on the edge of his seat, apparently internally debating whether to object or stay seated. Mr. Stanton continued:

"And that's because, in your experience, people who are guilty of crimes tend to want to escape from the police rather than be caught, right?"

"Well, sure."

"Were you one of the officers who originally arrested Professor Jackson outside of Dartmouth Hall?"

"Yes, I was."

"He was sitting there on the front steps when you arrived, correct?"

"Yes."

"When he saw your police car, he didn't make any effort to run away, did he?"

"No."

"In fact, he put his hands behind his head and laid on his stomach on the ground, didn't he?"

"Correct."

"Professor Jackson didn't attempt to resist, did he?"

"No."

"Did you accompany him in the police car to the police station?"

"I did."

"Did he seem sort of stunned to you?"

"I would have to say yes, he did."

"By the way, Sergeant Edwards, did you make any effort to investigate why Professor Jackson had purchased those two guns?"

"No."

"So as far as you know, he may have purchased them for self-defense, right?"

"I suppose so."

"I have nothing further for this witness."

Mr. Johnson had nothing further to ask Sergeant Edwards, who departed the witness stand. Mr. Johnson continued: "The State calls Carla Wilson to the stand."

Carla Wilson rose from the gallery and walked up towards the witness stand. She was tall and lean, and walked with a grace that was noticeable. Her long brown hair hung down around her shoulders, and framed a blemish-free face. She took the oath and was seated.

Mr. Stanton turned to me and whispered: "So what's her story?"

I whispered back: "Not one of my better students. Smart enough, but lazy. Was always trying to flirt with me after class to butter me up. I think she got a "D" on her first essay and was pissed at me. Even had her dad call me to complain that I was grading too hard."

Mr. Stanton held up his hand to stop me, and passed a note to his paralegal, who began rifling through the box of students records at her feet. Mr. Johnson began his examination:

"Please state your name for the record."

"Carla Wilson."

"You are a freshman at Dartmouth College, correct?"

"Yes, that's right."

"Were you in Professor Jackson's freshman English class last October?

"Yes I was."

"And you were present in the classroom on October 10 when Professor Jackson shot and killed fifteen students?"

Carla's lower lip trembled a bit, and she let out a deep breath. "Yes."

"Tell us what happened that morning."

"Well, I was sitting in my usual seat in the second row slightly to the right of Professor Jackson's desk. We were supposed to have a mid-term exam that day, so a lot of the kids in the class showed up a bit early to get ready. Anyway, I saw Professor Jackson come in and set his briefcase down on the desk. Then he opened it and stared into it for a few minutes, and the next thing I know he pulls out these two guns and starts shooting. I was shocked and initially didn't know what to do. But pretty quickly I got my act together and dove for the floor."

"Were you wounded during the shooting?"

Tears welled up in Carla's eyes, and her lips again quivered. "Yes, I got shot in the leg. The doctor thought it was probably a ricochet off something because of the angle of the bullet. But I just lay there on the floor with my hands over my head."

"Did you see anything else?"

"No, the shooting eventually stopped, but I stayed down on the floor with my head down until the police came."

"All right. Now had Professor Jackson ever gotten angry with the class prior to the day of the shooting?"

"Well, he had assigned an essay for the class to do, and we had turned them in at the end of September. And, like the first part of October, he passed them back to the class, and I think basically everybody had bombed."

"What do you mean, 'everybody had bombed?'"

"Well, Professor Jackson said that he was very disappointed with the essays, that, with a few exceptions, they were filled with spelling and grammatical errors and didn't show much understanding of the material. He was pretty upset with us."

Mr. Stanton jumped to his feet. "Move to strike the last sentence of the witness' testimony, 'he was pretty upset with us' as conclusory, without foundation and non-responsive."

"Sustained," bellowed Judge Winston. "That portion shall be stricken and the jury is instructed to disregard it."

Mr. Johnson continued: "Ms. Wilson, do you recall any of the exact words Professor Jackson used in describing the essays the day he passed them back?"

"Some of them. He said we were slovenly students. Lazy. Undisciplined. A disgrace to Dartmouth College, I think he said. He said that more than half of us didn't deserve to even be here, based on the essays."

"Ms. Wilson, you said Professor Jackson passed back the exams in early October — was that on October 1, do you recall?"

"Yes, I think it was October 1."

"Were you aware that October 1 was the day that Professor Jackson purchased the two guns from Hal's Gun Shop?"

"No. No I wasn't."

"That's all I have for this witness."

Mr. Stanton scribbled a few more notes on his legal pad. He leaned over to me and asked: "Is any of that true?" I whispered back "I did tell the class that I was disappointed in some of their performances, but a lot of the students did pretty well. I didn't say any of the rest of that nonsense. That's an out and out lie." Mr. Stanton got out of his chair and walked towards the witness box. "Ms.

Wilson, is it fair to say that Professor Jackson is not your favorite teacher?"

Carla squirmed a bit in the witness chair. "Well, no, he's not my favorite teacher."

"One of the reasons he is not your favorite is that you got a 'D' on that essay, didn't you?"

Carla blushed, and responded: "That's the grade he gave me."

"You felt that grade was unfair, didn't you?"

Carla stuck her chin out definitely: "Yes I did."

"You went and complained about that grade to Professor Jackson, didn't you?"

"I sure did. And he told me he wouldn't do anything about it."

"Well, actually didn't he tell you that you got the grade you deserved?"

Carla paused, and her eyes darted around the courtroom. "I don't remember his exact words."

Mr. Stanton turned and faced the jury, eyeing each juror for effect. "Really? You seemed to be able to recall with great specificity the derogatory things he said about the class when Mr. Johnson asked you. But you can't remember his exact words to you in a private meeting? Are you sure you don't remember Professor Jackson telling you that you got the grade you deserved?"

Carla's face was now turning beet red. "He might have."

"That made you mad, didn't it? So mad that you called your daddy and had him call Professor Jackson to complain, isn't that right?

"I was upset with Professor Jackson. He was being unfair. And yes, I told my father, and he said he would call Professor Jackson to straighten it out."

"Do you know whether your father called Professor Jackson?"

"He told me he did."

"Did Professor Jackson change your grade?"

"No."

"Now, you told the jury that you thought that the whole class had 'bombed' the essay, correct?"

"That's right."

"You don't actually know what grades were given out to the class, do you?"

"Well, not every one, no."

"How many students got 'A's' on the essays?"

"I don't know, but it couldn't have been many by the way Professor Jackson talked."

"How many got 'B's?'"

"I don't know the exact numbers. But most of the class did poorly."

"Define what you mean by poorly for me."

Carla again squirmed in her seat. "Oh, I don't know. C's or D's."

Mr. Stanton turned back to his paralegal who handed him a piece of paper. "Ms. Wilson, I am holding in my hands a certified copy of the grades given out by Professor Jackson for that first essay. How many people were in the class, do you know?"

Carla eyes were frantically darting back and forth. Sweat was beginning to show on her forehead. And she was slowly sinking further down in the witness chair, as if she could somehow escape Mr. Stanton. "I am not entirely sure. I think twenty-five."

"You are right, Ms. Wilson. There were twenty-five students in the class. Would it surprise you to learn that five students got either A's or A-'s?"

"Well, yes it would."

"That's about twenty-percent of the class, right?"

"I guess."

"Those five students didn't 'bomb' the essay, did they?"

"No."

"And would it surprise you to learn that eleven students got some kind of 'B' on the essay?"

"I didn't think that many people did that well."

"Those eleven students who got some kind of 'B' on the essay didn't 'bomb,' did they?"

"Well if that many got B's, then no."

"Do you want to look at the certified copy of the grades to see if I've counted correctly? I want to be fair with you."

Carla looked down at her hands. "No, I believe you."

"Good. Let me put it to you this way: were you aware that the lowest grade given on the essay was a 'D,' and that there was only one of those?"

Carla's jaw dropped and she turned deep crimson. She didn't respond to the question, but sank lower in the witness seat.

"Ms. Wilson, are you sure that Professor Jackson said all those derogatory things about the class, or did you perhaps just make that up because you had the worst essay in the class?" Mr. Stanton walked slowly closer to the witness box, and said in a softer, quieter voice: "I can call back Lilly Simpson and ask her if Professor Jackson said those things to the class, but it would be better, Carla, if you could clear this up for us. "

Tears again began to well up in Carla's eyes, she struggled to gain her composure, and finally whimpered: "I can't say for sure that Professor Jackson said all of those things about the class."

"Ms. Wilson, isn't it true that all Professor Jackson said was that he was disappointed in some of the essays?"

"Yes," Carla whispered.

"Thank you, Ms. Wilson. That's all I have."

Mr. Stanton turned and marched back to counsel table with a satisfied look on his face. I had to admit that he had done a masterful job of neutering Carla's testimony.

I looked over at the prosecution table and saw Mr. Johnson and his team engaged in heated discussion, presumably about whether to try to resurrect Carla's testimony. Ultimately, Mr. Johnson stood up and said "We have no further questions for Ms. Wilson." Judge Winston instructed her to step down from the witness stand, and she slinked out of the courtroom, head down. Things were looking up for the defense.

Chapter 19

Although Mr. Johnson had suffered a setback, he recovered quickly. With a small smirk on his face, Mr. Johnson bellowed: "The State calls Beth Williamson to the stand!"

My blood ran absolutely cold. I turned to look back at the crowd in the courtroom. From the back row, a figure rose and waddled towards the swinging wooden gate that separated the working courtroom from the peanut gallery. It couldn't be, but it was: Beth had come here all the way from France to testify against me. I would never have thought it possible. I nervously scanned the crowd to see if Nancy was with her. But Nancy was not in the courtroom, just Beth. I leaned over and whispered in Mr. Stanton's ear: "They can't call her, can they? I mean, she wasn't even around when the shootings occurred. Object. Do something to stop this."

Mr. Stanton leaned over and whispered in reply "Her name was on the witness list, but I never anticipated she would ever show up, based upon what you told me. As of right now, I don't have any basis to object to her being called as a witness. But I will do everything possible to limit her testimony. What do you think she will say?"

"I have no idea, but it won't be anything good, that's for sure."

Beth walked past counsel table without even throwing me a glance. She took the oath and then settled herself into the witness chair. Mr. Johnson began:

"Please tell the jury your name."

"Beth Williamson."

"Where do you currently reside?"

"Paris, France."

"Do you know the defendant, Daniel Jackson?"

"I certainly do."

"When did you first meet Mr. Jackson?"

"My freshman year in college. My roommate, Nancy, dated Dan all through college."

"Did you remain friendly with Dan and Nancy after college?"

Mr. Stanton jumped to his feet: "Objection! There was no testimony that the witness was 'friendly' with Mr. Jackson."

Judge Winston barked: "Sustained!"

Mr. Johnson sneered at Mr. Stanton over his shoulder, but it melted into a sickly smile as he returned his attention to Beth: "Ms. Williamson, did you maintain a relationship with Dan and Nancy after college?"

"Yes. Nancy and I corresponded regularly. After Nancy and Dan got married, I would stay at their home from time to time when my travels brought me in the area. Nancy and I also took some vacations together over the years."

"Are you currently living with Mr. Jackson's ex-wife, Nancy?"

"Yes, we share a flat together in Paris."

"Were you the reason that Nancy decided to divorce Mr. Jackson?"

"Objection!" bellowed Mr. Stanton. "Calls for speculation."

Before Judge Winston could rule, Mr. Johnson waived his hand and said "I'll re-phrase, your Honor. Did Nancy ever tell you why she had decided to divorce Mr. Jackson?"

"Objection!" Mr. Stanton was again on his feet. "Your Honor, could I be heard at a side-bar?"

Judge Winston motioned both counsel to approach the side of his desk. Again, although the jury could not hear the conversation, by leaning forward slightly I could hear everything. Mr. Stanton began: "Your Honor, we are not here trying Mr. Jackson's divorce case. This testimony is wholly irrelevant to the insanity defense, which is the only issue we are here to decide. This witness was not mentioned in the State's opening, and with good reason: she has nothing relevant to add. Her only purpose is to cast aspersions on my client to prejudice him with the jury."

Mr. Johnson replied: "Your Honor, if Mr. Stanton had just been a little patient, it would have become apparent why Ms. Williamson's testimony is relevant. If permitted, she will testify as to Mr. Jackson's propensity towards violence. Mr. Jackson is not insane, just a person with an uncontrollable temper — a temper that on October 10 he unleashed on his students."

Mr. Stanton face reddened deeply and he started to respond when Judge Winston held up his hand: "I've heard enough. I will permit this testimony to proceed, but if you can't make the link that you just indicated, Mr. Johnson, I will, upon motion by Mr. Stanton, strike the entire testimony and instruct the jury to disregard it. Do we understand each other?"

Mr. Johnson replied solemnly: "Yes. Thank you, Your Honor." As Mr. Johnson and Mr. Stanton each returned to their respective counsel tables, I could see Mr. Johnson smirk at Mr. Stanton, and then he looked at me, and mouthed "you're going down."

"Ms. Williamson, sorry for the interruption. I think I had asked you if Nancy had told you why she decided to divorce Mr. Jackson. Did she?"

"Yes."

"What did she tell you?"

Mr. Stanton was on his feet again. "Objection! Hearsay."

Judge Winston nodded his head affirmatively. "Mr. Johnson, it is hearsay, unless there is some exception to the rule that applies. Is there?"

Mr. Johnson fumbled with his notes for a moment. "Uhm, Your Honor, the hearsay rule only bars an out-of-court statement that is offered for its truth. We aren't

offering what Nancy told Ms. Williamson for its truth, only
for notice to this witness."

Mr. Stanton growled "Notice to Ms. Williamson is
not relevant to the defendant's insanity defense. And even
if it were relevant, its probative value is outweighed by the
prejudice to the defendant."

Judge Winston nodded in agreement. "Objection
sustained. Move along, Mr. Johnson."

Mr. Johnson shot a cold, hard stare at Mr. Stanton.
"Okay, Ms. Williamson, I had wanted to give the jury more
context in order to be fair, but let's get right to it. Did Mr.
Jackson ever beat Nancy, to your knowledge?"

Stanton bolted out of his seat. His objections were
coming so fast and furious that I wondered why he even
bothered sitting down. "Objection! There is no foundation
for this question, and I suspect that it is again calling for
hearsay testimony."

Judge Winston fidgeted in his chair and glowered
down at Mr. Johnson. "Mr. Johnson, can you lay a proper
foundation for the question — without relying upon
hearsay?"

But before Mr. Johnson could respond, Mr. Stanton
interrupted: "Your Honor, in light of the subject matter of
the question, and the prejudicial impact that a blurted out
answer might produce, I respectfully request the right to
voir dire the witness on this topic."

A wave of red was quickly rising up the back of Mr.
Johnson's neck, and his jaw muscles noticeably tightened.
He raised his voice: "Your Honor, this is my examination! I
don't need any help from Mr. Stanton to lay a proper
foundation!"

Judge Winston rubbed his chin thoughtfully. "I'm
not so sure that's correct. I am going to allow Mr. Stanton
to voir dire the witness on this topic, before ruling on his
objection."

Mr. Stanton pushed past Mr. Johnson, virtually elbowing him out of his way. Mr. Johnson gaped at this rudeness, but said nothing and returned to his counsel table, seething with anger.

"Now Ms. Williamson," Mr. Stanton began, "did you meet with Mr. Johnson to prepare to testify here today?"

Mr. Johnson stood to object, but Judge Winston simply motioned to Mr. Johnson with his hand to sit back down. Mr. Johnson plopped back into his chair, lips pressed together tightly in a deep frown.

Ms. Williamson replied: "Yes, I met with Mr. Johnson to discuss my testimony."

"Did Mr. Johnson ask you if you ever saw Professor Jackson hit his wife Nancy?"

"Yes, he did."

"What did you tell him?"

"No."

"So you never saw Professor Jackson hit Nancy, is that correct?"

"No."

"Did Mr. Johnson tell you that he wanted to ask you questions about what Nancy had told you about Professor Jackson?"

"Yes. Nancy had told me that...."

"Hold on, Ms. Williamson. I am sorry to interrupt, but that is precisely the type of hearsay testimony that Judge Winston has said is improper. Did Mr. Johnson tell you why he wanted to call you as a witness, and not Nancy?"

Now it was Mr. Johnson's turn to leap to his feet. "Objection! This is not proper voir dire. It goes way beyond what is necessary to rule on Mr. Stanton's objection."

Judge Winston smiled ruefully. "You are right, Mr. Johnson. The question is beyond what is necessary to rule on Mr. Stanton's objection. I have heard enough already to sustain his objection. But Mr. Stanton would be permitted on cross-examination to ask this question, and since he's already up here, I'm going to allow it — in part because I want to hear the answer."

Mr. Johnson slowly sunk back into his seat. "Well, Ms. Williamson," Mr. Stanton continued, "what about it? Did Mr. Johnson tell you why he wanted to call you as a witness, and not Nancy?"

"Yes."

"What did he tell you?"

"Objection!" Mr. Johnson was back on his feet. "This is hearsay! What's good for the goose is good for the gander. If Mr. Stanton won't let the jury hear what Nancy told Ms. Williamson about being beaten by Mr. Jackson, then he shouldn't be allowed to ask questions about what I said to this witness."

Mr. Stanton's jaw dropped open, and he stammered, "Your Honor, the prosecutor's speaking objection is totally improper, and unfortunately I now have to make a motion outside the presence of the jury."

Judge Winston nodded. "The bailiff will escort the jury back to the jury room, as we take a fifteen minute recess, so that I can discuss certain issues with counsel. Also, the deputy marshal shall clear the courtroom of spectators until the recess is over."

The bailiff sang out "All rise," and led the jury out of the courtroom. The deputy motioned for the crowd to exit the courtroom, and soon it was just Judge Winston, the lawyers and me left in the courtroom.

Judge Winston could barely control his anger. "Mr. Johnson, have you lost your mind? It was completely improper for you to suggest to this jury that Mr. Jackson's ex-wife told this witness that Mr. Jackson beat her. You know it, and I know it. And I suspect that Mr. Stanton wants to make a motion for a mistrial, am I right, Mr. Stanton?"

Mr. Stanton responded: "That's right, Your Honor. Mr. Johnson just polluted this jury with a factual statement predicated upon no admissible evidence. There is no way to un-ring that bell. You have to declare a mistrial. We'll have to start all over again. And I'll be filing a motion for the State to pay for my fees for the first trial, as a sanction for Mr. Johnson's egregious conduct. If the Court wants to report Mr. Johnson's misconduct to the appropriate state bar authorities for further discipline, that is, of course, entirely up to the Court." Mr. Stanton folded his arms over his chest, and glared at Mr. Johnson.

Mr. Johnson stammered "Your Honor, there is no reason to declare a mistrial. I can prove that Mr. Jackson beat his ex-wife. If you just grant me a continuance of three days, I will get the ex-wife here to testify herself. That won't be hearsay."

Before Mr. Stanton could respond, Judge Winston held up both of his hands, shaking his head negatively. "Oh no, Mr. Johnson. We're not going down that road. If the ex-wife was willing to testify, you could have called her instead of Ms. Williamson from the get go. But you made a tactical decision not to do that — or the ex-wife refused to voluntarily appear for trial, and we all know that you can't subpoena her from France. So we aren't going to be granting any continuances to try to solve this little problem you've created. On the other hand, we've invested a lot of time with this jury, and I am reluctant to grant a mistrial and start over. So here is what we are going to do."

Mr. Stanton lifted a hand said "Your Honor, could I be heard further before you rule?"

"No, Mr. Stanton. You've made your motion, and now I have to rule on it. The motion for mistrial is denied."

I looked over at Mr. Johnson, who sighed with relief. Mr. Stanton just frowned.

"Don't be so disappointed, Mr. Stanton. I'm denying the motion, but I will instruct the jury that there is not a scintilla of evidence that Mr. Jackson ever mistreated his ex-wife, and any suggestion of that by the prosecutor should be ignored. Now, Mr. Johnson, is there any further testimony that you wish to elicit from Ms. Williamson that would be admissible — in other words, not based on something she was supposedly told by Mr. Jackson's ex-wife? Please don't mince words with me, because you are perilously near disbarment as it is."

Mr. Johnson hesitated a moment. "No, Your Honor."

"All right. I am also going to allow Mr. Stanton to complete his cross-examination of Ms. Williamson, and then she will be excused from the stand with no re-direct. Understood?"

Both Mr. Johnson and Mr. Stanton nodded affirmatively.

"Bailiff, let's get the jury back in here and get back to work. Deputy, you may open the courtroom to the public again."

After the spectators and jury were seated, Judge Winston addressed the jury:

"Ladies and gentlemen of the jury, I want your full and complete attention for a moment. Before we took our recess, Mr. Johnson had made an objection to a question Mr. Stanton asked. In making his objection, he suggested that Mr. Jackson's ex-wife had told this witness that she had been beaten. This witness would not be allowed to testify to any such conversation, if it occurred, because it is deemed to be hearsay. We don't allow hearsay testimony in a trial because it is inherently unfair to the other party, who can't cross-examine the supposed speaker about the statement. If the prosecution wanted to try to prove that Mr. Jackson mistreated his ex-wife, he should have made the ex-wife a witness, if he could, or find a witness who saw Mr. Jackson abusing his ex-wife. As we have all heard, this witness never saw Mr. Jackson strike his wife. So I instruct you that there is not a scintilla of admissible evidence to support any suggestion that Mr. Jackson mistreated his ex-wife. You are to ignore the suggestion that Mr. Jackson in any way mistreated his wife, unless and until some witness gets on this stand and is allowed to testify to that, and be cross-examined by Mr. Stanton. This is very important. Do you all understand my instruction?"

The jurors all shook their heads affirmatively.

"Now, Mr. Stanton. Do you have some additional questions for this witness?"

"Well, Your Honor, I think I would like an answer to my last question, which was: did Mr. Johnson tell you, Ms. Williamson, why he decided to call you and not Nancy as a witness?"

Ms. Williamson frowned slightly. "Well, he said that Nancy was not willing to say that Dan had abused her. But she had told me . . . ."

Judge Winston slammed down his gavel. "Ms. Williamson. Mr. Stanton did not ask you what Nancy told you, and as you've undoubtedly figured out from how I just instructed the jury, such testimony is improper. Just answer Mr. Stanton's questions."

Beth shook her head sheepishly.

"That's all I have for this witness," Mr. Stanton said. He took a long look at the jury, then slowly retired to his seat at counsel table. I leaned over to Mr. Stanton, whose face was covered with beads of sweat, and patted him on the arm. "You saved the day. You made Beth and Mr. Johnson look like assholes. Great job."

Mr. Stanton smiled slightly, but replied: "Don't get too cocky yet. The prosecution is about to put its best witness on the stand, and it's probably the one that will make or break our case."

Chapter 20

"Mr. Johnson, call your next witness," Judge Winston directed.

"The State calls Dr. Paige Wells to the stand." Dr. Wells got up from the prosecution table and strode up to the witness box, took the oath and was seated. Mr. Johnson began:

"Please state your name and address for the record."

"My name is Paige Wells, and I live at 3715 Meadow Lane, Concord, New Hampshire."

"By whom are you currently employed?"

"The New Hampshire State Police."

"What is your position or title?"

"I am designated as the Department's psychiatrist."

"Please describe your duties."

"I provide psychiatric care for officers who need it. And I am also called upon to consult with regard to crimes involving potentially mentally ill suspects to evaluate their mental states."

"How long have you held that position?"

"About four years."

"Prior to that, where were you employed?"

"I taught abnormal psychology at Amherst College for about five years."

"Where did you get your medical training?"

"I took my pre-med courses at Brown University, and then attended Harvard University for a combined M.D. /Ph.D. program, specializing in psychiatry."

"Dr. Wells, are you familiar with dissociative disorders?"

"Yes I am."

"Could you explain to the jury what dissociative disorders are?"

"Yes. Dissociative disorders generally impair the normal state of awareness and limit or alter a person's sense of identity, memory or consciousness. There are essentially five recognized dissociative disorders: dissociative amnesia, which involves the inability to recall important personal information, dissociative fugue, which involves the creation of a new, either partial or complete identity to replace the personal details that have been forgotten, depersonalization disorder, which involves the feeling that one's body or self is disconnected or unreal, dissociative identity disorder, which involves the development of multiple personalities, and finally dissociative disorders not otherwise specified, which is where a person displays characteristics very similar to some of the previously discussed disorders, but not severe enough to receive their diagnosis."

"What causes a dissociative disorder?"

"That is a complicated question, and one upon which there is substantial debate. Traditionally, it was thought that dissociation was a defense reaction to stressful or traumatic situations, usually involving some childhood trauma, often sexual abuse. This is called the Post-traumatic Model. But more recent research is beginning to suggest that might be a flawed understanding of the disorder."

"Have you written any scholarly articles discussing the causes of dissociative disorders?"

"Yes. My article entitled 'Re-thinking Diagnosis and Treatment of Dissociative Disorders" was published in the New England Psychiatric Journal about three years ago."

"In that article, did you discuss some of this more recent research you mentioned?"

"Yes. The problem with the traditional, Post-traumatic Model was that researchers went to patients with dissociative disorders and asked them if they remembered being subjected to child abuse. This is called a retrospective study. This type of approach suffers from two flaws, I believe. First, you are depending upon the recollection of someone whose memory and mental functioning is impaired to report accurately on events that may have happened decades ago. Second, it is highly suggestive. When more recent researchers adopted a prospective approach — that is, following the development through adulthood of a child who was subjected to documented abuse — virtually no correlation was found between child abuse and the onset of a dissociative disorder. Prospective studies of persons who suffered emotional traumatic events in adulthood also did not support the notion that emotional trauma is necessarily a trigger for dissociative disorders."

"If emotional trauma does not cause dissociative disorders, what does?"

"Recent studies suggest a link between sleep-related disorders and dissociation. But while emotional trauma cannot, and should not be ruled out as a possible trigger, other factors, including sleep-related problems, may be more important in causing the development of dissociation disorders."

"Dr. Wells, did you examine Professor Jackson?"

"Yes I did."

"How long was your examination?"

"Approximately four to five hours."

"Based upon that examination, and your knowledge and understanding of dissociative disorders, did you arrive at an opinion to a reasonable medical certainty concerning whether Professor Jackson was suffering from a 'depersonalization disorder' on October 10 at the time of the killings?"

"Yes, I did."

"What is that opinion, Dr. Wells?"

"My opinion is that although Professor Jackson had an emotionally unsatisfying childhood, has suffered through some personally traumatic events, and may, indeed, benefit from psychiatric counseling, he was not suffering from a depersonalization disorder — or any other dissociative disorder — on October 10 at the time of the shootings."

"Why did you arrive at this conclusion?"

"Professor Jackson is an intelligent, articulate man. He knows who he is and has highly developed coping skills to deal with difficult events in life. He understands his emotional shortcomings, and has made peace with them. He does not exhibit any sleep-related disorders. In short, I would characterize him as a normal person dealing with life issues in a normal way."

"You are aware that Dr. Van DeMere's opinion is that Professor Jackson's divorce triggered a depersonalization disorder?"

"Yes, I am aware of that."

"You apparently disagree with that view — please tell the jury why."

Dr. Wells turned slightly, so that she was facing me. "Professor Jackson's divorce was undoubtedly traumatic for him. But he dealt with it. He sought marriage counseling, and when he could see that wasn't going to save the marriage, he gave in to the divorce and moved on. If that was a trigger, or a partial trigger, for a depersonalization disorder, I would have expected it to be accompanied by sleep-related issues. Professor Jackson had no such sleep-related issues."

"Do you have an opinion as to whether he was sane at the time of the shootings?"

"Yes. My opinion is that he was sane, meaning he was rational and understood the nature and consequences of his acts."

"Thank you, Dr. Wells. That's all I have for now."

Mr. Johnson sauntered confidently back to the prosecution table and sat down. Mr. Stanton finished jotting some notes on his legal pad, got out of his chair, and approached Dr. Wells.

"Dr. Wells, you heard Mr. Johnson's cross-examination of Dr. Van DeMere, didn't you?"

"Yes I did."

"He criticized Dr. Van DeMere for not using the Clinical Structured Interview to examine Professor Jackson, do you remember that?"

"I do."

"You didn't use the Clinical Structured Interview questions to examine Professor Jackson, did you?"

"Not all of them, but many of them."

"But you didn't use all of them, did you?"

"No I didn't."

"Now, in your testimony today, you have said that you believe the Post-traumatic Model is flawed, correct?"

"I do not believe that it adequately explains the causative factors for dissociative disorders."

"In other words, Doctor, you don't think that emotional traumas cause depersonalization disorder, correct?"

"Not alone, no."

"Yet you spent most of your interview of Professor Jackson delving into his relationship with his parents, the death of his brother and his divorce, didn't you?

"We did spend a substantial amount of time exploring those areas, yes."

"And that's because emotional trauma could cause a depersonalization disorder, isn't that right?"

"Medical science can't rule out that possibility at this time."

"So the answer to my question is yes, right?"

"Yes."

"How many questions did you ask him about his sleeping patterns?"

"I know we discussed it, but I'm not sure right now how many questions I asked about it."

"I was present for the entire interview, wasn't I?"

"Yes you were."

"If I were to tell you that according to my notes, you asked exactly one question about sleeping habits, would you be able to dispute that?"

"I know that I didn't ask very many questions about that, but I thought it was more than just one."

"But you can't say for certain how many questions you asked regarding sleep-related difficulties, can you?"

"No, I can't."

"You said that Professor Jackson was a normal person dealing with life issues in a normal way, is that right?"

"Yes, I think so."

"Is it normal for a person to shoot fifteen people to death for no reason?"

Dr. Wells hesitated for a moment. "Well, no, that's not normal"

"Thank you Dr. Wells. That's all the questions I have at this time."

Mr. Johnson shot up for his re-direct examination. "Dr. Wells, why didn't you ask all of the recommended Clinical Structure Interview questions?"

"Because Professor Jackson's answers obviated the need to ask some of those questions."

"Can you give us an example?"

"Sure. I asked Professor Jackson if he had ever suffered any physical or sexual abuse from his parents or any other relative. He said no. If he had said yes, there was a series of additional questions to ask. But since he said no, I didn't ask the additional follow-up questions."

"Why didn't you ask more questions about sleep-related problems?"

"Because Professor Jackson was very clear that he was having no issues with his sleep patterns. If he was, then, of course, there would have been additional questions to ask."

"Thank you Dr. Wells, that's all I have. Your Honor, the prosecution rests."

Judge Winston looked towards our counsel table. "Mr. Stanton, does the defense have a rebuttal case to put on?"

Mr. Stanton rose from his chair: "Your Honor, I would like to have the opportunity to consult with my client and would therefore request a continuance until tomorrow morning, at which time the defense will either put on a short rebuttal case, or rest. With the Court's permission, I would ask that my client be allowed to meet with me after adjournment in the witness room, before he is transported back to his cell."

Judge Winston shook his head affirmatively. "Very well. The request for continuance is granted. The defendant and counsel may use the witness room to confer after court is adjourned. Court is adjourned until 10:00 o'clock tomorrow morning." Judge Winston got up to leave, and everyone jumped to their feet as he exited.

Chapter 21

After the jury was escorted out of the courtroom, the deputy came and hand-cuffed my hands and led me to the witness room, while Mr. Stanton gathered up his papers. Within a few minutes, Mr. Stanton joined me. I started the conversation:

"Can you ask the deputy to ask my friend Tim to wait in the courtroom? I'd like to talk with him for a few minutes after we are done."

"Sure." Mr. Stanton stuck his head out of the witness room door, got the deputy's attention and pointed out Tim in the courtroom. "Okay, done."

"Well, what's your assessment of where we are?"

"I think we did all right today. The blow-ups certainly hurt us with the jury. But I think we did get the sergeant to give some helpful testimony about your behavior after the shooting. I think the jury thinks Carla was a lying little bitch out for revenge, and will give her testimony no credence. In fact, I think Carla may actually help us. And Beth Williamson was a complete bust for the prosecution, and in fact, I think calling her ended up undermining the prosecution's credibility. The fact that the prosecution went to such lengths to try to jimmy-up a reason for the shooting actually plays into our theme: sane people don't shoot people for no reason, and you had none. Now, I have to admit that Dr. Wells was impressive. But even she admitted that shooting fifteen people wasn't normal, and she offered no explanation for why you would do it. I think we have a fighting chance."

"I think I should testify."

"Why? I've already told you that a lot of bad things can happen if you do."

"I think the jury gives Dr. Van DeMere zero credit. That means it all turns on Dr. Wells' testimony, and I thought she was very impressive. So if it goes to the jury like this, I think I'm a goner. I think the jury wants me to testify. To have me look them in the eye and hear from my own lips that I was as surprised as anyone to find those guns in the briefcase, that I was horrified at what I was doing but unable to stop myself, and still to this day, after being examined by shirks from both sides, I don't know why I did this, and neither does anyone else. Maybe I can't make the jury like me — after all, I admit I killed fifteen people — but at least maybe I can get them to not want to kill me. My friend Tim, who has been here every day watching the trial, also thinks that the best way for me to avoid the death penalty is for me to testify."

Mr. Stanton sat quietly, thinking it through. Finally, he said: "Listen, Dan. I'm getting a little tired of your friend Tim whispering in your ear and acting like an arm-chair quarterback. I don't recommend that you take the stand for all of the reasons that we previously discussed. And believe me, despite what Father Tim thinks, the jury is never, ever going to like you or want to help you. Those blow-ups are seared in their memories forever. But at the end of the day, it's your call to make. If you insist on taking the stand, I'll put you on. But I am going to give you a letter stating that it was my advice that you not take the stand, and I will ask the judge to let me put that on the record outside of the presence of the jury so my malpractice insurance company won't cancel my policy. Do you want to talk about it with your buddy Tim after this, think about it overnight, and let me know in the morning? I'll prepare some questions that will let you say what you've just told me, as well as work on my closing argument, so that we will be ready to go whichever way you decide. Okay?"

"All right. I appreciate your advice, Mr. Stanton, and won't disregard it lightly. I will think about it overnight. Should we meet here at 9:00 a.m. tomorrow morning?"

"That's a plan." Mr. Stanton gave me a clasp on the shoulder and shook it gently. He knocked on the door, and the deputy appeared. Shortly after Mr. Stanton left, the door opened again and Tim walked in. We embraced and then sat opposite each other across the table. I began the conversation:

"I thought today went pretty well. What did it look like from your vantage point?"

"Well, I have to admit that your Mr. Stanton did a pretty good job on cross with the police officer, Carla and Beth. By the way, did you have any idea that Beth would be testifying?"

"Nope. Complete surprise. The bitch."

"Well apparently she was prepared to testify that you beat Nancy. Would that have been true?"

"Of course not. I never laid a hand on Nancy in anger. Hell, towards the end, she wouldn't even let me touch her affectionately. It would have been a complete lie, but it would have been hard for Mr. Stanton to cross-examine her on it, so I was glad that he was able to keep it out of evidence."

"Yeah, but the jury heard those questions, and heard the prosecutor blurt out that Nancy told Beth that you beat her. That worries me some."

"But the judge instructed the jury to disregard that, in pretty strong language."

"Do you really think that they can forget something like that? I'm afraid that will lurk around in their minds."

"Well, Mr. Stanton did what he could. I mean, he objected, moved for a mistrial, and got an instruction from the judge. That's going to have to be good enough. What did you think of Dr. Wells?"

Tim sighed. "She was terrific. Well-credentialed, good experience. She even wrote an article on depersonalization disorders. I think the jury loved her, and

believed her. Dr. Van DeMere looked like a joke compared
to her."

I shook my head in agreement. "Yes, that's sort of
the way I felt, too. Still Mr. Stanton thinks he can still win
this thing."

"Dan, I hate to sound like a broken record. This
isn't all about winning. I still feel that the best way to save
your life — and your soul — is for you to take the stand,
admit the shootings, express remorse, and seek forgiveness.
What does Mr. Stanton think now about you taking the
stand?"

"Still against it, but said it was my decision. He
says that if I decide to take the stand, he will make me sign
a letter saying I decided to do so against his advice, and he
also wants to put it on the record outside the presence of the
jury."

"He's just trying to intimidate you into not
testifying."

"Just like you are trying to intimidate me by saying
that I'll lose my soul if I don't testify."

"You know it's not the same thing. I'll support you
no matter what. But I am trying to help you reach the right
decision."

"I know, Tim. I think that this is a decision that I
am going to have to make on my own, though. Thanks for
the insights."

With that, we both got up and embraced again. As
the deputy came to handcuff me for the return trip to
prison, I knew that I would be in for a long night thinking
this through, but at least tomorrow the ordeal would be
over.

Chapter 22

I arrived at the courthouse the next morning tired, anxious and irritable. I had barely slept at all, tossing and turning, engaged in a debate with myself about the best course of action. Mr. Stanton, who made his living trying criminal cases, recommended that I not take the stand and take my chances with the jury. After all, even if the jury convicted me, it might sentence me to life imprisonment, rather than death. Mr. Stanton had explained that New Hampshire had not executed a person since 1939. I had initially been willing to plead guilty when I thought that life imprisonment was the punishment. If the jury went against me, that was the most likely sentence. But something deep inside me urged me to take the stand, and make the jury understand that I didn't know why this had all happened. Maybe I could convince them that in a strange way, I, too, was a victim here of circumstances beyond my control. Or maybe I would so piss them off that they'd take only five minutes to convict and sentence me to death. After hours of going back and forth, I had finally decided that I wanted to testify. Tim's views ultimately persuaded me. If I testified, and could successfully convey my own bewilderment at my actions, my sincere remorse and desire for forgiveness, I was more likely to get a life sentence than the death penalty. That was about the best result I could hope for at this point, so I was going to go for it.

When the sheriff took me to the witness room, Mr. Stanton was already there. Unlike the other day, Mr. Stanton looked well rested and well groomed. He had on a different suit, this one a deep navy blue, and wore a sharp, "power" red tie with his white button down shirt. He stood and shook my hand, and gestured for me to take a seat.

He sat down himself, and looked me in the eyes.

"You've decided that you want to testify, haven't you?"

"Yes."

Mr. Stanton sighed deeply. "All right. Here's a letter that I prepared. It says that I have advised you of all the possible negative repercussions from taking the stand, and advised you against testifying. The letter further says that you have decided to testify. I've signed the letter, and there is a place for your signature. If that's really what you want to do, please sign it. I'll keep the original and get you a copy."

I read and signed the letter and gave it back to Mr. Stanton. He continued:

"'I have prepared a short series of questions to ask you that will essentially let you tell the jury a little about your upbringing and background, to humanize you a bit. I'll also ask you about the divorce."

"Do we have to go into that in front of the jury? I really would rather not get into the details of the failure of my marriage."

"Look, Professor. In for a penny, in for a pound. If you're going to testify, then it's for all the marbles. Besides, if we don't bring it up, the prosecution may get into it anyway. So best for us to introduce it first. Besides, it's possible that the circumstances surrounding the divorce will evoke some sympathy for you, and also help buttress Dr. Van DeMere's testimony a bit. Okay?"

I nodded my head, reluctantly. Mr. Stanton continued: "I will question you in a way that will allow you to tell the jury that you don't deny that you bought the guns, but have no recollection doing so, were surprised to find them in your briefcase, and what happened thereafter. Remember, when I am questioning you, answer like you and I were having a friendly conversation. Get it all out there. Now on cross, the prosecutor will hammer you, again and again, that you bought the guns, knew that shooting the students was wrong and yet you did it anyway. There's not much we can do about that. But the thing that the prosecution will still be lacking is a reason for the killings, and I am going to pound that theme home in my closing argument."

"But I thought you told me that motive is only important in a circumstantial evidence case — which this is not."

"That's what the general learning is. But as this case has unfolded, particularly with the prosecution's failed attempt to establish a motive with Clara's and Beth's testimony, the absence of a motive plays directly into our overall theme: sane people don't kill people for no reason; but insane people may. No offense, Professor."

I nodded. "Any tips for answering Mr. Johnson's questions?"

"Listen carefully to his questions. Keep your answers short. Take your time. Don't panic. I get to ask questions after he is done, and I will try my best to clean up anything that doesn't help us. Any other questions?"

I shook my head no. I wanted to get this over with.

The deputy came and escorted me into the courtroom. It was packed with people. Apparently word had gotten out that I might testify, or that in any event, the closing arguments would be given and the case would go to the jury today. I glanced over at the prosecution table. Mr. Johnson was pouring over notes on several different legal pads. Dr. Wells was there, too, wearing a white skirt and jacket. Our eyes met briefly. Her eyes conveyed a slightly sad visage, as if she was sorry that I was in this position, and for what was to come. I scanned the crowd and found Tim sitting in his customary seat on the aisle. Our eyes met briefly, and I nodded slightly to him. He nodded back, as if he understood that I had decided to testify. He gave me a thumbs up signal. I looked away and tried to focus myself at the task at hand.

Mr. Stanton had told the bailiff that there was something that he wanted to put on the record before the jury was brought into the courtroom. After about five minutes, the bailiff returned to the courtroom, announced the entry of the judge, everyone in the courtroom jumped to their feet and Judge Winston climbed up to the bench.

"Ladies and gentlemen, please be seated and come to order. Mr. Stanton, my bailiff tells me that there is something that you wish to put on the record before we bring in the jury?"

Mr. Stanton rose from his chair. "Yes Your Honor. My client has decided that he wants to testify on his own behalf." A murmur ran through the audience. Judge Winston pounded his gavel for silence. "Order in the Court! If there is another outburst, I will clear the courtroom. There will be no further warning!" Judge Winston glared around the gallery to drive home his point. "Mr. Stanton, you may continue."

"Well, Your Honor, I just wanted to make a record that I have advised Professor Jackson that he is not required to testify and of the possible negative consequences that could accompany a decision to take the stand."

Judge Winston leaned over the bench and looked directly at me. "Professor Jackson, has Mr. Stanton advised you that you cannot be made to testify."

I stood up. "Yes, Your Honor."

"Has he informed you of the pluses and minuses of a decision on your part to testify?"

"Yes, we have discussed it at length, and I understood everything he said."

"Did Mr. Stanton tell you that by taking the stand, you waive your right against self-incrimination guaranteed to you by the Fifth Amendment? In other words, once you take the stand and start testifying, you can't refuse to answer questions on the grounds that the answers may incriminate you?"

"Yes, Mr. Stanton has explained that."

"And you have made the informed decision to testify on your own behalf?"

"Yes."

"You realize that Mr. Johnson will have the chance to cross-examine you if you testify?"

"Yes, of course, Your Honor."

"All right then. Mr. Stanton, you have discharged your professional responsibility and made your record. Let's bring in the jury and get going."

The jurors were ushered into the courtroom by the bailiff, and took their seats. Judge Winston addressed Mr. Stanton:

"Does the defense wish to offer a rebuttal case?"

"We do, Your Honor. The defense calls Professor Dan Jackson to the stand."

I rose from my chair to walk to the witness stand, but felt the room spin a bit, and grabbed the edge of counsel table to stabilize myself. I quickly gathered myself and strode slowly to the witness stand, staring straight ahead. When I got there, the clerk asked me to place my hand on the Bible and swear to tell the truth. I said that I would and sat down in the chair. I looked out at the courtroom. To my right sat the jurors, all intently looking at me with blank expressions, neither hostile nor friendly. To the left of jurors sat Mr. Johnson and Dr. Wells at the prosecution counsel table. Mr. Johnson had a small sneer on his face, and looked like he was trying to stare me down. Dr. Wells was also looking at me, but with a more consoling demeanor. Behind the counsel tables I saw what seemed to be hundreds of faces, all with scowls or frowns. And, of course, there was Tim with a small smile on his face. I took a deep breath and let it out, and then looked at Mr. Stanton, who was standing in the center of the courtroom waiting for me to calm myself.

"Could you please state your name for the record?"

"Dan Jackson."

"You are a visiting professor at Dartmouth College?"

"Yes."

"How long have you held that position?"

"About two, two and one-half years."

"Professor Jackson, tell the jury a little bit about your personal background."

"I was born and raised in River Falls, Wisconsin. Went to Dartmouth College, and then went on to get my Ph.D. in comparative literature from Harvard. I've taught at University of New Hampshire, and a number of small, liberal arts colleges in New England before coming back to Dartmouth to teach."

"Professor, were you married?"

"Yes, I was until about nine months ago."

"What was your wife's name?"

"Nancy."

"Where did you meet each other?"

"Back in River Falls, Wisconsin. We were high school sweethearts."

"How long had you been married?"

"Twenty-five years."

"What caused the divorce?"

"Well, one night last year right after dinner, my wife confronted me with the fact that she had been having an affair for years with someone else, had fallen in love with that person, and wanted a divorce." I could feel myself blushing in embarrassment, and looked down at my clasped hands in my lap.

"Professor Jackson, I now this is a hurtful subject, but the jury needs to know the full truth. Your wife told you that she had been having an affair and had fallen in love with another woman, right?"

I took a deep breath, and slowly let it out. Without looking up, I said in a soft voice: "Yes, that's right. She was in love with Beth Williamson."

The courtroom was dead silent. A tear developed in my left eye, and I could feel it seep slowly down my cheek. Mr. Stanton stood like a statute, letting the moment take effect.

"Did you do anything to try to save the marriage?"

I looked up, slightly bleary-eyed. "Yes. We went to marriage counseling. But after a while, it was clear that the marriage couldn't be saved, and we got divorced."

"How did those series of events make you feel?"

"Hurt. Betrayed. Inadequate. A failure."

"Did you seek any other psychiatric help at that time?"

"No, I didn't realize I needed any."

"Professor, I want to shift gears here now. I want to show you what has been marked as State Exhibit 4, which purports to be a receipt for the purchase of the two pistols used in the shooting. Is that your signature on the bottom of the receipt?"

"Yes it is."

"Do you remember buying the two pistols?"

"No I don't. I know that I must have, but I have no recollection of it."

"Why did you buy two pistols?"

"I don't know."

"All right, I want to draw your attention to the night before the shootings, the evening of October 9. Do you remember what you were doing that night?"

"I remember putting the finishing touches on a mid-term exam that I was going to give my freshman English class the next morning. I remember working fairly late into the evening completing it."

"Professor, if you were planning to shoot your students, why were you working so hard on the mid-term exams?"

"I had no idea that the shooting was going to happen. It was nothing that I planned to do."

"Then, when you came to class the next day to administer the exam, tell the jury what happened."

I took another deep breath and let it out. "I got to class and opened my briefcase and saw the two guns sitting on top of the mid-term exams. I had no recollection of putting the guns into the briefcase, or any idea why they would be there. But as I stared at them, I could feel my hands reach out for the pistols. In my mind, I kept trying to tell my hands to stop, but nothing I did seemed to be able to control them. Then, almost before I knew it, my fingers were pulling the triggers and the guns were blazing away. I was horrified, but I couldn't get my body to stop. Then it was all over. I couldn't believe that I was responsible for such a despicable act. I think I went into shock, because everything after that is sort of a blur, until I woke up the next morning in the police station."

I looked over at the jurors to see what their reaction was. Some jurors sat with their arms crossed over their chests, jaws clenched. They clearly weren't buying it. But other jurors sat with slightly raised eyebrows and parted lips. I think they were trying to decide if what I was saying was the truth, or just so much bullshit.

Mr. Stanton continued:

"Professor Jackson, do you have any idea why this happened?"

"I don't know why I did this. I know that Dr. Van DeMere thinks that I have a depersonalization disorder triggered by my divorce. I don't know if that's true or not. All I do know is that I have never killed or injured anyone before in my life. It's just not in my nature. So maybe I am crazy. I just don't know." I looked down at my hands in my lap again, my face reddening again. Mr. Stanton again let the silence linger.

"Do you feel any remorse for you have done?'

I looked up. "Oh my God. Yes. Yes. Yes." Tears welled up in my eyes, and my voice came haltingly: "If there was anything I could do to turn back the clock and avoid shooting those students, I would do so. I am so sorry that I have visited such sadness on these students and their families. So sorry."

"That's all I have for Professor Jackson at this time."

Mr. Stanton returned to counsel table. Mr. Johnson grabbed up his legal pad and virtually leapt to the center of the courtroom.

"So, Professor Jackson, you're 'sorry,' are you?" Mr. Johnson made quotation marks in the air with the first two fingers of each hand.

"Yes."

"So 'sorry' that the instant that you ran out of ammunition, you turned and left the class room, isn't that right?"

"I told you I think I must have gone into shock. I really don't remember much of what happened after the shooting stopped."

"You mean after you stopped shooting, right?"

"That's right."

"Well, you remember that you didn't lift a finger to try to help any of your students that you shot, don't you?"

"I remember just leaving the class room, yes."

"Leaving without trying in any way to help any of the students you'd shot, right?"

"That's right."

"Professor, you knew at the time that you pulled the triggers on those guns that bullets were going to fire, correct?"

"I don't know that I was thinking of that at that moment."

"Well, you told this jury that you were trying to tell your hands and fingers to stop what they were doing, correct?"

"Yes, that's what I remember going through my mind."

"And the reason you wanted to stop your hands and fingers was that you realized that firing those guns was going to harm, and possibly kill, your students, isn't that right?"

I gulped slightly and shifted in my chair. "Yes, that's true."

"So, at the time you pulled the triggers, you realized that people were going to be hurt and possibly die, didn't you?"

"At some level, I must have."

"Isn't it true that at the time you pulled the triggers, you knew that hurting and killing people was wrong?"

My head was beginning to spin. This is precisely what Mr. Stanton had warned me about. Well, there was no backing out now. "I have always known that hurting and killing people was wrong."

"All right, Professor, let's talk a minute about your testimony concerning why you killed these students. You claim that you don't know why you did it, right?

"That's right."

"You don't think that the way your parents brought you up caused you to kill those students, do you?"

"Certainly not."

"And you don't think that your divorce caused you to kill your students, do you?"

"No, I don't. But Dr. Van DeMere thinks that it may have triggered this depersonalization disorder that led to the shootings."

"Well, the jury has already had a chance to hear Dr. Van DeMere and his theories," Mr. Johnson virtually sneered. "I am interested in what you think, and you don't think the divorce caused you to shoot your students, correct?"

"That's correct."

"All right, Professor. Now, in one of your answers to Mr. Stanton's questions, you said that you had never hurt or killed anyone before, isn't that true?"

"Yes."

"That's not entirely true, is it?"

My heart started to beat a little faster. Where in the world was he going with this? I had no prior criminal record, and no involvement with any kind of violence. "I don't know what you are talking about."

"Well, Professor Jackson, while you were a student at Dartmouth, weren't you involved in a serious car crash on the road from Hanover to Lebanon when you were driving?"

I felt as if someone had just punched me in the stomach. My God. He was going to dredge up the car accident? "That was a long time ago, and it was an accident."

"Professor, I don't care how long ago it was. Were you involved in a serious car crash when you were a student at Dartmouth, yes or no?"

"Yes."

"You were driving a car with your twin brother in the front seat, correct?"

I could feel the sweat bead up on my forehead. My right knee began to jiggle involuntarily. "We were on our way to Boston."

"You'd been drinking, isn't that right?"

"I'd had a few beers before we took off."

"It was snowing heavily that evening, wasn't it?"

"Yes, it was."

"Somewhere between Hanover and Lebanon, your car crossed the center line into oncoming traffic, didn't it?"

"Yes."

"And as result, your car crashed into an eighteen-wheeler, isn't that true?"

"There was a terrible car accident."

"Your own twin brother was killed isn't that true?

This wasn't fair. It was an accident — not my fault. "Yes, but it was an accident. I never intended for it to happen."

"You'd been drinking before the accident, right?"

"I already said that I had a couple of beers."

"You weren't tested for blood alcohol level, were you?"

"No."

"So, as far you know, you might have been over the legal limit, right?"

Mr. Stanton jumped to his feet. "Objection. Calls for speculation."

"Sustained," Judge Winston declared.

"Let's go at it this way, Professor. I have the police report from the accident right here. It says that according to the truck driver, your car swerved into his lane, causing him to slam on the breaks, and go into an uncontrollable skid. Is that what happened?"

I swallowed hard. My heart was beginning to race. I could feel the sweat dripping down the side of my face. "It was a long time ago, but I think that's right."

"The reason your car crossed the center line was that you had been drinking, isn't that right?"

"No, that's not true. The road was slippery and I just skidded across into the other lane. It could have happened to anyone."

"The fact is, Professor, whether legally drunk or not, you were responsible for your twin brother's death by letting the car cross the center line, isn't that true?"

I jumped to my feet, with my fists clenched at my side and shouted at Mr. Johnson, "It was his own damn fault!! He'd been an asshole the whole weekend, had embarrassed me in front of my girlfriend and fraternity brothers, and then was blabbing all during the drive. He deserved to be slapped. If he hadn't grabbed my arm, I never would have over steered into the oncoming traffic."

Judge Winston pounded his gavel on the bench and looked sternly at me. "Professor Jackson, be seated immediately. Your job is to answer questions respectfully, not to make a scene. And if you use profanity in my courtroom again, I will hold you in contempt. Do you understand?"

I was breathing heavily as I sat back down in the witness chair. I looked meekly over at the judge, and said "Yes Your Honor. I am sorry."

When I looked back at Mr. Johnson, he had an evil grin on his face, suggesting that he enjoyed the fact that I had lost my cool. But I also saw Dr. Wells, feverishly writing a note on a legal pad, ripping off the page, and taking it up to Mr. Johnson. Mr. Johnson read it quickly and his jaw dropped. He turned towards the judge: "Your Honor, may I request a five minute recess to confer with my colleagues before finishing up?"

Judge Winston glanced up at the clock on the wall and nodded his head affirmatively. "Court will stand in recess for ten minutes."

Chapter 23

I was taken to the witness room, with Mr. Stanton in hot pursuit. When the door was closed, Mr. Stanton stammered: "Good God, Professor. What are you doing up there?"

I just shook my head and said nothing for a moment. But then I responded: "I just lost it there for a moment. I wasn't expecting that we'd get into the accident. I really don't see how that is inconsistent with my testimony that I never hurt or killed anyone. I think it was pretty clear that I meant intentionally hurt or killed."

Mr. Stanton just stood there for a moment, lips pursed. He then said in a quiet voice: "But you made it sound like you wanted to hurt your brother."

I looked at him in disbelief. "No, I didn't."

"You said it was his fault, and that he had been bugging you the whole weekend, and he deserved to be slapped."

"That doesn't mean that I caused the accident on purpose."

Mr. Stanton lowered his chin to his chest, and was silent again. "Look, Professor, when it's my turn to ask questions again, I'll ask you some questions to make it clear it was an accident. But Mr. Johnson may not be done with this area. He got some note from Dr. Wells, which makes me nervous. So stay on your toes out there, and calm down. No more outbursts or jumping around on the witness stand."

I exhaled and nodded my head. Mr. Stanton knocked on the door and got the sheriff's attention. We were escorted back into the courtroom, where I mounted the witness stand. After the judge and jury re-entered the courtroom, and people took their seats, Mr. Johnson continued:

"Professor, before we recessed, I was asking you about the crash that killed your twin brother, do you remember that line of questions?"

"Yes, I do."

"You said that the crash was your brother's own fault, and that he'd been bugging you the whole weekend, right?"

Just the point Mr. Stanton had made minutes earlier in the witness room. I guess it was possible that the jury would misunderstand and think that I wanted to hurt David. I better get that straightened out. I sighed, and then answered: "Look, I got a little exasperated with that whole line of questioning, and I apologize. Yes, I said those things, but they really don't have anything to do with what we're talking about here. I loved my brother, and would never have done anything to harm him intentionally. It was an accident."

"Really. The truth of the matter is that you were envious of your brother's close relationship with your father, isn't that right?"

"He had a closer relationship than I did with my father, because he was good at the things my father was good at. I had a closer relationship with my mother. I don't think I was envious."

"You were also jealous of him because he was a better athlete, isn't that right?"

"He was a better athlete, but no, I don't think I was jealous."

"He had more friends and was more popular than you, right?"

"That's true. He was more of an extrovert. I was an introvert. That doesn't mean I wanted to hurt him."

"He invited himself up to Dartmouth for Winter Carnival, didn't he?"

"Yes, he did."

"And you resented that, didn't you?"

"I guess I was slightly annoyed."

"He interfered with your studying the whole weekend, didn't he?"

"Some."

"He walked in on you and your girlfriend making love, didn't he, and then teased you about it in front of your fraternity brothers?"

I slammed my hands down on the arms of the witness chair, the muscles in my jaw tensing. "Who told you that? I never mentioned that to anyone!"

"Never mind who told me that. It's true, isn't it?"

Now I was steaming mad. I could feel my teeth grinding together, and my breathing accelerate. "Yea, that happened. So what does that have to do with anything?"

"And in front of some of your fraternity brothers, you told your brother that you were going to kill him for that, didn't you?"

I exploded: "Who told you that! That never came up in the psychiatric interviews. I didn't mean it. I was just mad at David and wanted him to back off."

The courtroom was dead quiet.

"Look, Professor, let's cut to chase: you threatened to kill your brother, and not more than a few hours later, he dies in a crash where you drove your car over the center line in front of an eighteen-wheeler. You blame yourself for your brother's death, isn't that the long and short of it?"

The volume of my response increased: "It was an accident."

"Professor, I didn't ask you if it was an accident. You blame yourself for your twin brother's death, yes or no?"

I sat there breathing hard, sweating profusely. I looked up at Mr. Johnson and said in slow, distinct voice: "Yes, I do blame myself for his death. I probably shouldn't, but I do."

Mr. Johnson unfolded Dr. Wells' note and read the following question from the sheet of paper: "And the reason that you bought those guns and shot those students was because you wanted to be caught and punished for a crime that you believed you had committed, but for which you had never been punished — killing your brother — isn't that right, Professor?"

It was as if a giant vacuum had sucked all of the air from the courtroom. A gasp ran through the gallery. Even Judge Winston seemed stunned by the question, unable to strike his gavel for silence. Mr. Stanton was on his feet, searching for an objection to make, but finding none. I looked over at Dr. Wells, who had tears in her eyes, and was silently shaking her ahead affirmatively. I looked over at the jurors, who sat with their eyes wide open, eyebrows arched. I looked over at Tim, whose head was down, as if in prayer. My God. It couldn't be true, could it? Although I hadn't consciously shot my students in the hopes that I would be punished, I had to admit that there was a certain perverse logic to it. I did hold myself responsible for David's death. And in my heart, I knew that David's death had led to the death of my mother and father. I was responsible for their deaths, too. At some subconscious level, maybe I did buy the guns and shoot my students to get the punishment I deserved.

I sat there without responding for what seemed like an eternity. Tears were streaming down both cheeks. Finally, I looked right at Mr. Johnson and replied: "Maybe subconsciously that was the reason. I had never thought about it that way until just now. But it makes more sense than any of the other explanations."

I could hear Mr. Stanton collapse into his chair. I looked over at him and saw that he had his head in both hands, staring down at the counsel table. Even Mr. Johnson seemed overwhelmed. He slowly walked back to the prosecution counsel table saying "That's all the questions I have for this witness."

Mr. Stanton sat in his chair with his head in his hands for several more seconds. Then he took a deep breath and got to his feet. "Professor, the crash that killed your brother occurred because of the snow storm, correct?"

"Yes."

"You were never given any traffic citation, were you?"

"No."

"Because you loved your brother, you may blame yourself, but intellectually you understand that it wasn't your fault, right?"

"That's what I always thought, until today."

"And prior to today, did it ever cross your mind that the accident that killed your brother and the shootings that bring us here today were related?"

"No."

"That's all the questions I have for you, Professor."

Mr. Johnson indicated that he had no further questions, and I returned to the counsel table. I looked over at the jury, once I was seated. I saw a lot of stern looks. But I didn't care. I had finally found out why this terrible event had happened. I did deserve punishment for David's death. I just hoped it wouldn't be my own death.

Mr. Stanton stood again: "Your Honor. The defense rests."

Judge Winston nodded his head. "Thank you, Mr. Stanton. The court will stand in recess until two o'clock, when we will hear closing arguments." The judge pounded his gavel and left the bench.

Chapter 24

Mr. Stanton said that he had work to do to get ready for the closing argument, so I was taken to a holding cell near the courtroom where my lunch was waiting. But I couldn't eat much. There was a gnawing feeling in the pit of my stomach that wouldn't go away. I was just plain scared, and there was now nothing I could do to alter my fate, one way or the other. I wouldn't mind be punished for what I had done — to the students and to David — but I didn't want to die.

Fifteen minutes before court was to resume, the deputy led me to the witness room, where Mr. Stanton was waiting for me. I sat down across the table from him, and asked him: "So where do we stand now? Does the fact that I did have a reason for shooting my students mean that I wasn't suffering from a mental defect or illness at the time of the shooting?"

Mr. Stanton quickly responded: "Nope, we're still in the ballgame, I think. Our closing theme has to be altered a bit, but it's still basically the same: sane people don't gun down people with whom they have no quarrel; insane people may. Look, we thought that maybe it was your divorce that caused this depersonalization disorder, but actually it appears to have been the death of your brother. That fits better into the model that Dr. Wells testified was the majority view — a childhood or adolescent trauma. That trauma lay dormant for years, festering and going unresolved. It finally popped up, causing you to behalf in an irrational way. You had no reason to want to hurt those students. It's irrational. You need treatment, not punishment."

That all sounded right to me, but would it fly with the jury? I sat quietly for a moment, and then took both of Mr. Stanton's hands in mine. "Look, Mr. Stanton, no matter how this comes out, I want to thank you for your efforts on my behalf. I know you tried your hardest to save me. And I realize that I may have screwed it all up by taking the stand. But I can't change that now. Thanks."

Mr. Stanton nodded his head and said "It has been my pleasure to represent you. But don't give up the ship just yet. I think I can persuade the jury. If not all of them, at least a few, so we could get a hung jury and a mistrial. If that were to happen, I bet the prosecution might be willing to agree to a plea deal of life imprisonment, rather than re-try the whole damn case."

"What do you mean by mistrial?"

"A verdict must be unanimous. If the jurors can't all agree, it's called a mistrial — a do over, if you will — and the case has to start all over again with the selection of a new jury and the presentation of the evidence."

"But it's our burden to prove that I am insane, right?"

"Yes, but only by a preponderance of the evidence, meaning more likely than not. Think of it like 50.1%. If I can convince any of the jurors that you were insane, we at least have a mistrial. That would be a victory, of sorts."

At that point, the deputy knocked on the door, indicating that court was about to resume. The deputy led me back in to counsel table and I took my seat. I looked over at the prosecution table to see Mr. Johnson busily scribbling notes on a legal pad. Dr. Wells sat next to Mr. Johnson, but she was pensively staring off into space. I knew that she was the one who had figured it all out and handed Mr. Johnson the note. Although her insight may have doomed me, I was grateful that she had helped me understand why this had all occurred.

The bailiff announced Judge Winston's entry into the courtroom, everyone stood, and the judge proceeded to take his place on the bench. He pounded his gavel and brought the courtroom to order. "Mr. Stanton, you may proceed with your closing argument."

Mr. Stanton rose and strode to a spot directly in front of the jury box. He had no notes. He briefly looked around the jury box at each juror, and then began:

"May it please the Court," he said turning slightly towards Judge Winston, "counsel," he said turning back towards the prosecution table, "ladies and gentlemen of the jury," he said solemnly, facing back towards the jury box. "It has been my great privilege to appear before you these last few days representing Professor Jackson in this tragic case. And I want to thank each and every one of you for the courtesy that you have shown me and Professor Jackson in paying careful attention to the testimony and evidence that has been presented in this case. I know that at times it has been difficult to do, and my client and I are grateful for your service."

Mr. Stanton paused for a moment, took a deep breath, and let it out. "Why are we here today, and what are you called upon to decide? We are here today because of a tragedy that occurred on October 10 last year at Dartmouth College. Fifteen students were killed; five others wounded. It was a terrible, terrible event. Nothing we do here today can change that awful reality." Mr. Stanton paused, looking at each juror.

"You will not be called upon to decide whether a crime was committed. Professor Jackson has admitted to that. He is filled with remorse for the shootings. So is every right-minded human being with an ounce of empathy. The question you must decide is far more complex: was Professor Jackson suffering from a mental defect or illness at the time of the shootings? Judge Winston will be instructing you on New Hampshire law on this question, and listen to his instructions carefully. I think you will hear Judge Winston tell you that if you find that Professor Jackson was suffering from a mental defect or illness at the time of the shootings, then he is not legally responsible for his actions, and should not be punished. If that was your finding, Professor Jackson would be turned over to the New Hampshire State Hospital and receive treatment for his illness until such time that state psychiatrists and a judge determined that he was not a threat to anyone."

"Now let's look at the evidence that has been presented to you on this question. I put Professor Jackson's boss, Katie Smith, on the stand. You remember her testimony: she said that Professor Jackson had a fine reputation as a teacher and no violent tendencies had been apparent in his prior employment or while at Dartmouth. What does this prove? This violent act was completely contrary to Professor Jackson's true nature and character. The normal Professor Jackson would never have randomly shot his students. Only the mentally ill Professor Jackson could have done that."

"I also put Lilly Simpson on the stand. Her testimony, as an eye witness to the shootings, was remarkable. She described Professor Jackson's actions with stunning detail. Remember what she said: he looked surprised when he opened his briefcase, and stood there staring into it. He withdrew the pistols robotically. And after the shooting, he stared at his hands, as if he could barely believe they were his, and muttered 'Oh my God. How did this happen?' That is the portrayal of a tormented man not in control of his actions because of some mental affliction."

"Now you also heard Dr. Van DeMere testify that in his expert opinion, Professor Jackson was suffering from a depersonalization disorder triggered by the traumatic events surrounding his divorce. That's easy enough to understand, isn't it ladies and gentlemen? A person's spouse of twenty-five years suddenly confesses that she has been having a long-term affair with another woman and wants to leave to pursue a relationship with her — that could send anyone into a mental and emotional tailspin. The prosecution has criticized Dr. Van DeMere for focusing on so recent a trauma because supposedly most scholars believe that it is childhood or adolescent traumas that bring on dissociative disorders. Well, let's assume that's true. We now know that Professor Jackson was also profoundly affected by the death of his twin brother, David, back in college. And that he, in fact, blames himself for his death, although he shouldn't because it was just an accident. But regardless, that incredibly traumatic event obviously continues to affect Professor Jackson to this very day. It could have triggered his depersonalization disorder."

"Finally, you heard and saw Professor Jackson testify. He testified that when he shot those students, he didn't want to do it, but couldn't seem to stop himself. That is consistent with what Lilly Simpson saw. It's also consistent with both Dr. Van DeMere's and Dr. Wells' description of how a person suffering from a depersonalization disorder perceives the world — as if watching oneself in a dream. Professor Jackson is a troubled, mentally ill man. That's what the evidence shows."

"Now what did the prosecution offer to try to rebut our evidence? Not much, really. Mr. Johnson put on Sargent Edwards. Did he have anything to tell you about whether Professor Jackson was suffering from a mental illness? Not really. Why was he called? So that the prosecution could parade before you those horrible photographs of the crime scene, to enrage you and make you want to punish Professor Jackson. I could see that many of you were angered or outraged. And I certainly understand why. But the issue isn't whether a crime was committed. It's whether a person suffering from a mental illness should be held responsible for actions he could not control. Did Sargent Edwards shed any light on that question? A little, but it favored the defense. He testified that in his experience, people guilty of crimes run away from the police. He testified that Professor Jackson made no effort to evade arrest. Why? Because in his mind, he didn't shoot those students, some alien force controlling his body did. He wanted to find out why this had happened, not try to evade arrest."

"Who else did the prosecution call? Carla Wilson. Why did they call her? Because they wanted to have her testify that Professor Jackson shot his students because he was angry with them. Was that true? No, even Ms. Wilson eventually had to recant that testimony. If the prosecution thought they had a strong case showing Professor Jackson wasn't suffering from a mental illness, it never would have called Carla Wilson to try to establish some motive for the crime. That was an act of desperation, and it totally failed."

"And then there was Ms. Williamson. You and I know why the prosecution called her: the prosecution wanted to use hearsay testimony to suggest that Professor Jackson mistreated his ex-wife, and therefore had a violent nature. But Judge Winston put a stop to that. You remember his instruction: you are to disregard any such suggestion. Indeed, Ms. Williamson admitted that the reason the prosecution wanted her to testify instead of Professor Jackson's ex-wife is that his ex-wife refused to testify that he had abused her. Again, if the prosecution thought it had a strong case showing that Professor Jackson wasn't suffering from a mental illness when he shot those students, it would never have tried to call Ms. Williamson as a witness."

"Finally, the prosecution called Dr. Wells. She's well qualified and well intentioned, but her conclusion that Professor Jackson was not suffering from a depersonalization disorder now has to be seriously questioned by each one of you. Why? Because even after her examination of Professor Jackson, she underestimated the traumatic impact of his twin brother's death. She reached her conclusion without the benefit of hearing

Professor Jackson's testimony here in court. In light of that testimony, it should be clear to you that Professor Jackson was deeply traumatized by his twin brother's death, and that is what probably triggered his depersonalization disorder."

"In summary, whatever label you slap on Professor Jackson's state of mind — dissociative disorder, depersonalization disorder, depression or whatever — it should be clear to you that he was suffering from some mental defect or illness that prevented him from stopping what occurred. Judge Winston won't be giving you an instruction defining what constitutes a mental defect or illness. That's because New Hampshire law leaves it up to you, the jury, to use your everyday, good common sense to make that determination. And every day, good common sense teaches us this simple truism: Sane people don't randomly shoot fifteen people with whom they have no quarrel. A person suffering from a mental defect or illness, however, might do so. Judge Winston will instruct you that it is our burden to prove that Professor Jackson was suffering from a mental defect or illness by a preponderance of the evidence, which means more likely than not, or by 50.1 percent — not beyond a reasonable doubt. Ladies and gentlemen of the jury, I submit to you that it is more likely than not that a person who randomly shoots fifteen people is suffering from a mental defect or illness."

"Professor Jackson is sorry for what he did. But he suffers from a mental illness. He needs treatment, not punishment. I ask you, when you retire to the jury room, carefully consider all of the evidence, and to bring a verdict of not guilty by reason of insanity. Thank you for your time and attention."

Mr. Stanton turned and walked slowly back to counsel table. He looked exhausted. He sat down and folded his hands on his legal pad and waited for Mr. Johnson to begin.

Chapter 25

Mr. Johnson stood and marched to the center of the courtroom. He, too, had no notes to speak from. He confidently looked around the courtroom and took careful stock of each juror. He then started:

"Ladies and gentlemen of the jury, the prosecution joins Mr. Stanton in thanking you for your service. Judge Winston told you before the trial began what an important civic duty it is to be a juror, and I hope you can now appreciate how right he was."

"As the defense has admitted, the defendant, Professor Jackson, slaughtered fifteen of his students, and wounded five others. He committed the crime of capital murder. But the defendant claims that he should not be held responsible for this terrible crime because he was mentally ill. As the defense has also admitted, it is their burden to prove that Professor Jackson was mentally ill. And Judge Winston will instruct you that the defendant had to be mentally ill at the time of the shooting. We don't care if the defendant was sane or insane the day before the shooting, or five minutes after the shooting occurred. The law is only interested in Professor Jackson's mental state at the time of the shooting."

"Did the defense sustain its burden of proving the defendant was mentally ill at the time of the shooting? Absolutely not. Katie Smith, the defendant's boss, didn't shed any light on his mental condition at the time of the shooting. She testified about his mental state before the shootings, and that testimony didn't help the defense: she testified that the defendant acted and seemed perfectly sane. And poor Lilly Simpson. She was called to testify concerning what she saw at the crime scene. But let's be honest: she's not a trained psychiatrist or psychologist. She is not qualified to offer opinions about the defendant's sanity or insanity. She was a frightened teenage girl, whose

memory under those trying circumstances is quite frankly
not trustworthy. In any event, her opinion that the
defendant looked surprised while looking in his briefcase is
a far cry from evidence that he was mentally ill. To use the
defense analogy, if that was the case, every person who
looked surprised when they opened a birthday present
would be put in the looney bin."

"And the defense had the unmitigated gall to call
Dr. Van DeMere as a so-called psychiatric expert. You
saw and heard him. He is certainly not a well-qualified
expert. The medical school he graduated from lost its
accreditation and went out of business two years after he
left. He hasn't written any scholarly articles on the subject
of depersonalization disorders, or even treated any patients
suffering from that malady. Simply put, he's a hack. You
should disregard everything he said."

"Now compare him to Dr. Wells, the prosecution's
expert. She is well educated, credentialed, a teacher and
writer in the area. She examined the defendant and
concluded that he was not suffering from a
depersonalization disorder. Now, it is true that she didn't
get to hear the defendant's testimony here in this courtroom
before arriving at her opinion, but nothing he testified to
would alter that opinion. Why? Because she testified that
in her opinion, depersonalization disorder is closely linked
with sleep-related disorders. Did the defendant say that he
was having trouble sleeping in the weeks or days leading
up to the shooting? No. Did the defendant say that he had
trouble sleeping after the shootings? No. The fact that he
may have shot his students out of some subconscious desire
to be punished does not transform his volitional act into the
product of a depersonalization disorder. Dr. Wells' opinion
is as valid now as it was when she first developed it after
extensively interviewing the defendant."

"In summary, in this phase of the trial, it is your
duty to determine whether the defendant's murdering of

fifteen students should be excused because he was mentally ill. That is the only question before you — not what the penalty should be, if you find him to be guilty. That will be decided in another phase of the trial, if the defendant is convicted."

"The evidence overwhelmingly demonstrates that the defendant was sane at the time of these murders. The defendant may have personal issues to deal with. We all have personal issues to deal with. But that does not make him mentally ill, or excuse him for these fifteen terrible murders. When you go back to the jury room, I urge you to bring back a verdict of guilty. Thank you for your attention." With that, Mr. Johnson returned to counsel table and sat down.

At that point Judge Winston took control of the process, reading a long series of instructions to the jury, informing them of what they were to decide and other things of a legal nature. Then the jurors were removed from the courtroom to deliberate in the jury room, the door guarded by a deputy. Mr. Stanton and I were escorted to the witness room next to the courtroom to await the jury's decision.

Chapter 26

When the door to the witness room closed, I took a seat and asked: "So, Mr. Stanton, is now the time for you to approach Mr. Johnson about a plea deal?"

"Are you kidding? Why would you want me to do that now? I think we're winning. Even if the jury convicts you, that doesn't mean that it will vote for the death penalty. I admit that waiting for the jury takes some balls, but don't give up now."

"If we're winning, maybe you can get a better deal than a guilty plea for life imprisonment. Maybe he'll go for a life sentence with the possibility of parole or maybe a twenty year sentence. How are we ever going to know if you don't ask? You're gambling with my life, you know. It's not just about winning and losing." I could hear an echo of Tim in my words, and self-consciously looked down at my hands for a moment.

Mr. Stanton stared at me silently. Then he spoke softly: "Professor, if you want me to go out there and ask Mr. Johnson what sort of plea deal he'd be willing to do, I will. I realize that I get caught up with thrill of battle sometimes, but I never forget who the boss is: the client. If that's what you want, I'll do it." Mr. Stanton sighed heavily and looked down at the floor.

I looked at Mr. Stanton. I was suddenly struck by the thought that his reticence to ask for a plea deal may also stem from the fact that if his approach was unsuccessful, he is afraid that I may second-guess him like his client did in the Milford People Movers case. "Mr. Stanton, I appreciate everything you've done for me, but I do want to find out if some plea deal is possible. Taking the death penalty off the table would be a big relief for me. And don't worry, if Mr. Johnson rejects a plea deal, I won't later blame you for that. This is all on me — you won't hear any recriminations from me."

Mr. Stanton looked at me strangely. "Why do you say that?"

I blushed slightly, realizing that I had never told Mr. Stanton that I had Tim do some background checking, nor had I ever acknowledged that I knew anything about Mr. Stanton's past. Time for some back peddling. "Um, no reason. Just wanted to acknowledge that this was my decision, just like it was my decision to take the stand. No matter what happens, I am accepting responsibility for it, that's all."

Mr. Stanton nodded affirmatively, apparently satisfied, and left the room. He was gone for almost one half hour. When he returned, I couldn't initially tell from his demeanor whether his conversation with Mr. Johnson had gone well or poorly.

"Well, I spoke with Mr. Johnson. The guy is a complete prick. He says that he has orders from on high to see this thing through to the bitter end, and push hard for the death penalty. I tried every alternative I could think of, but it was a complete bust. Better settle in and see how the jury comes out."

I thanked Mr. Stanton, and went back to drumming my fingers on the table. Mr. Stanton paced back and forth, hands in a ball, with a stern look on his face. After a while, it became annoying and nerve-wracking, so I broke the silence:

"Mr. Stanton, please sit down. Your pacing is making me dizzy. Come on. Take a rest. How long do you think we'll have to wait for a verdict?"

Mr. Stanton sank down in a chair on the other side of the table, and exhaled profusely. "No way to tell for sure. The learning is that a quick verdict favors the defense; people say that if the prosecution hasn't proven its case, then the jury comes back fast. But here, we have the burden of proof on the insanity defense, so I would think that a quick verdict would favor the prosecution.

Therefore, I think the longer they are out, the better off for us."

"If they do find me guilty, what happens next?"

"Well, we will go to the sentencing phase. And the judge will ask the prosecution if they have any further evidence that they want to introduce on the subject of penalty, and will ask us if we have any evidence to offer in mitigation of the offense. Frankly, I don't think that the prosecution will offer anything else, and I don't have anything else to offer. If you hadn't testified, I probably would have put you on to say that you were sorry and remorseful, but you've already done that. So I expect that both sides will rest and the jury will adjourn to consider the death penalty versus life imprisonment."

I nodded, but didn't know what else to say. So I just sat there to await my fate.

Twenty minutes later, a knock came on the door. Mr. Stanton opened the door to find a deputy there who whispered something in Mr. Stanton's ear. Mr. Stanton's face went slack and lost all its color. He turned to me and said in a quiet voice: "The jury's back with a verdict. We need to go back into the courtroom."

I got up from my chair. As I tried to start the procession back into the courtroom, my legs felt like they weighed one thousand pounds each. I dragged myself back to counsel table. It had been less than one hour. One way or the other, the jury had found this to be an easy case. I fell into my chair and felt all of the air leave my chest. This was going to be it.

The bailiff sang out "All rise for the jury!"

Everyone in the courtroom dutifully got to their feet. As the jurors processed into the courtroom, I looked at each one. Not one of them would look at me. That couldn't be a good sign. After the jurors were seated, Judge Winston asked: "Has the jury reached a verdict?"

Juror number seven stood. "We have, Your Honor."

"The bailiff will take the verdict form from the jury foreman and read it aloud. I again warn those in the courtroom that there are to be no outbursts," Judge Winston directed.

The bailiff slowly marched over to the jury foreman, who handed him a piece of paper. The bailiff retraced his steps, and while standing in front of the judge's bench virtually shouted: "The jury finds the defendant, Dan Jackson, GUILTY of fifteen counts of murder in the first degree, GUILTY of five counts of attempted murder in the first degree, and GUILTY of twenty-five counts of kidnapping."

I sank back into my chair. There it was. All that was left was life imprisonment or death.

Despite Judge Winston's admonition, there was a rising crescendo of noise in the courtroom. He pounded his gavel several times to quiet the crowd, and then continued:

"Very well. We will now proceed to the sentencing phase of the trial. Does the prosecution wish to offer any further evidence at this time?"

Mr. Johnson stood, with a smile on his face: "No, Your Honor. We have no further evidence to offer, although we will have a brief argument to make to the jury on the appropriate sentence."

"All right, thank you Mr. Johnson. Mr. Stanton, does the defense wish to offer any evidence in mitigation?"

Mr. Stanton started to get up, and I knew from our prior discussion that his answer would be "no," but I suddenly heard another voice coming from my left:

"Your Honor, I have some further evidence to offer in mitigation."

I turned my head and saw Dr. Wells standing by the prosecution counsel table. Mr. Johnson had jumped up as well, and grabbed her arm, but she shook it free and stepped a few steps further away from counsel table.

This development caught Mr. Stanton completely by surprise. "Your Honor, I didn't have any further evidence to offer, and it is not appropriate for Dr. Wells to interfere at this point."

Mr. Johnson snarled: "I agree. She can't decide for herself that she wants to testify."

Judge Winston scratched his chin and shook his head slightly, as if trying to clear out some mental cobwebs. "This is highly unusual. I am going to order a short recess, so that I may discuss this with counsel. Bailiff, please escort the jury back to the jury room." Everyone stood as the jurors filed out, and finally the courtroom came back to order.

Judge Winston continued: "Well, gentlemen what are we going to do about this?"

Mr. Stanton began: "Dr. Wells just can't decide on her own that she wants to offer testimony in mitigation. I have no idea what she is going to say. Let Mr. Johnson call her if she wants to testify."

Frowning, with a deeply furled brow, Mr. Johnson responded: "I don't want to call her. I don't need anything further from her. If Mr. Stanton doesn't want to call her, then she shouldn't be permitted to testify."

Judge Winston tented his fingers in front of his face, knocking them together. "Well, gentlemen, here's the problem as I see it. The jury has heard that Dr. Wells wants to offer some testimony in mitigation. The jury has heard that you both object to it. If I keep her from testifying, the jury is going to be left to wonder what that testimony might be. That could hurt the prosecution, or that could hurt the defense. And whichever side is unhappy with the sentence handed down by the jury will use this whole incident as a grounds for appeal, and if they convince the appellate court that Dr. Wells' outburst was prejudicial, we could all be back here next year to do this all over again."

"That is a result that I want to avoid. Also, a man's life is at stake. I believe that a trial is a search for the truth, not just gamesmanship between the prosecution and the defense. So here is what I am going to do. I am going to make Dr. Wells a court appointed expert. She's certainly qualified — you both admitted as much in your closing arguments. I will inform the jury of my action, and allow Dr. Wells to offer testimony on the issue of an appropriate sentence as a court-appointed neutral — not on behalf of either the prosecution or the defense. You can object to that procedure for the record if you want, but we all know that I am well within my discretion to do this."

I could tell that Mr. Stanton was hopping mad and about to explode, so I grabbed his sleeve and gave it a tug. He looked down at me, and I half stood up and whispered in his ear: "Let her do it. I think it may help. It certainly won't hurt. Let it go."

Mr. Stanton heaved a sigh, and said "Very well, Your Honor. The defense has no objection to the proposed procedure."

Mr. Johnson's face was still creased by a deep frown, but he finally said "The prosecution does not object."

When the jury was back in the courtroom, Judge Winston explained what was about to occur, and Dr. Wells again took the witness stand and was sworn. Judge Winston undertook her examination:

"Dr. Wells, you said that you wanted to offer some evidence pertaining to the sentencing phase of this case. What would you like the jury to know?"

"Thank you, Your Honor. I wanted to let the jury to know that, contrary to what Mr. Johnson told them in his closing argument, I do believe that Professor Jackson's testimony alters my opinion somewhat in this case. I am still not convinced that he is suffering from a depersonalization disorder, but I do believe that he is a deeply troubled individual who momentarily was probably unable to control his actions. Not maybe insane, but also not fully responsible for his actions. I think it would not be appropriate to put such an individual to death. If he gets a life sentence, he will fall under my jurisdiction, and I can assure this jury that I will make sure that he gets adequate treatment, and hopefully someday he will be able to rejoin society. That's all that I have to say."

Judge Winston looked down at Mr. Johnson: "Any questions, Mr. Johnson?"

"No, Your Honor."

"Mr. Stanton, any questions?"

"No, Your Honor."

Dr. Wells was excused, and she walked right past the prosecution table and out of the courtroom, glancing at me with a small smile as she went past. Strangely, I always knew that she had been trying to help me.

Judge Winston turned to Mr. Johnson and said: "Any further closing arguments on the sentencing phase, Mr. Johnson?"

"Yes, Your Honor, just a few additional thoughts. Ladies and gentlemen, by the quickness of your verdict, it is clear to me that you understand that the defendant is responsible for these heinous crimes. The only question left is should he forfeit his life for his terrible deeds."

"Taking a human life is not a decision to be made lightly. But the law permits you to make that decision in a capital murder case like this one. And justice cries out for the death penalty here. As the Bible teaches, 'an eye for an eye.'" Only the death penalty will offer closure for the parents and loved ones of the slaughtered students. If you only sentence the defendant to life imprisonment, he will be a burden on the State for the next twenty-five years. He will get three meals a day, and rent-free accommodations.

True, his freedom will be curtailed, but that is nothing compared to the curtailment of the young lives of the fifteen students he massacred. Do justice. Bring back a sentence of death, by lethal injection, and end this awful ordeal for the families and friends of these students."

Judge Winston nodded to Mr. Stanton: "Mr. Stanton, any further remarks?"

"Yes, Your Honor. Ladies and gentlemen, Professor Jackson has heard your verdict loud and clear, respects it and accepts it. But even if you don't believe that he was mentally ill, you have to believe that he is a mentally troubled individual. That's what Dr. Wells testified to during the sentencing phase. You know that he is sorry for this tragedy."

"Killing Professor Jackson will not bring back those students. Even Mr. Johnson didn't claim that killing Professor Jackson would deter future mass murders. Killing Professor Jackson accomplishes one thing, and one thing only: revenge. But as a society, haven't we grown beyond the need to kill people for simple retribution? Aren't we more advanced than that? Mr. Johnson quoted the Bible about an 'eye for an eye,' but that passage comes from the Old Testament. Some of you may remember what Jesus said to an assembled mob who was about to stone to death a prostitute: 'let he who is without sin cast the first stone.' None of us are without our own sins — certainly not as grievous as Professor Jackson's — but sins nonetheless. Mercy is an attribute of advanced societies, and that is what I am here asking for today: mercy for Professor Jackson. He needs treatment. A life sentence will allow him to get the help he needs, while protecting society. And a life sentence is no walk in the park. Serving time in our penal system is not like living in a hotel, I assure you. No one tries to break into prison. It is serious and significant punishment. So I ask you, show mercy and compassion, and return a verdict of life imprisonment. Thank you."

The jury was again instructed by Judge Winston on the law concerning sentencing, and the factors that they could take into account. The jurors were then led back to the jury room to deliberate. Mr. Stanton and I retired to the witness room. We both sat silently in our chairs, lost in our own thoughts. After about thirty minutes, the silence was broken by a rapping on the door. I now knew what that meant: the jury was back.

We were led back into the courtroom and took our seats at counsel table. The jurors filed back in, again not looking at me. When everyone was seated, Judge Winston directed the bailiff to get the verdict form from the jury foreman. He did so, and returned to his spot in front of the bench. Judge Winston solemnly said "The defendant will please rise and face the jury." Both Mr. Stanton and I got slowly up from our chairs. Sweat was pouring down my face, and I felt slightly nauseous. In a loud, clear voice the bailiff read the verdict form: "We the jury find that the defendant, Dan Jackson, should be sentenced to death."

I fainted.

Chapter 27

I awoke with a start from the sharp smell of ammonia. A paramedic was waiving a broken capsule under my nose. I found myself sitting in a chair in the witness room. The paramedic administering the smelling salts was also checking my vital signs. I looked around and saw Mr. Stanton, his lips pushed firmly together.

"Professor Jackson, are you okay?"

I answered feebly, "I guess so."

The paramedic left and Mr. Stanton pulled up a chair next to me. "Look, Professor, we still have some moves to make. We have thirty days to appeal. If we appeal, that acts as a stay of execution until the state appellate process is completed. That could take two to three years. And if we still don't get the sentence thrown out at the state level, we could try a habeas corpus action in the federal court, which could take another couple of years. During that time, we could also petition the governor of New Hampshire for clemency. So the fight isn't over."

I thought carefully about what Mr. Stanton said, and asked, "What would be the grounds for an appeal?"

Mr. Stanton sat quietly, staring down at his hands. "I'm not entirely sure at this point, but three things immediately jump to mind. First, I think that allowing the crime scene photos into evidence was prejudicial. Second, I think that the judge erred when he denied my motion for a mistrial. Third, I intend to interview as many of the jurors as possible who will talk to me, which is permitted under New Hampshire law; maybe I'll find out that something went amiss in the jury room during deliberations. Admittedly, the first ground is a long shot, but I really do think that Johnson polluted the jury with his outburst about you beating Nancy. I mean, look at what a short time the jury was out, both on the conviction and the sentencing. They were riled up. And it's possible that the jury interviews will show that, despite the judge's instruction to ignore the suggestion that you abused your ex-wife, the jury members just couldn't get that out of their minds. That could be our best basis for appeal. But at worst, an appeal will buy us some time."

"I think I need to think about this, and discuss it with Tim. On the one hand, I am guilty. I shot those students. And I caused the accident that killed David. But, on the other hand, I don't think that I deserve to die. I'm willing to be punished, but not killed."

"Well, you have some time to think about it. As I said, we have thirty days to appeal, and I will get right to work on interviewing the jurors. The guard will be here in a few moments to take you back to the prison. I'll be up to see you in a couple days, and we can discuss it further then." Mr. Stanton came over and took my hand in both of his and looked me square in the eyes: "This isn't over yet. I'm going to be here for you every step of the way. We'll be talking." The deputy came and escorted me back to the van for the return trip to the prison.

Chapter 28

New Hampshire hadn't executed a person for over seventy years, so it had no death row to house soon-to-be executed inmates. I was therefore allowed to stay in the cell that I had been occupying for the past two months. I had a restless night of tossing and turning, thinking about whether to appeal, or just accept the jury's verdict.

The next morning, Tim came to visit. He entered the interview room dressed in his priest's black uniform and white collar. He grabbed me in a big bear hug, which gave me a feeling of calm that I hadn't had in days. We then sat across from each other, staring silently at each other for a moment. Tim finally broke the silence:

"Tough break on the death penalty. I was hoping that they'd give you life imprisonment. Your testimony on the stand conveyed real remorse and contrition. I thought for sure the jury would see that and show some clemency. But I was wrong about that. What happens next?"

"Mr. Stanton says that I have thirty days in which to appeal, and if I do, it operates as an automatic stay of execution until the appellate process is over. He also says that if the appeal to the state Supreme Court didn't work, I could also file some kind of action in the federal court challenging the verdict. He says the whole process could take two to three years. And he says that we could petition the governor for clemency, if the appeals aren't successful."

Tim frowned. "Is that really what you want to do? Drag this whole process out for several years?"

My jaw clenched and I pounded my hands on the table. "What the hell do you want me to do? Just accept the death penalty? Look, I admit I killed those students, and my own twin brother, for God's sake! I am willing to be punished. But don't tell me that I have to just willingly go to my death."

Tim was silent for a moment, but his gaze never left mine. "Dan. I love you. I think you know that. I don't want to see you die. But let's be honest with each other: you shot those students. I don't know what happened in that car accident with David. Only you know for sure whether you're responsible for his death. But stop thinking about yourself for a minute. What do you think the families of your dead students are going through? How do you think a lengthy appeal process will affect them?"

I struggled to get control of my breathing, which was now racing. I really hadn't given much thought to the families of the dead students. Of course, the trial must have been like pouring salt into an open sore. They would feel the same deep sense of loss that I felt over David's death. "I guess those families are pretty torn up over the loss of their children. But I told them that I was sorry and never intended to hurt anyone."

"Look, Dan. As I said, I thought your testimony on the stand was heartfelt and sincere. But it was not a one-on-one, personal conveyance of regret and request for forgiveness. I think that the only hope for closure for those families is some kind of redemptive event, where their loss is acknowledged and they actively forgive you. Until you can tell each one of them how sorry you are and seek their forgiveness, the only redemptive event will be your execution. It may not be fair, but that's human nature. Until those families feel that justice has been done, and are able to forgive, their wounds will never heal."

I sat quietly, pondering what Tim had just said. I hated to admit it, but he was right. Those families were suffering. I was sure that the appeal process would be painful and result in repeated dredging up of painful memories. There had to be some way to try to assuage the families' feelings that did not require me accepting a death sentence.

"Tim, I see your point. I would be very willing to tell each family how sorry I was and ask for their forgiveness. But realistically, I can't give a personal apology to each of the families. Probably none of them would agree to come here to see me. And I'm only allowed to use the phone one time a week. Have any other ideas on how I could personally apologize?"

Tim thought for a moment. "Sure. Write each family a personal letter, telling them what you remember about their child, how sorry you are, asking for their forgiveness and letting them know why you feel that you need to appeal. In fact, you might ask their permission for you to appeal."

"Do you really think that any of those families are going to say that it's okay for me to appeal — if they even acknowledge and respond to my letter? I mean, I shot their children."

"Forgiveness is a powerful medicine. It not only helps salve the conscious of the person seeking forgiveness, it also helps the person who forgives to move on and leave behind his anger. As the saying goes, 'forgiveness is the gift you give yourself.' You might be surprised at how many of the families would react positively to such a personal letter from you. Writing those letters might also give you insight into whether you can justify a decision to appeal."

"Well, I'm willing to give it a try. Can you ask Mr. Stanton to get me the addresses of the families? I'll start writing today. That way, I'll get all of the letters written within the thirty days I have to decide whether to appeal. Maybe some of the answers I get to my letters — if I get any — will help me decide what to do."

Tim nodded his head in agreement and smiled slightly. "Good choice, Dan. I'll talk to Mr. Stanton as soon as I leave. Do you want a list of the students' names?"

"No, I saw the list at the trial. I remember each one of them. Thanks, Tim, for helping me think this thing through."

We both stood and hugged each other again. As Tim turned to leave, he said softly: "Remember, Dan. Even if you decide to appeal, odds are the verdict isn't going to be reversed. So don't get your hopes up too high."

Chapter 29

I started writing the letters to the families of my dead students the afternoon after Tim's visit. It proved to be more difficult than I thought it would be. I remembered little anecdotes about each student easily enough. In fact, tears filled my eyes as I wrote something special about each student. Each of them, in their own ways, had been full of promise, I realized. I was able to convey that to each of the families in prose that would have made Shelly proud. Expressing remorse and asking for forgiveness was also easy enough. I desperately wanted to be forgiven. In each of the letters I was eloquent in my pleas for the families' pardon. But the difficult part was trying to explain why I wanted to appeal the verdict.

So ten days after Tim's visit, I had fifteen letters written containing the easy parts, but no letters completed yet with the hard part — justifying the appeal. I had tried to think of hundreds of different ways to explain why I might appeal, but they all rang hollow to me. If Dr. Wells was right, I killed those students because I wanted subconsciously to be punished for killing my own twin brother. But if that was true, why didn't I just shoot myself as punishment? Why use those innocent lives as a vehicle to secure my own punishment? All I could think of was that I was a coward, unable to pull the trigger of a pistol firmly inserted into my own mouth; I was going to make someone else kill me. But that didn't entirely ring true: I was more than willing to be punished, just not executed. If my subconscious mind was seeking a way to insure that I would be punished, it must have overlooked the possibility of the death sentence. So the truth of the matter was that I wanted to appeal because my subconscious mind had misunderstood that the likely penalty for fifteen murders was death. That just didn't seem right. I couldn't send out letters with that flimsy of an explanation. So the unfinished letters sat on my little table in my cell unsent.

Fifteen days after the verdict had been returned, Mr. Stanton came to the prison for a visit. A guard took me to the interview room, where Mr. Stanton was waiting. We shook hands and took our respective seats.

"Professor, I think I have some good news. I've completed the interviews of the jurors who would talk to me, and I think I've come up with some interesting things."

"How many jurors agreed to talk with you?"

"Five. Six of the other jurors flat out refused to talk to me, saying that they had performed their 'civic duty' and didn't want anything else to do with the case. One juror apparently is on an extended vacation to Mexico, so I couldn't track her down."

"So what did you learn from the five who talked to you?"

"Well, just as I suspected, Beth's appearance at the trial, and her attempts to testify that you beat Nancy loomed large in the jury room, notwithstanding the judge's instruction."

"But Beth never testified that I beat Nancy. In fact, you got her to admit that she never saw me lay a hand on Nancy. How could the jury be confused about that?"

"There's an old saying among trial lawyers: innuendo is more powerful than direct proof. According to two of the jurors I spoke to, a majority of the jurors concluded that you did beat Nancy and were a person prone to violence, precisely because we wouldn't let Beth testify about what Nancy supposedly told her about the beatings."

I was flabbergasted. "Beth admitted that she was testifying because Nancy wouldn't take the stand and say that I beat her. How could they ignore that?"

"According to two of the jurors, the majority of the jury interpreted that statement to mean that Nancy was too nice of a person to accuse her ex-husband of abuse. I know it seems like a ridiculous inference, but that's what they said."

"What about the other three jurors who you spoke to. Did they corroborate this?"

"Well, yes and no. The other three recalled that the subject of you beating Nancy came up, but weren't sure if a majority of the other jurors took a firm position on whether they thought you did, or did not, beat Nancy."

"But that's what they were talking about when they decided to reject my insanity plea and sentence me to death?"

"Well, it was part of the narrative. The five jurors also said that you looked and sounded 'too normal' to be insane. Nobody in the jury room thought Dr. Van DeMere knew what he was talking about, so that's on me. I picked the wrong expert. On the other hand, the jurors loved Dr. Wells. But the long and the short of it was the jury thought you were just a person prone to violence, in light of the Nancy-beating non-testimony, and flew off the handle for some reason. The jurors didn't accept Carla's explanation that you were mad at the class, but they sort of agreed that your divorce probably pushed you over the edge. In their minds, you were a ticking bomb, waiting to go off."

I was not surprised that the jury didn't think that I was insane. Hell, I didn't think that I was insane either, and had never really thought much of Dr. Van DeMere or his 'depersonalization disorder' nonsense. "Can't say that I blame them on the insanity defense issue, although I am puzzled how they decided that the divorce pushed me over the edge. There just wasn't that much testimony about that, other than from Dr. Van DeMere, whom they didn't believe. What about the death penalty. Didn't my testimony help at all on that point?"

"Nope. Once they decided that you weren't insane, and that you had killed fifteen kids, they really didn't have much trouble in concluding that you deserved the death penalty. You weren't sick, just angry for some reason. You didn't need treatment, just punishment. Eye for an eye type of thinking."

"So, overall, do the juror interviews help or hurt?"

"Well, New Hampshire law is different than a lot of other states regarding what you can and can't do with post-verdict jury interviews. In most states, you can't use affidavits from jurors to impeach or challenge the verdict, unless you can show bribery or some other improper outside influence on the jury. A simple failure to follow the judge's instructions, for example, can't be used to overturn what the jury has done."

"But that doesn't seem fair. If you can prove that the jury didn't do what the judge told them to do, that would seem to undermine the verdict."

"The problem is that in most states, and even in New Hampshire to a certain extent, there is a strong public policy favoring the sanctity of the jury's deliberations and the finality of judgments. Now, New Hampshire is a little bit different than a lot of states. In New Hampshire, a trial court is given more discretion to allow evidence of juror misconduct in deciding whether to grant a new trial. Here, we have an argument that the jury was improperly influenced by Beth's appearance as a witness and Johnson's improper suggestion to the jury that you beat Nancy. It could support our position that the judge should have granted our motion for a mistrial."

"Will the five jurors agree to submit affidavits saying that they voted to find me guilty because of Beth's appearance and Mr. Johnson's statements?"

"I'm not sure yet. They were prepared to say that *other* jurors seemed to vote for your guilt on that basis, but they weren't so willing to admit that *they* had done so. But even if I can get only one of them to acknowledge that, it would still support our position that a mistrial should have been declared. The jury verdict has to be unanimous. If there would have been one hold out because of Johnson's improper conduct, arguably we should still get a new trial."

"When will you know if you can get one of the five to give you an affidavit to that effect? I need to decide whether to appeal in the next two weeks."

"I've given my paralegal a draft affidavit for each of the five jurors to look at to see if they are willing to sign it. Should know in the next couple of days. But listen, we're not under any time constraint here, as far as I'm concerned. To appeal, all we have to do is file a simple notice of appeal that specifies, in general terms, the grounds for the appeal. That's a no brainer. We don't even technically have to have the juror's affidavits at the time we file the notice. We can move for leave to supplement the record later, if we have to. So don't worry: we can get the appeal on file within the thirty days, no problem."

"But I have to decide whether I want to appeal. I've spoken with my friend Tim, and he's suggested that I write letters of apology to the families of the students I killed, ask them to forgive me, explain why I want to appeal, and ask for their permission."

Stanton slammed his fist down on the table, startling me. "God damn it! That is probably the worst fucking idea that I have ever heard. Why in the world would you want to do that? The families aren't going to 'forgive' you for slaughtering their children, and they sure as hell won't give you their 'permission' to appeal. I don't know what planet your buddy Tim is on, but on planet Earth, things don't work that way. All you are doing is admitting your guilt, and possibly providing the prosecution with more evidence as to why your appeal should be denied. He might move to supplement the record with copies of those letters. It's a terrible idea. Just forget that nonsense."

"Look, Mr. Stanton. I am sorry for what I have done. It's too late for me to tell my brother that I didn't mean to cause his death, and that I am sorry, but I can still provide some measure of comfort to those families. I asked Tim to get the families' addresses from you. Did you bring them?"

"So that's why he asked for the addresses. Yeah, I brought them, but I never thought you were going to use them to write letters asking for permission from the victims' families to appeal. I'm begging you, Professor. Don't do this. We still have a fighting chance, but if you do this, I'm not sure what impact it will have on our appeal."

I thought for a moment. The problem was that both Mr. Stanton and Tim were right, but they were operating in different realms. Render unto Caesar what is Caesar's, and unto God what is God's. Mr. Stanton was primarily concerned with winning, which, of course, also benefited me. Tim, on the other hand, had larger concerns: my salvation, even if it came at the cost of my life. I wasn't sure that I had a soul, but in the event that Tim was right about that, it was something to keep in mind.

"I hear what you are saying Mr. Stanton, and I will think some more about whether to send the letters. But let me ask you this: why do you think I should appeal, and what do you think is the likely outcome of such an appeal?"

Mr. Stanton's lower lip rose up over his mustache and his eyes widened, as if surprised by the question. "Well, one reason to appeal is to try to get the death sentence thrown out. I am assuming that you don't want to die."

"Of course I don't."

"And then, there is the whole notion of a fair trial. Maybe the judge was within proper limits when he allowed the photographs of the crime scene to be displayed to the jury. But he should have granted my motion for a mistrial. That God damn Johnson deliberately blurted out that you had beaten Nancy. That's not a fair trial. You should appeal to protect the sanctity of the judicial system."

It seemed to me that was a bit hyperbolic, but it did have an element of truth to it. Mr. Johnson hadn't played fair. When Mr. Stanton successfully blocked him from getting the testimony he wanted from Beth, he simply essentially testified to it himself. I'd have to try writing up that as an explanation in my letters. Maybe that would be convincing.

"Okay, fair enough, Mr. Stanton. Now, realistically, what are the chances of success on appeal?"

"Well, it depends on how you define 'success.' I think that there is about a fifty-fifty chance that we could get a new trial because of prosecutorial misconduct."

"Any chance the New Hampshire Supreme Court would throw out the verdict and set me free?"

"Zero chance of that. The best we could hope for was a new trial."

"But I seem to remember something from the criminal procedure summer school class about the Constitution prohibiting being tried twice for the same crime."

"You're talking about what's called double jeopardy. The Fifth Amendment to the Constitution says that 'no person shall be subject for the same offence to be twice put in jeopardy of life or limb.' It applies in both state and federal cases. But generally, it doesn't apply when the defense makes the motion for mistrial, because by making the motion, the defendant is deemed to have waived the protection of the double jeopardy clause. In rare cases, double jeopardy may bar a re-trial, even when the defense moves for a mistrial, but only if we could show that the prosecutor intentionally 'goaded' us into making the motion. It's a pretty tough test to satisfy, and we'd be hard pressed to meet it here. So our best outcome is a new trial. Period."

"So if we are 'successful,' all we get is a chance to do the trial all over again?'"

"That's right, but remember that we've learned a lot from the first trial. I won't use Dr. Van DeMere again, that's for sure. And we'll be better prepared to deal with the other prosecution witnesses as well. If the case is reversed, and a new trial granted because of prosecutorial misconduct, there's a good chance that Mr. Johnson will be removed from the case, and we'll get a new prosecutor who may be willing to make a plea deal. A new trial would open up several new possible avenues to pursue."

But at the end of the day, the pivotal facts would remain the same. I killed fifteen of my students. I am not insane. Even with a new expert — assuming that Mr. Stanton could find one to testify that I suffered from some mental illness — I was not at all confident that the result would be any different.

"Okay, thanks Mr. Stanton. You've given me a lot to think about. Come see me in a week or so, and I will let you know about my decision on the appeal."

Mr. Stanton sighed, nodded his head and rose to shake my hand. "Okay, Professor. But please give this careful thought. We can still win this." Mr. Stanton left, and I was escorted back to my cell, where I immediately went back to working on my letters to the family, to see if I could write a compelling reason why I should appeal.

Chapter 30

A few days after my discussion with Mr. Stanton, and while I was still in the throes of trying to complete my letters to the families, I was told that I had an unexpected visitor: Dr. Wells. A guard escorted me to the interview room, where Dr. Wells was already seated and waiting. Dr. Wells rose from her seat and extended her hand. I reached over and shook it. She placed her left hand over our right hands in a soft embrace, and looked deeply into my eyes. There was both warmth and sadness in her visage. We both sat down.

"Dr. Wells, this is an unexpected surprise. Is it okay for us to be meeting like this, without the lawyers?"

Dr. Wells smiled warmly. "Yes, it's okay. And I would prefer, now that the trial is over, that you call me Paige, Dan."

I could feel a brief flash of heat rise up my neck, and responded, "Sure. Eh, okay. I guess that I was still caught up with your courtroom persona. Which, by the way, was very impressive. But you know, I am still considering whether or not to appeal. If I do appeal and win, the case could be tried all over again. Are you sure that it's okay for us to be talking?"

"Dan, if the case is tried again, I will not participate, so rest assured, there is nothing improper about my being here or us talking."

"But why wouldn't you testify again at a new trial. You were a terrific witness. If I were the prosecutor, I sure would want to use you again."

Paige smiled. "Dan, I don't want to testify against you again. Sitting through the trial made me realize that I don't truly believe that the death sentence is an appropriate punishment for you — or any other mass murderer. I will not serve as an expert witness in a capital case again."

"Why not?"

"Since the trial, I have pored over my research on other mass killings over the last two decades. I have come to the conclusion that virtually all of these other shooters suffered, to one degree or another, from some overwhelming psychosis that caused them to hurt others. Not all of them may have been technically insane, but, at a minimum, they were not in full control of their faculties. As I recall, Mr. Stanton told the jury that sane people don't engage in mass killings for no reason. I would re-phrase that concept slightly: people who are not suffering from some mental infirmity do not randomly kill other people. I don't think it is right to execute such people. They need treatment. In fact, I think as a society we need to do a better job of identifying people in need of treatment before they finally lose control. I now believe that if you had gotten appropriate grief counseling after your brother's death, you and I wouldn't be sitting here now."

I nodded. "Unfortunately, there's not much we can do about that now."

"Well, that's one of the reasons that I came to see you today. I wanted to talk with you about David's death, and your role in it. It's still important for you to come to grips with what happened that night, understand it for what it is, and move on. You do realize that it was an accident?"

I stared down at my hands for a moment and sighed. I hated talking about this. Paige was going to ruin what had otherwise been a very nice visit. Why would she want to do that?

"Do we really have to go over this again? I mean, if my guilt over David's death is what lead to the whole shooting thing, don't you think its run its course and I'm through with it?"

Paige shook her head negatively. "Dan, the fact that you still find it so difficult to talk about David's death is the best evidence that your guilt remains unresolved. I want to help you get past this."

"Why?"

"Because I have come to be very fond of you and care about what happens to you. Although I recognize that you are not technically my patient, I feel like you are my patient. I realize that you will probably appeal, so there may be several years before this is done, but that time could be spent in a happier and healthier state of mind if you can understand what happened. So, I ask again: you do realize that David died in an accident, don't you?"

"Yes, he died in an accident. An accident that I caused."

"How did you cause it?"

"You heard the testimony at trial. I was mad at David and slapped him while I was driving. That provoked his response, and I drove over the center line. How is that not my fault? Even you thought so, when you passed up that note to Mr. Johnson, feeding him that question about how I shot the students to make sure I'd be punished for killing David."

Paige was quiet for a moment. "Dan, my note was a top-of-the-mind response to what I was hearing from your testimony. But I've had some time to think about the totality of what I know about your situation, and now I have a slightly different view. I don't think that your guilt is about slapping your brother in the car. You may feel badly about doing that, but not because you really think that you caused the accident. During our interview you told me that you were not jealous of David. But I think you were. And for years and years before the accident, you felt guilty about being jealous. That's the real guilt that you couldn't get past, and once David was dead, you had no way to resolve that guilt. I think that is the guilt that may have provoked your subconscious mind to find a way to make sure that you would be punished. But you should not have felt guilt about being jealous of David. It's normal for siblings to be jealous of one another."

"There were other things I didn't tell you during that interview. I wasn't just jealous of David. There were times that I loathed him. I mean, really hated the way he treated me. That's not normal. Especially for a twin. Twins are supposed to be closer than normal siblings. I now realize that part of me wanted to hurt David, so that he would know what it felt like. That's what must have caused me to slap him in the car, resulting in the accident."

"Dan, you're reasoning is flawed. Fraternal twins are not some kind of 'super siblings.' Research is now suggesting that while identical twins may share a special cooperative bond because of their identical genetic make-up, fraternal twins may actually be super-competitive with each other, at least fraternal twins that are the same gender. Look at it this way: you and David shared a womb for nine months. Space in there got cramped, and you were in constant competition for elbow room and nourishment. One of you had to come down that birth canal first, so there was competition even to get born. Some research suggests that a 'womb memory' is created of such competition that never really goes away. So it is perfectly natural that you would feel some jealousy and competitiveness with David. He probably also felt the same sort of thing about you. Remember he called you 'Professor' when he wanted to get your goat; but that was really a sign of his insecurity regarding his own intellect. You didn't really hate each other. You were both just acting out a competition that began at conception."

I thought about that for a minute. There was some truth to what Paige was saying. David and I had always been competitive. I always did feel a little guilty about being jealous of David's exploits. "But I was mad at him and if I hadn't acted on my anger by slapping him, he'd be alive today."

"Would he? How do you know that you might not have skidded on the ice and snow regardless of the slap?

And how do you know that the truck might not have jack-knifed and blocked the road in any event. Some things are just accidents. If you re-played what happened in your car ten times, it might produce the crash only once. That's an accident— not a premeditated attempt to harm David."

I sat back in my chair. My eyes narrowed and my mouth dropped open slightly. God, I wanted to believe what Paige was saying. I tried to speak, but couldn't find the words. Finally, Paige filled the void:

"Listen, Dan. You need to forgive yourself over David's death. You didn't mean for it to happen, it just did. Forgiveness is the gift we give to ourselves. Forgive David for sometimes being a jerk, and forgive yourself for being human, and having the normal human responses of jealousy and anger." Paige looked intently at me, waiting for a reply.

"You know, my friend Father Tim said the same thing about forgiveness."

"Was that the priest who was at trial every day in the first row?"

"Yes, that was him. Because of the things I've discussed with him, I have been thinking a lot about forgiveness recently, because I am trying to write letters to the families of the students I killed to apologize to them and ask for their forgiveness. Maybe to get forgiveness, I have to be willing to give it as well, even if it's to myself."

"I'm curious. How did you decide to write letters to the families of the slain student?"

"Well, that was Father Tim's idea. He said that in order for the families to get closure, he felt that they would need some acknowledgement from me of the wrong I had done them, and of the remorse I feel, as well as a request for their forgiveness. I am also trying to explain to them why I might want to appeal, and asking for their permission."

"Do you have any responses back from the families?"

I shifted uncomfortably in my chair. "No, because I haven't been able to finish any of the letters and send them out yet."

"Why not?"

"I am having trouble coming up with a good explanation for why I might want to appeal, other than the obvious one that I don't want to die. But that sort of excuse isn't going to bring any comfort to the families: their children didn't want to die either, but I took their lives. I realize that if I appeal, it will drag out the agony for these families for several years. Maybe the only way for closure for these people is my execution. I don't know. But that's what I am wrestling with."

Paige bit her lip, and was quiet for a while. "Dan, I don't know the answer either. I certainly understand your desire to live, and I also understand the sorrow and anger that the families must be feeling. Under these circumstances, it seems so unfair that this is the choice you are left with. Doesn't Mr. Stanton want you to appeal?"

"Yeah, he does. He thinks we have a pretty good shot based upon his motion for mistrial, but I am not so sure. Even if I could get a new trial, the result might well be the same. I've got to decide in a few more days what to do. Frankly, our discussion today about David may help me decide the right thing to do, and help me finish those letters."

"I hope so, Dan. If there's anything else that I can do, please feel free to call me. I'll come back to talk any time you want."

Paige rose to leave, and we clasped hands again. She disappeared out the door, and I was led back to my cell.

Chapter 31

The days flew by. I tried over and over to finish the letters, but couldn't find a reason that I thought adequately explained why I should appeal. In fact, what I had learned from Mr. Stanton about the likely outcome of an appeal had made the task significantly harder: "success" meant doing the trial all over again, and thus putting the families through that agony one more time, probably with the same result. It was becoming increasing difficult for me to reconcile appealing with the unalterable fact that I had committed these murders. No letters from me would change that fact, and everyone knew that.

I had also used the time to think through my feelings about David and his death. What Paige had said about forgiveness made sense, and it was consistent with what Tim was constantly preaching. But both of them had left a few things out of the equation. Forgiving doesn't mean forgetting, and forgiving doesn't eliminate responsibility for one's actions. In fact, forgiving means acknowledging that a wrong has been done, and asking someone's pardon nonetheless. After much struggle, I had reached peace on the issue of David. I had forgiven his competitiveness and sometimes hurtful behavior towards me. And I had also forgiven myself for my competitiveness and jealousy towards him. However, I had to face up to the fact that, although it may have been an accident, I was responsible for David's death. The time for excuses was over. The time to accept responsibility for my actions had come.

Tim had come to visit me almost every day. We chatted about our memories of college days, and Tim's plans for the Rutland parish. Tim didn't bring up the subject of the letters, and whether I had sent them out, and I decided not to bring up the topic either. This was a decision that I was going to have to make on my own. As

Tim had said at his very first visit at the Hanover jail, I was going to have to save my own soul. He couldn't do it for me.

When Mr. Stanton came for his next visit, I had made up my mind.

"Professor, you have that look on your face. You've made a decision, haven't you?"

"Yes," I replied softly.

"Well?"

I bowed my head slightly and quietly replied: "I sent the letters out to the families yesterday. But I didn't include the part about explaining why I wanted to appeal and asking for the families' permission. I told each family something special about their child, and how sorry I was that I had shot him or her. Then I told them that although there were portions of the trial that were not fair, I had decided that I would not appeal, and would instead accept my punishment. I asked them to pray for me."

Mr. Stanton sat dumbfounded, his mouth open and his eyebrows arched. When he finally recovered from his surprise, he said: "I'm not completely surprised. I respect your decision. It takes real courage to face up to something like this. I will still be here every step of the way, to do whatever I can to help you."

"Thank you, Mr. Stanton. I appreciate that."

"Professor, is there anything I can do for you now?"

I smiled and sighed. "Not really. I guess I'd like to know how the execution will occur, so that I can get mentally prepared."

"Sure, sure. Well, as I've told you, there hasn't been an execution in New Hampshire in a long, long time. The method of execution used to be by hanging, but now it is prescribed to be done either by lethal injection or hanging. I assume that you'd prefer lethal injection, right?"

I nodded, and Mr. Stanton continued: "Well, because there's been no executions in New Hampshire for so long, the state prison doesn't have a 'death chamber,' or anything like that. I think that what they will have to do is set up a clear plastic tent in the prison gym and administer the lethal injection there. By state law, the murder victims' immediate families have the right to witness the execution, so the Warden will also set up a small grand stand near the tent so that the families will be able to view the execution."

I interrupted Mr. Stanton's explanation: "Do you really think very many people will come to watch an execution?"

"I don't know for sure, but I think that there will be several families who will want to do that. You have the right to have someone present in the room with you. I know that your family is all deceased. Is there someone else you'd like to be with you?"

"Well, I hope you aren't insulted, Mr. Stanton, but I would like it if Dr. Wells and Tim would agree to be present with me. Could you ask them?"

Mr. Stanton smiled slightly. "Sure, I can do that. And don't worry Professor. I'm not insulted. I'd pick Dr. Wells over me in a heartbeat. And your friend Tim is a priest. It makes sense for him to be there, too."

"Thanks, Mr. Stanton."

"Now the way the execution will occur is that you will be led into the tent, and there will be a hospital gurney with two perpendicular extensions to strap your arms down on. You will be strapped to the bed and an intravenous line will be set up in your arm. It's connected to three vials. The contents of the first vial contains a strong sedative that will relax you, the next vial contains a pain killer, and the final vial contains a drug that will cause your heart to stop. It's supposed to be painless."

I gulped a couple times. "Okay. Anything else I should know?"

"Well, once we know when the execution is scheduled, you'll be entitled to a last meal. What should I tell the guards you want for your last meal?"

"Sausage and onion pizza."

"You got it. Anything else you need?"

I rose from my chair. "No, I think that's it. Will you be there at the execution?"

"Do you want me to be?"

"I guess so, if you don't mind."

"Sure. I'll be there." We shook hands, and I was escorted back to my cell.

Chapter 32

The authorities were apparently caught off guard when the thirty-day time to appeal passed with no notice of appeal being filed. They had assumed that an appeal was a certainty, and thus had not made any plans for the execution. However, things got moving quickly, and the execution was ultimately scheduled for the following month. The Warden told me that the additional thirty days would give me adequate time, in the event that I changed my mind and wanted to pursue a federal habeas corpus appeal. I thanked the Warden, but assured him that there would be no appeals of any kind.

While I waited for the execution day, I spent my time enjoying the simple things that had always brought me pleasure. I worked on completing the scholarly paper that I had begun well before the shootings. I re-read old favorite books. And I also had the time to mull over the letters that I received from some of the families to whom I had written. I received ten response letters, and they were about evenly split. About half of them thanked me for my letter and expression of remorse, and said that although it would be difficult, they would try to forgive me and remember me in their prayers. The other half of the responses were filled with vitriol, and best wishes for a swift journey to hell. I was buoyed by the positive responses, but not overly affected by the negative ones. I did not blame the naysayers. Apparently I had been unable to forgive myself for David's death for years. I knew exactly where they were coming from.

Finally, execution day arrived. I got up at my normal time, showered, shaved and dressed as usual. I skipped breakfast. My stomach was rumbling, but it wasn't from hunger.

Two guards came to my cell to get me. They handcuffed me and led me to the prison gym. As I entered

the room, the glare of two large banks of lights that had
been set up in the gym assaulted my eyes, causing me to
momentarily squint and turn my head away. As my eyes
adjusted to the brightness, I saw the execution tent directly
ahead of me. It was made of clear plastic. The hospital
gurney, intravenous contraption and the three vials were all
plainly visible. The bleachers that Mr. Stanton had
described were immediately to the left of the entrance of
the execution tent. They were filled to the gills with
mothers, fathers, sisters and brothers of the dead students.
The guards ushered me into the tent.

The Warden, Dr. Wells, Tim and a medical
technician were already inside the tent waiting for me. My
handcuffs were removed, and the guards escorted me
towards the gurney. The medical technician said to me in a
low voice: "Professor Jackson. Could you please lay down
on the gurney, and place each of your arms on the
supports?"

I looked at the gurney. The arm supports made it
look like a cross. This was going to be my crucifixion.
With shaking legs I turned and lifted myself up on to the
gurney and lay down. I spread both arms out on the
supports. I could feel the sweat dripping from under my
arms. The guards strapped down my ankles, and the
medical technician strapped both arms to the supports. Dr.
Wells was then allowed to approach me. She bent over the
gurney and spoke quietly in my ear: "Dan, I know that you
are scared. But you will not feel any pain."

I smiled weakly. "Thank you for coming, Paige. I
know that you were trying to help me throughout this
whole thing. I wanted to let you know that I really
appreciate everything you did for me." I held my breath
momentarily, fighting back tears.

"It's going to be all right, Dan. You're going to be
all right." Dr. Wells stepped back away from the gurney.

Then Tim came over, dressed in his priestly garments. "Dan, you are doing the right thing. I saw one of the letters you wrote to the families. It was beautiful, and I am sure brought that family great comfort. You deserve the same comfort. Please accept Jesus into your heart now, and ask him for forgiveness. It's yours for the asking, and it will bring you everlasting peace. Will you do that, if not for yourself, for me?"

I looked up into Tim's eyes. They were radiant, and conveyed great warmth and sadness. "I will," I gulped. "Goodbye, and thanks for everything," I whispered.

The Warden then walked over and stood next to the gurney. He turned towards the audience in the bleachers, and in a deep baritone voice pronounced: "Dan Jackson. You have been found guilty of capital murder and sentenced to death by a jury of your peers. Do you have any last words that you'd like to say?"

I had thought about that for a long time. What profound last words could I utter that would make any difference? The only thing I could come up with was not so profound: "I am sorry."

The Warden stepped away from the gurney. The medical technician stuck the intravenous needle in my arm. I winced from the pain. I glanced over at the bleachers. The faces of the onlookers were distorted somewhat by the clear plastic, and they took on a hideous, amusement park/fun house appearance. I quickly looked away. I saw the Warden nod his head up and down. A cool feeling began creeping up my arm and I looked over at the vials. A plunger in vial number one was slowly being depressed, driving the fluid through the intravenous device. I was beginning to feel a bit sleepy, and could feel my eyelids becoming heavy. Could it really be happening so quickly? I glanced over at the vials again, willing my eyes to stay open. The plunger in vial number two was slowly pushing the liquid into my arm. I looked at Dr. Wells, whose lips were tightly locked in a frown, and her forehead creased with worry lines. I looked over at Tim. His eyes were closed, his hands folded in front of him, and his lips moving in silent prayer. This was it. I looked over at vial number three. The plunger had already done its work. The vial was empty. I felt my eye lids falling down like broken garage doors. My breathing became labored. I wanted to fight, but couldn't muster any more energy to resist the inevitable.

Suddenly, I began to see a bright white light in the distance. I had read about near-death experiences. Often people reported being drawn to a white light. It was the white light of eternity. It was my final destination. I hoped it was heaven and not hell. Maybe I should have been more religious during my lifetime to hedge my bets, but I would soon have the answer in any event. As I approached it, the light became even more glaring and harsh. It was hurting my eyes. I could feel myself squinting, and my eyelids were fluttering. Then, almost involuntarily, I began opening my eyes.

Chapter 33

All I could see initially were bright lights overhead. I closed my eyes again, and tried to get a better feeling of the environment around me. I seemed to be in a bed, but I could feel my arms at my side, and they didn't feel like they were strapped down anymore. I could move my legs; they weren't strapped down either. I heard a soft, constant beeping nearby. It seemed somehow comforting, not threatening. I then heard something in the distance. It sounded like footsteps. Then I sensed the rustle of clothing near my bed.

I squinted open my eyes to see what was around me. Everything was blurry. I saw a young woman dressed in a blue top and pants. She looked like a nurse. What was going on? I slurred out a few words: "Am I dead? Is this heaven?"

The nurse shrieked in surprise and ran to the door. She screamed down the hall: "Call Dr. Wells! Tell her Dan Jackson is awake!"

She returned to my bedside. My vision was slowly improving, and it appeared that I was in a hospital room of some sort. I was confused. Had something gone wrong with the execution? Was I going to have to go through that all over again, or would I be hung the next time? I grabbed the nurse's wrist and looked her in the eye: "Am I dead, or did something go wrong with the execution?"

The nurse cocked her head, with a quizzical look on her face. "No, you're not dead. You are at Mary Hitchcock Hospital in Hanover. You were in a serious car accident and have been in and out of a coma ever since. I don't understand what you mean by 'execution.'"

In a coma since the car accident? I couldn't have been in a coma for all these years. It didn't make any sense. And what about the shootings, trial and execution? What the hell had happened to me?

"Can you please help me sit up? I need to sit up." The nurse obliged my request and raised the head portion of the bed. "Now please get me a mirror." The nurse went into the bathroom that adjoined my room and returned with a hand-held mirror. I looked at the mirror. It was me, but I looked like I did as a college student. No age lines around the mouth. No graying hair. What in the world was going on? I felt a little vertigo, and slightly dizzy.

At that moment, an attractive blond woman dressed in a white smock and pants hurried into the room, carrying a clipboard with a thick stash of papers attached. I recognized her instantly. It seemed impossible, but a glance at the name tag on her smock confirmed it: Dr. Wells! She came quickly to my bedside, took my pulse, and looked into each eye with the aid of a penlight.

"How are you feeling?" Dr. Wells asked.

"God, Dr. Wells, it's good to see you. What happened to me — was there some screw up with the execution? And why do I look so young again. I don't understand what is happening."

"Slow down, Dan," Dr. Wells said in a soft, comforting voice as she placed her hand on my arm. "It's perfectly normal for someone coming out of a coma to be disoriented at first. It's going to be all right. You're going to be all right."

"That's exactly what you told me at the execution. Don't you remember everything that's happened to me? You were there every step of the way, trying to help me."

"Dan, I don't know anything about any execution. However, I do remember everything about your case. You were brought into the emergency room pretty banged up from the accident. I was one of the neurosurgeons summoned by the emergency room staff to help stabilize your condition, and determine whether immediate surgery was required. Thankfully, it wasn't. But you did slip into a coma and were admitted to this hospital room for further care. Over the last six weeks, I have visited you almost every day, and while there were some other times that we thought you were coming out of the coma, each previous time you slipped back. I'm glad this time you've stayed with us."

My head was spinning. This just didn't make any sense. While I was still trying to sort this out, I heard a voice from behind Dr. Wells:

"Hey, Professor — nice to have you back among the living!"

Dr. Wells moved aside. My brother David was standing in the doorway to my hospital room with a shit-eating grin on his face. Tears began streaming down my face, and I began sobbing uncontrollably. David rushed to my side. Apparently trying to lighten the mood, David said "Hey, if you're not as glad to see me as I am you, I can leave, you know." I sat upright in the bed and wrapped my arms around him, giving him a big squeeze. When I eventually let David go, I exclaimed:

"Thank God you are alive. I didn't kill you. I have never been so happy to see anyone in my whole life."

"Whoa, bro. What are you talking about? I was never in any danger from that car accident. Hell, I walked out of the emergency room the next morning with a few bandages and some aches and pains."

"But I saw you at the accident scene. You had been thrown through the windshield and were covered with blood. And I woke up for a moment in the emergency room and saw a doctor taking your pulse and shaking his head. I was sure you were dead."

"I guess I led with my head — the one part of my body which is hardest to damage any more than it already is. You know scalp wounds. They bleed like hell, but really don't amount to much. I think you saw one of the ER doctors getting me ready to have my head stitched up. But that was no big deal. You were the one that we were all worried about. Mom and Dad have been sick with worry that you'd never wake up."

"Mom and Dad are alive?"

David raised his eyebrows and looked over at Dr. Wells, who shrugged her shoulders. David then looked back at me. "Dan, are you feeling all right? Yes, Mom and Dad are alive. They flew out here after the accident and stayed for ten days. But eventually, they had to go back home to their jobs. And since the doctors couldn't say when you'd wake up, it seemed like the only practical thing to do. Dad calls me twice a day for updates on your condition. Mom tells me that he cries every night, afraid that you wouldn't wake up."

"But what about you? You had school you needed to finish."

"I dropped out for the semester. I'll pick up the classes I missed in summer school. No big deal. There was no way I was going to leave you here all alone in the hospital." A sly grin crossed David's face: "After all, if Batman's hurt, Robin isn't going to run away."

"But I don't understand. What about the students I shot, and the trial, and the execution?"

David and Dr. Wells looked at each other with arched eyebrows. David spoke in a slow, deliberate fashion: "Dan, maybe you should tell us what is going on inside that head of yours."

I answered in a clipped, fast-paced fashion: "I was mad at you for ruining Winter Carnival weekend for me, and insisted that you leave, and that's how we ended up driving down to Boston. I caused the car accident by trying to slap you, and crossing over the center line. You were killed in the accident, and it turns out that subconsciously I spent the rest of my life trying to punish myself for killing you. Eventually, I was a professor here at Dartmouth, and I went into my class room to administer a mid-term exam, found two pistols in my briefcase, and then couldn't stop myself from pulling them out of the briefcase and shooting them at my students, killing fifteen of them. But at the time, I didn't know why I did it, and I needed to find out why. I had to retain a criminal defense lawyer, and eventually had to plead not guilty by reason of insanity to try to avoid the death penalty. My lawyer retained a quack of an expert, and Dr. Wells was the expert shrink for the prosecution — but all along, I felt like she was trying to help me. In fact, Dr. Wells was the one who figured out why I shot those students — it was a way to make sure that I would be punished for killing you. Anyway, I got convicted and sentenced to death. Oh, and my best friend Tim was with me throughout the ordeal. He had become a priest, and ultimately convinced me to accept my punishment. At the moment of the lethal injection, I woke up here in the hospital room."

David and Dr. Wells stood there with blank looks on their faces in absolute silence. David let out a long, low whistle, and then looked me directly in the eyes:

"Dude, they must be giving you some pretty good drugs in here for you to have dreamed that one up. You are a student here, man. Not a professor. And, if I recall our hunting experiences together, you'd be lucky to hit one student if you fired a thousand bullets in a classroom. But more importantly, you didn't cause that accident."

I looked at David in disbelief. I started to rebut his statement when David held up his hand and asked:

"Dr. Wells, could you give us a few moments together alone."

"Sure, I'll be right out here in the hall. But just for five minutes, no longer. I still need to examine Dan."

After Dr. Wells had existed, David began again:

"Look, Dan. The lawyer told me not to talk about the accident with anyone. I don't think he meant with you, though. So whatever you have to say has to stay between us."

"David, you know and I know that I had been drinking that night. I let myself get distracted. I was mad at you and hit you with my right hand. That caused the car to cross the white line. That's what caused the accident. I was responsible."

David stared down at the floor, and said in a low voice: "No, bro. That's not what caused the accident. I had been an asshole, and deserved to get kicked off campus. I was teasing you while you were trying to drive in a blinding snow storm. I am the biggest dick in history. I caused the accident, and almost killed you. If you had died, I don't know what I would have done. Life would have been over for me."

I could see tears falling to the floor from David's downward-tilted face. I spoke slowly: "It wasn't your fault. And you know what? Now I realize it wasn't my fault either. It was just an accident. Isn't it ironic that I wanted to punish myself for killing you, and you were punishing yourself about possibly killing me? I guess we can stop punishing ourselves now, because we're both going to live a long life."

David looked up, and quickly wiped away the tears from his eyes with the backs of his hands. He smiled weakly. "Sounds good to me."

Dr. Wells knocked on the side of the door. "Time's up. I need to see my patient." She re-entered the room, and David stepped back from the bed. Dr. Wells started poking and prodding my abdomen, raising and lowering my legs and arms, and rotating my head. When she had finished that, she started scribbling some notes on her charts. I broke in:

"Dr. Wells, can you explain to me what happened? Why did I have such a vivid experience — I can't really call it a dream. It was too real. There was too much detail. It all felt real."

Dr. Wells sat down on the edge of my bed and gathered her thoughts for a moment. Then she began her explanation.

"We don't completely understand what happens to the brain when a person goes into a coma. It often times depends on what area of the brain has suffered trauma, and a number of other factors. Some research suggests that the part of the brain that is normally involved when we dream actually experiences a decrease in activity during comas, while other, deeper areas of the brain are stimulated. That research would seem to indicate that it is less likely that you would dream in the classic sense. On the other hand, it is very common for coma victims who are in a 'light' coma to report, upon awakening, that they were aware of what was going on around them, in terms of hearing people speaking to them. The fact that you incorporated your friend Tim and me into your coma experience tells me that there were times during the past six weeks when you were in a 'light coma,' and able to hear and understand at least some of what was going on around you. Tim visited you frequently, and I often saw him talking to you, even though you seemed non-responsive. I was constantly talking to you when I would visit your room to check on you. And I know for a fact that I would often tell you that everything would work out all right."

"But the research on comas is very incomplete. The 'dream area' of the brain is not always 'turned off' in coma victims. And even when it is, we don't have a good understanding of precisely how the deeper areas of the brain function. Some researchers believe that these deeper parts of the brain may replicate the function of the higher "dream areas," but in slightly different ways. Some people who are in long-term comas report an almost total absence of dream-like states. Others report incredibly vivid experiences, like yours. I like to think of it as creating a 'coma reality.' These 'coma realities' may play a vital role in brain healing that we don't yet understand."

"So, if I were to guess, I'd say that when you were in a deeper coma, these deeper parts of the brain took over and functioned in some way to try to help your mind and body recover. You thought you killed your brother, and felt guilty. You wanted to be punished. So you were. But luckily, the shock of the 'execution' re-engaged the higher functioning part of your brain, bringing you out of the coma. That's the best I can come up with."

I sat quietly taking this all in. "I think I understand what you are saying. But still, it seemed so life-like, so real. I don't suppose it is possible that this deeper part of the brain has some clairvoyant capabilities? An ability to see into the future?"

"Dan, if you're asking me do I think that twenty-five years from now you will become a Dartmouth professor and shoot your students, happily I am pretty sure the answer is no. Clairvoyance is not a scientifically well documented ability under any circumstances, much less coma induced. I wouldn't worry much about that. Now, I think it is time for you to get some rest. Say good-bye to your brother, for now."

David crossed back over to my bed and gave me a big hug, and then left the room, followed by Dr. Wells. Although I was certain that I would be unable to sleep, having just aroused from a six week nap, I was asleep almost the moment that my head hit the pillow. It was a deep and this time dreamless sleep.

Chapter 34

My great awakening had taken place on a Thursday morning. When I next awoke, it was Friday. The nurses came and poked and prodded me, drawing blood, taking my pulse, checking my lung function and ultimately freeing me from a catheter. The nurses then gently, at first, began manipulating my legs and arms to limber them up. Finally, just before lunch time, with the aid of a walker, I was allowed to walk down the hall for a short stroll. Although I was still pretty weak, it felt wonderful to be on my feet and moving. It felt great to be alive.

The rest of the day I spent sitting in a chair in my room, reading and seeing occasional visitors. Several of my friends from the frat and the dorm had stopped by to say hello. Apparently my coming out of the coma was big news on campus, and I was even visited by a reporter for the Daily Dartmouth to schedule an interview for the following week when I would feel stronger and more like talking.

David showed up at my room around lunch time and hung around for the rest of the day, either sitting on my bed or on the arm of my chair, watching the parade of visitors. He smiled and laughed with my friends, but seemed to be taking care not to take the spotlight off me. I caught him a couple times, just sitting and staring at me with a huge grin on his face. Whatever our differences had been before, it was clear to me that the accident and coma had forever altered our relationship. We both now knew that the bond between us was indeed special, and that despite our different personalities and abilities, we both loved and needed each other. When I had thought that I had lost David, I was lost and desperate to punish myself. When David thought I might never wake up, he was agonized. Starting life fighting for space with each other in a uterus is an experience that leads to both competition and also companionship. The truth is, we completed each other.

On Saturday morning, as I stirred groggily from my sleep, I was startled awake by an unexpected sight: Mom and Dad were standing at the foot of my bed. I bolted upright in my bed, struggling to free myself from the sheets to get out of bed, unable to even utter a word in my excitement. Mom rushed over to the side of the bed and threw her arms around me, and in a sobbing voice said:

"Oh, Dan! My darling boy! I was sure that we'd lost you! And that thought was unbearable."

I was hugging her back so hard I was afraid I might break her ribs, so I relaxed my grip and pushed her gently away from me, still holding on to her shoulders with my hands. "Mom, I can't tell you how much I missed you. While I was in the coma, I had this terrible dream — no, it wasn't a dream, more like a vision. And in it, I was a grown man and you and Dad were dead." I looked over Mom's shoulder at my father, who was standing stoically behind her. "I thought I had killed David in the accident, and that you two had died shortly after that from the grief you felt over David's death. In a way, in this vision, I had killed you, too." I could feel hot tears running down my own cheeks. My father approached the bed, gently moved Mom to the side and gave me a quick hug. He whispered softly in my ear:

"Dan, we were afraid that we had lost you. Thank God you're back."

Dad let the brief hug dissipate. But he stood holding my shoulders and shaking his head. "Your mother and I have had lots of discussions while you were in your coma, and she told me things about myself that I never really thought about or understood before. Like the fact that I seemed to enjoy being with David more than with you. Did you feel that way, Dan?"

I looked down at the bed for a moment. With a lump in my throat, I said in a low voice: "Maybe a little."

"I can now understand how you might. I mean, I went to all of David's athletic stuff, but didn't follow your activities as much. But honestly, I didn't understand what you did — it was way above me. I guess I could have asked you to explain it, but I didn't want you to think your father was dumb. I shouldn't have been that way. But it didn't mean that I loved you any less."

I looked up at my father, who was smiling broadly. This was the first time since that time in my room after the barber shop incident that my father had told me he loved me. In a quivering voice I responded: "Dad, I always knew that. It's just I've always wanted you to be proud of me, like you were of David."

At this point, Mom chimed in: "Dan, you don't know it, but when you are away at Dartmouth, you are all your father talks about — to me, the neighbors, and the men around town. How smart you are, how well you are doing at an Ivy League school. He beams with pride every time someone asks about you. Of course, so do I." Mom smiled warmly.

Dad broke back in: "She's right, Dan. I just was never very good at expressing my feelings. I wish that I could say that will all change because of the accident. But you can't undo a lifetime of upbringing and habit overnight. But I am going to try. I now realize that I want both you boys to know how important you are to me. Someday, I won't be here to tell you, and then it will be too late. The accident showed me that none of us really know when our time will be up, so we better not put off until tomorrow what we should do today."

The three of us were silent for a moment, each, I think, savoring a new understanding between us. Mom and Dad then settled into the chairs in my room, and I began peppering them with questions about back home, the relatives, and what I had missed while I was in my coma. After about an hour or so, someone knocked on the door to my room, and a head poked through. It was Tim. My parents had known Tim since freshman year, and greeted him warmly. Tim came over to my bedside and gave me his signature bear hug.

"Dan, man it's good to have you back. You had a lot of us worried as hell — oh, sorry Mr. and Mrs. Jackson," Tim said sheepishly. Mom and Dad just laughed and nodded.

"Tim, it was the most amazing thing. I had this coma experience where I was a professor here and murdered my students. I had to stand trial, and you came to visit me in jail and help me figure out what do to. You were a priest of the Episcopal Church over in Rutland. You kept telling me about the importance of accepting responsibility and seeking forgiveness. In the end, that's what I was about to do: accept the death penalty and seek forgiveness. I have to admit, there were times when I thought you were a pain in the ass for riding me so hard."

At first, Tim was completely silent, with a stern look on his face. Then he began laughing so hard, tears came to his eyes and he was gasping to catch his breath. "Let me get this right: you were a professor and killed your students? What a ridiculous premise for a dream — although you got me being the priest part right."

"It wasn't a dream. Dr. Wells called it a 'coma reality.' I probably included you because I was aware that you were visiting me here in the hospital."

Tim smiled. "That's what friends are for. You'd have done the same for me."

We chatted for a while longer, with Mom and Dad asking Tim questions about his family and Tim's plans for the future. Then there was another knock on the door, and a familiar face peered around the door. It was Nancy. My parents and Tim greeted Nancy, made up some excuse about something that they had to attend to, and left. I think they thought Nancy and I should have some time alone.

Nancy approached my bedside cautiously. She was wearing a tight red sweater that hugged her breasts. She sat on the edge of my bed, leaned over and gently kissed me on the lips. As I kissed her back, I felt a chill run up my spine, and goose bumps rise on my arms. I did not open my mouth to invite her tongue in, nor did my tongue venture forth from its moorings.

"Oh Dan. I was so worried. David called me on Thursday when you woke up, but I had classes all day Friday, so I couldn't get up here until today." She grabbed both of my hands in hers with a big smile on her face. "Are you all right?"

"Yea, I am all right. Still a little weak from being in bed for six weeks, but the doctors say that I'll be up and around in a week or so."

Nancy lowered her eyes and stared at her hands. "Dan, after I heard about the accident, I felt so badly that our last words at Winter Carnival had been angry ones. I shouldn't have left you that Sunday morning. If I had stayed, you probably wouldn't have ended up driving David down to Boston and there wouldn't have been any car accident. I'm really sorry for the way I acted. I hope you'll forgive me."

There was something about Nancy's presence that was making me feel uncomfortable, but it wasn't how we had parted on Winter Carnival weekend. "Look, Nancy, I understand why you got so upset and left. Hell, I was pretty angry myself. But the accident wasn't your fault. It was just an accident, so don't give it another thought."

Nancy looked up at me, and smiled broadly. "Thanks, Dan. That makes me feel a lot better."

I found myself unable to hold Nancy's gaze. An awkward silence descended upon us, with neither of us apparently able to carry the conversation forward. To break the silence, I asked: "By the way, how did you get up here so quickly this morning?"

"I got a ride."

"From whom?"

"Why, from Beth of course. She's waiting in the hall to say hello, too." Nancy called out over her shoulder: "Beth? Beth? It's okay for you to come in now and say hello."

The door opened and in walked Beth. Her hair looked like a bird's nest, and she wore a pair of worn bib overalls over a ratty T-shirt. She stumbled over to my bedside, and stood beside Nancy. I saw her place her hand gently on Nancy's hip, and with a small smile and a wave of her other hand, she said: "Hi Dan. How are you doing?"

The sight of them together gave me the creeps. The vision of them naked together, locked in their lover's embrace, aroused anger in me that I fought to control. I suddenly knew with certainty that while not everything in the "coma reality" was a foretelling of the future, my failed marriage to Nancy — and its cause — were right on the money. It was a future that was not for me. Forgiveness had its limits. After a few seconds of awkward silence, I responded:

"Uh, hi Beth. Thanks for driving Nancy up here. You know, I hate to be a spoiled sport, but I am beginning to feel really exhausted. Mom and Dad were here for a while, and now this, well I think that I need some rest. So maybe you two better go. Thanks for coming. Nancy, I'll give you a call when I get out of this place." But I knew that I never would.

Nancy crinkled up her face and parted her lips slightly, her face a study of confusion and hurt. She leaned over and quickly gave me a peck on the cheek. "Sure Dan. I understand. Give me a call when you're feeling better." Nancy turned and marched out of the room, with Beth in tow. As Beth got to the door, I could have sworn that she turned her head slightly towards me, and with a small grin on her face, winked at me. The door closed and they were gone.

Later that afternoon, as I lay in my bed watching television, a nurse came into my room and said that my faculty adviser was here to see me, if I was up to it. Honestly, I didn't know who my faculty adviser even was, so as much out of curiosity as anything else, I told the nurse to send him in. The door opened, and in walked a man in his late sixties dressed in a rumpled gray suit. His gray streaked hair was pulled back into a pony tail. He had a mustache that seemed to engulf his mouth.

"Dan? My name is Gus Stanton, I am the head of the Government department and your faculty adviser."

The room began to spin, and I felt my hands clutching the sides of the bed in a death grip. I could feel the color leave my face, and again I felt a chill — no, more like a glacier — run down my spine. I began gasping for air, my breathing coming quickly and in an irregular pattern.

Professor Stanton turned and ran quickly to the door: "Nurse! Nurse! I think something is wrong with Dan! Please hurry!"

The nurse quickly scurried into my room, took my pulse and felt my forehead, which by this time, was covered with a gleaming sheen of sweat.

My breathing started to return to normal. My heart stopped pounding in my chest. I took a deep breath, and then let it out, and looked up at the nurse and Professor Stanton:

"I'm all right. I'm all right. Sorry, I don't know what came over me. But it's okay now."

The nurse nodded and said: "Dan, I think you need to rest. I'm going to have to ask your visitor to come back tomorrow or on Monday."

"No, please. I would like to hear what Professor Stanton has to say. Just five minutes and I will rest, I promise."

"All right, Dan. But I will be back here in five minutes and Professor Stanton had better be gone."

I nodded my agreement, and the nurse turned and left the room.

I sat for a moment looking at Professor Stanton. I knew that I had never met him before. But I might have seen him around campus, or at one of the Government department functions. I never knew that he was my faculty adviser. How he got into my "coma reality" was a mystery. If parts of that experience really were a vision of the future, Professor Stanton's role in them was certainly not apparent to me.

"Why are you here, Professor? I don't think we have ever met."

"We haven't met, Dan. That's one of the reasons I am here. You had declared Government as your major, and indicated an interest in law school. Are you still interested in law school?"

I thought for a moment. I had wanted to go to law school, based upon the summer school criminal procedure class. If anything, my "coma reality" experience with the trial had showed me how exciting a trial could really be.

"Yes, I am still interested. In fact, I know for certain that I want to be a lawyer."

"Why?"

"It's hard to explain, but I like the strategy and tactics of trials, and the fact that lawyers can help people through some very difficult times."

Professor Stanton smiled. "Yes they can. I was a practicing lawyer once, down in Boston. But I had always wanted to teach, so after about ten years of practice, I went back to grad school, got my Ph.D., and after bouncing around at a few different schools, ended up here. But there are days when I miss the thrill of trial work, so I know what you mean. Anyway, the reason I am here is that I heard about your accident, and the fact that you couldn't complete the winter trimester. I want to help you get back on track so that you can graduate on time with your class, and also help you get ready for the LSAT tests that you should take this May."

I smiled slightly. "That sounds great, Professor. Thank you so much. But I am a little tired just now. Could we talk about this next week?"

"That would be fine, Dan. I'll get back in touch next week. But in the meantime, don't worry. If you are willing to work hard, I will stay with you every step of the way, and make sure that everything works out as it should."

I said goodbye, and Professor Stanton left the room. I settled back into my bed and closed my eyes. Professor Stanton would be there every step of the way for me. Just like my own Mr. Stanton in my "coma reality" took care of me at every step. Dream or vision, I couldn't be sure. But I was certain that fate had been altered, and my future changed. I just couldn't be sure as to why.

ACKNOWLEDGMENTS

There have been too many mass shootings in this country. Inevitably, when one occurs the media reports are filled with talking-heads speculating on why the shooter committed the crime. It caused me to wonder what might motivate such a killer. So about five years ago I began thinking of writing a fictional novel about a mass shooting at a college from the perspective of the shooter. The project languished under the press of other demands until the Aurora, Colorado theatre shootings. That event sparked renewed interest on my part in the subject matter, and I began writing in earnest. But I found that I was coming quickly to agree with Gus Stanton's world-view: sane people don't randomly kill other people.

I wasn't sure that I was qualified to write about what motivates truly insane people; indeed, that whole notion may be oxymoronic. Then I remembered a talk that Scott Turow, the highly acclaimed lawyer and author, gave to a group of lawyers in my firm shortly after his first book *Presumed Innocent*, was published. He told the story of how he was unable to get his first novella published, which was about a young man's coming of age in New Orleans. In retrospect, he said he realized that the book suffered from two fundamental flaws: he had never been to New Orleans, and he had never had a "coming of age" experience. The lesson I took from Scott's story: at least start writing about something you know, even if it eventually leads you into unfamiliar territory.

I know something about litigation and trials. I have had the opportunity over a thirty-five year career to participate in some pretty interesting legal proceedings with some pretty unusual characters. So the focus of my story changed, drawing upon the things I knew and venturing into the uncharted waters of the vagaries of New Hampshire law and what might cause a sane person to consider such a heinous act. Ultimately, of course, the story took on a life of its own.

I am grateful for the help and insight of several "beta readers" who provided suggestions to improve the story along the way, including: Susan Kornfield, Nicole Pakkala, Judy Frumm, Chip Champagne, Art Fogel, Dale Reid, Jane Kerr, Steve Houghton, Peg Sickeler, Penny Gundry, my twin sister Kathy Kyr, and my adult children, Ryan, Morgan and Andrew. The flaws remaining are my doing, not theirs. I am also very grateful to my assistant Sheila who helped me edit and format the book (on her own time), and acted as my principle cheerleader when I had doubts about finishing. Special thanks also goes to Robin Katz of Blackbird Design for the great cover design, and to Suzy Halpin of Suzy Halpin Photography for the photo used on the back cover of the paperback version. But I am most appreciative for my "alpha reader," Robin, my wife of over thirty years. Without her, this book would never have been written.

CPSIA information can be obtained at www.ICGtesting.com
Printed in the USA
BVOW07s1413091114

374350BV00001B/169/P